HEROIN
An Illustrated History

HEROIN

AN ILLUSTRATED HISTORY

SUSAN BOYD

FERNWOOD PUBLISHING
HALIFAX & WINNIPEG

Copyediting: Jessica Antony
Cover design: David Lester
Interior design: David Lester

Printed and bound in Canada

Published by Fernwood Publishing
32 Oceanvista Lane, Black Point, Nova Scotia, B0J 1B0
and 748 Broadway Avenue, Winnipeg, Manitoba, R3G 0X3
www.fernwoodpublishing.ca

Fernwood Publishing Company Limited gratefully acknowledges the financial support of the Government of Canada, the Manitoba Department of Culture, Heritage and Tourism under the Manitoba Publishers Marketing Assistance Program and the Province of Manitoba, through the Book Publishing Tax Credit, for our publishing program. We are pleased to work in partnership with the Province of Nova Scotia to develop and promote our creative industries for the benefit of all Nova Scotians. We acknowledge the support of the Canada Council for the Arts, which last year invested $153 million to bring the arts to Canadians throughout the country.

Library and Archives Canada Cataloguing in Publication

Title: Heroin : an illustrated history / by Susan Boyd.
Names: Boyd, Susan C., 1953- author.

Description: Includes bibliographical references and index.
Identifiers: Canadiana (print) 20210354003 | Canadiana (ebook) 20210363126 | ISBN 9781773635163 (softcover) | ISBN 9781773635347 (EPUB) | ISBN 9781773635354 (PDF)

Subjects: LCSH: Heroin—Canada. | LCSH: Heroin—Canada—Pictorial works. | LCSH: Heroin abuse—Canada. | LCSH: Drug control—Canada—History.

Classification: LCC HV5822.H4 B69 2022 | DDC 362.29/30971—dc23

Contents

Acknowledgements

I WOULD LIKE TO THANK FERNWOOD PUBLISHING AND THEIR STAFF FOR TAKING on this book project, especially Wayne Antony, Beverley Rach, Anumeha Gokhale, Jessica Antony and Jessica Herdman. Thank you to David Lester for creating the book cover and beautiful book design. Due to their commitment to social justice, I am grateful to work with Fernwood and David Lester. As well, thank you to Zoe Gram and her staff for providing publicity with Fernwood for the book. I am grateful to the University of Victoria and to the Canadian Social Science and Humanities Research Council for funding my Insite grant to examine heroin regulation more fully. These supports made the publication of *Heroin: An Illustrated History* possible.

Thank you to all of the city, provincial and federal archives staff across Canada. Your assistance was invaluable. I am deeply grateful to a number of people who contributed to this book, especially Donald MacPherson, who provided endless feedback, Peter Kim, Jean-François Mary, Steve Rolles, Dr. Scott MacDonald, Frank Crichlow, Natasha Touesnard and Zoë Dodd. Thank you to the many other people and organizations who contributed to this book: Aiyanas Ormond, Brittany Graham, VANDU, WAHRS, DULF, Canadian Drug Policy Coalition, Moms Stop the Harm, Pivot Legal Society, Crackdown, CAPUD, Portland Hotel Society, Jonny Mexico, Elaine Briere, Neil Magnuson, Karen Ward, Janice Abbott and Sisterspace, Ann Gibbon, Shelley West and Robert Nightingale, Trey Agnew, Maggie MacPherson, the LeDain family, Leslie Ottavi, Brian Murphy, John Olson, Bob Masse, Elaine Alfoldy, Kent Monkman and Henri Robideau.

Over the last six years, a number of other people contributed to my earlier SSHRC research on heroin regulation. Thank you to Beth Abbott for her critical editing skills on earlier heroin-related papers, Lydia Lobbezoo, Sarah Wojcik, Alexa Norton and Andrew Ivsins, who were Research Assistants on my SSHRC grant, and SNAP members for inviting me to collaborate with them for nine years. Thank you to Jeremy Kalicum, Eris Nyx, John Conroy, Jade Boyd, Iain Mitchell-Boyd, Sunera Thobani, Dara Culhane, Kristen Mattison, Emily Nickerson, Akwasi Owusu-Bempah, Jean Swanson, Ann Livingston, Dean Wilson, Kathleen Kenny, Women's Committee for BCYADWS, Erica Thomson, Shohan Illsley, Manitoba Harm Reduction Network, Bruce Alexander, Anna-Karin Ahlman, Perry Kendall, Marliss Taylor, Shay Vanderschaeghe, Rebecca Haines-Saah, Petra Schulz and Jess McEachern, all of whom provided input. Although, all omissions and mistakes are of my own making.

As well, this book could not have been written without the support of my loving family and extended family, especially little River Mae Boyd. Thank you.

I respectfully acknowledge that I live and work on unceded Indigenous territories; and I thank the Squamish (*Sḵwx̱wú7mesh Úxwumixw*), Tsleil-Waututh, and Musqueam (*xʷməθkʷəy̓əm*) First Nations for their hospitality.

For SNAP *and in memory of Dave Murray,*
Canada's distinguished advocate for flexible,
less medicalized, heroin-assisted treatment
and an end to drug prohibition.

1

Heroin, Addiction and Harm Reduction

In July 2021 I was standing on a busy retail street corner in Vancouver. I noticed that within a two-block radius there were four legal retail shops selling drugs: a liquor store, a pharmacy, a convenience store selling tobacco products and a cannabis shop. All of these outlets were busy with customers going in and out. A few blocks away is a large hospital and three more pharmacies. All of a person's legal drug needs could be met on these few blocks, yet none of these sites stock legal heroin, even though the drug is similar to a plethora of other opioids available in Canada. I have long been curious why the drug heroin, especially illegal heroin, is vilified and why many Canadian health providers and the public fail to recognize its therapeutic value, especially given the illegal overdose death epidemic in Canada.

THE OVERDOSE CRISIS

Canada is experiencing the worst illegal drug overdose death epidemic in its history. Between 2016 and 2021, over 24,626 people in Canada have died from an overdose of illegal drugs. These are entirely preventable deaths. Yet, since 2010, preventable illegal overdose deaths have steadily risen in Canada. These deaths are due to prohibitionist drug policies and practices, a poisoned illegal drug supply (for example, heroin, unknown to the buyer, may contain illegal fentanyl and its analogues and/or benzodiazepines) and inadequate access to flexible and culturally appropriate drug substitution programs. Over a century of punitive, racialized, gendered and class-biased drug policy has produced immeasurable harm.

A sharp increase in illegal overdose deaths in British Columbia (BC) led to a public health emergency being declared in April 2016. In January 2022, the Yukon declared a public health emergency. Yet the epidemic continues in and outside of BC and the Yukon. The province of BC has the highest illegal overdose death rate (deaths per 100,000 people) in Canada. From 2010 to 2021 over 11,028 people died in BC alone from a preventable illegal drug overdose.[1] Ontario, with a much larger population than BC, recorded 2,426 illegal drug overdose deaths in 2020 alone, a sharp increase from 1,517 deaths in 2019. In Alberta — from January 1, 2016, to June 30, 2020 — 3,139 people have died from an illegal drug overdose.[2] Although overdose deaths and related hospitalizations and emergency room visits have risen across Canada, outside of BC and the Yukon no other public health emergencies have been declared. In fact, in 2019 Alberta's Conservative-led government ordered that life-saving programs such as iOAT (injectable opioid agonist treatment) be shut down.

In contrast, people who use drugs, activists and allies were quick to address the overdose death crisis early on, speaking publicly about the ongoing preventable tragedy and the loss of loved ones. They also set up sanctioned and unsanctioned harm reduction services, such as overdose prevention sites where people could consume their drugs safely. In responding to the poisoned illegal drug supply, some activists even provided packaged, labelled, individual doses of

A safe supply box of heroin distributed by the Drug User Liberation Front (DULF) with Vancouver Area Network of Drug Users (VANDU) at the April 14, 2021 No Compromise for Safe Supply rally in Vancouver. (Photo by Henri Robideau, reprinted with permission.)

safe (drug tested) illegal heroin to be distributed with drug user unions and their members, along with packaged doses of cocaine and methamphetamine.

Dave Murray of SALOME/NAOMI Association of Patients (SNAP), formally NAOMI Patient Association (NPA), at the four-year anniversary celebration on February 28, 2015, at Woodward's in Vancouver. (Photo by Jade Boyd, reprinted with permission.)

Yet, with neither adequate safe legal drug supplies nor health, social and legal resources, efforts are limited and some workers are at risk of arrest. The question that looms large is why all levels of government failed to act quickly to prevent these deaths early on. Are these lives not worthy?

As I worked on this book in 2020, the global COVID-19 pandemic emerged. In stark contrast to the few or no measures taken by local, provincial and federal governments in Canada to stem illegal overdose deaths, all provinces and territories declared a state of emergency or a public health emergency to address COVID-19. All levels of government acted swiftly setting up COVID-19 safety measures (including economic support, social distancing, online schooling, travel restrictions, testing). The province of BC quickly declared a public health emergency on March 17, 2020, in order to address the pandemic. In contrast, it took about six years for the province of BC to declare the rising overdose deaths (since 2010) a public health emergency. As the two public health emergencies coalesced in BC, a steep increase in illegal drug overdose deaths was reported in the months following the beginning of the COVID-19 pandemic.[3] Similar increases occurred in Ontario and Alberta. In the pages of this book, I try to make sense of our failure to address the illegal overdose death epidemic by examining the history of heroin prohibition, our punitive and flawed drug policies and the decades of resistance to these policies. Aided by more than one hundred images, the story of heroin prohibition unfolds. Drawing from primary and secondary sources, this book provides an illustrated history of the regulation of heroin in Canada.[4]

Although I have written about Canadian drug prohibition and its manifestations for decades, I began to focus more closely on heroin regulation in 2011. My interest was spurred on after participating in a Canadian drug reform meeting in January 2011, organized by what was to become the Canadian Drug Policy Coalition. A number of long-time activists were there, including Dave Murray. At a break, Dave told me about a new peer-led group that had just started meeting weekly at the Vancouver Area Network of Drug Users (VANDU) in the Downtown Eastside (DTES) of Vancouver, BC. Dave was facilitating these meetings with the support of VANDU. At that time, the independent group called themselves the NAOMI Patients Association (NPA). Dave invited me to meet with the members of NPA. After meeting with the NPA, they invited me to collaborate with them to tell their own story as the first people in North America to receive heroin-assisted treatment. Thus began a nine-year collaboration.

NAOMI recruitment poster on a wall inside of the Vancouver Area Network of Drug Users (VANDU) site in 2005. (Photo by the author.)

Every member of NPA had been a research participant in Canada's first heroin-assisted treatment (HAT) clinical trial, the North American Opiate Medication Initiative (NAOMI), which recruited 251 research subjects from February 2005 to March 2007 in Vancouver and Montreal. The NPA members and other NAOMI participants were the only people in North America to receive heroin-assisted treatment (HAT) at that time. However, even though the trial results were positive, once the clinical trial ended, a permanent heroin-assisted treatment program was not established. At the end of the trial, NAOMI participants had the option to either return to conventional treatments that had previously failed them or to buy heroin from the illegal market where they were once again vulnerable to overdose death, infection and arrest. Given the success of the trial, it was surprising that a permanent HAT program was not set up in Canada at the end of that first trial. It was also surprising given that HAT is and continues to be available in numerous other countries and is an effective and safe drug substitution treatment for long-time opioid users for whom conventional treatments such as abstinence-based treatments or methadone maintenance therapy have failed.

After much struggle and advocacy, including a second clinical trial in Vancouver and a challenge under the *Canadian Charter of Rights and Freedoms*, a small number of people now receive HAT at four clinics in Canada, all in BC. Approximately 160 people benefit from these HAT programs. Even in the face of two public health emergencies, HAT has not expanded in Canada, even though it saves lives. If we look at the history of heroin over the last century, it may not be that surprising that so many people are confused about the drug and its therapeutic value.

WHAT IS HEROIN?

Heroin (diacetylmorphine) is an opioid, a semi-synthetic drug derived from the compound morphine found in the opium poppy plant. In 1898 Frederick Bayer and Company marketed diacetylmorphine as a pain reliever and cough suppressant and branded it as "heroin." Bayer advertised heroin as superior to morphine because a smaller dose was needed for the same effect. Heroin was never as popular as opium-based medicines or morphine, possibly because in the early 1900s it was most often advertised for respiratory problems rather than wider applications associated with opium. Heroin is a central nervous system depressant, as are all opioids (such as morphine, codeine and Demerol) and alcohol. Although heroin and other opioids produce similar effects, there are differences in how people respond to them, and they differ in relation to potency, duration of effects and administration (oral, injecting, smoking). Large doses of potent opioids like heroin can lead to respiratory failure and death. Because illegal heroin sold on the illegal market is not regulated, potency and quality are never assured, and a poisoned drug supply puts people who use heroin (and other illegal drugs) at greater risk of adverse effects, including overdose death. Although heroin continues to be prescribed safely for therapeutic use in the UK and other countries, the demonization of *illegal* heroin users and the drug in North America, especially since the 1940s and 1950s, has altered our opinions.

THEN CAME THE "JUNKIE" AND THE WAR ON DRUGS

Prior to the 1900s, people who used heroin were not seen as criminal or pathological. Rather, people were able to buy the drug legally with or without a prescription. The transition from law-abiding citizen to "junkie" or "criminal addict" is a product of drug prohibition. For over a century, heroin has been portrayed as highly addictive and destructive. In Canada, heroin has long been deemed, until recently, as having no therapeutic value. Lurid representations of alleged junkies and addicts have been produced and disseminated by law enforcement, politicians, medical professionals and others through film, print and other media, language, theory and texts, producing a constellation of myths and stereotypes that contribute to legal and social discrimination and stigma. Stereotypes, says critical race theorist Stuart Hall, reduce people to a few essentialist characteristics, accomplished partially through representation (in visual images and texts). Hall is referring specifically to Black people; however, his analysis is relevant to people who use illegal heroin. Hall also explains that stereotyping occurs most often when there are "gross inequalities of power,"[5] so that some meanings of an image are privileged over others. Images accumulate meanings over time and play off one another, but often one image is repeated over and over again in texts and visual representations (in print, television and online news, police reports and popular media and films). Think of the negative images and stereotypes that you have been exposed to over time about people who use illegal heroin. Most often they are poor and racialized people, and equally often include the iconic image of "shooting up." This image is now associated with deviance and degradation.

Following the criminalization of narcotics in the early 1900s, the heroin user was transformed from a patient in need, to a weak-willed individual, a "dope fiend" and then a "junkie," symbolizing degradation, deviance, addiction and death. For decades following criminalization, ideas about out-of-control and criminal "junkies" informed drug law and policy. In Canada, people who used heroin would also be labelled as "criminal addicts" in order to emphasize their supposed criminal nature. Over time, recurring stereotypical images of ruined people who used heroin and racialized violent traffickers have an effect.[6] Since the late nineteenth and early twentieth century, people have been horrified and entertained by stories about drugs, immorality, degradation, addiction and traffickers. As we will see, international and domestic prohibition, white supremacy, colonialism, racial and gendered violence, social and legal discrimination and stereotyping and othering all shape drug policy and have terrible consequences.

"Shooting-up" scene in the 1971 film, *The Panic in Needle Park*. (Reprinted with permission from Photofest.)

A CRIMINAL JUSTICE APPROACH

Drug prohibition refers to international and national drug control systems that nations, including Canada, adopted and refined for over a century. Drug prohibition is a set of international treaties, domestic laws and policies that criminalizes some drugs and the people who possess, produce, sell, or import them for non-medical or non-scientific reasons. Canadian drug laws also shape the type of services that can be provided to people. For example, publicly funded drug treatment and heroin or narcotic clinics were not set up following prohibition in Canada. In the 1920s it became illegal for doctors to prescribe drugs like morphine or heroin as treatment for those labelled addicted. In order to set up the first official supervised injection site in Canada, Insite, in Vancouver in 2003, a section 56(1) exemption from the Controlled Drugs and Substances Act (CDSA) was necessary. The CDSA is our most current federal drug law. The CDSA also fulfills Canada's international drug control obligations set out in three United Nations drug control treaties. Along with the new Cannabis Act and the Food and Drug Act, the CDSA and other federal acts detail what substances are illegal or legal to possess, produce, sell, import or export in Canada, and the associated criminal offences and penalties.

The CDSA also includes a series of lists or "drug schedules" of criminalized drugs. Schedule 1 includes the most highly restricted drugs, such as opium, heroin, morphine, cocaine, codeine, oxycodone and hydromorphone, among others. Many drugs included in Schedule 1 can be legally prescribed by a doctor; however, they are criminalized when bought on the illegal market or given to a person without a prescription. Possession of illegal heroin can lead to a prison sentence of up to seven years. Trafficking illegal heroin can lead to imprisonment for life. Although many people in Canada receive lesser sentences for Schedule 1 offences, the CDSA is harsh, and the accumulation of lesser offences — even fines — can snowball into prison time.

Rather than adopting a health and social approach to drug regulation early on — an approach that would allow for personal possession and focus more on education, based on civil fines and less punitive sanctions for illegally selling small amounts (similar to tobacco regulation) — drug prohibition in Canada started out with and is still primarily uses a criminal justice approach. In the early 1900s some drugs, such as opium (in smoking form) and later heroin, became constructed as evil and dangerous. So, too, were the people who were thought to use and sell these drugs. Over the years, new drugs were added to the drug schedules — thereby criminalizing them and their users. With little evidence of the harm of the drugs themselves, drug prohibition is actually tied up with colonization and systemic racism, as well class and gender injustice, both in Canada and globally.

Over the last century, lives have been destroyed — literally — due to what is often referred to as the "war on drugs." That is, it is the prohibition itself, not the drug or effects of its use, that causes the most harm. As Steve Rolles, an internationally renowned UK senior policy analyst at Transform Drug Policy Foundation, explains:

> Consider, for example, two injecting heroin users; the first is … using 'street' heroin (of unknown strength and purity) with dirty, possibly shared needles in unsupervised and unsanitary environments. Their supplies are purchased from a criminal dealing/trafficking infrastructure that can be traced back to illicit production in Afghanistan. They have HIV, Hepatitis C and a long, and growing, criminal record. The second uses legally manufactured and prescribed pharmaceutical diamorphine of known strength and purity in a supervised, clinical setting, with clean injecting paraphernalia. There is no link to failing drug producer states; no criminality, profiteering or violence involved at any stage of the drug's production, supply or use; no blood borne disease transmission risk; a near zero risk of overdose death; and no offending to fund use.[7]

Drug prohibition as a whole is not driven by evidence of its efficacy in dealing with drug use nor "addiction" but rather by structural violence, including colonialism, gendered and racial violence, legal and social discrimination and stigma, a growing global illegal and sometimes violent market, a poisoned drug supply, racial profiling by law enforcement and healthcare professionals, incarceration, child apprehension, loss of custody, experimental drug treatment and compulsory drug treatment. As Steve Rolles makes clear above, many of the outcomes we associate with heroin are actually the result of drug prohibitionist laws and policies coupled with structural violence. By examining the past — the reports, policies and practices that support heroin criminalization and drug prohibition — the drivers of the current illegal drug-overdose death epidemic in Canada are brought more clearly into focus. We need to know the history of heroin and drug prohibition in order to understand its present and its future.

RESISTANCE TO CRIMINALIZATION

The heroin story is also one of resistance to criminalization. The impact of drug prohibition and resistance to it takes many forms. Each province and territory, city or region has its own important story to tell. Since the late 1940s, drug reform advocates in Canada have called for a health and social approach rather than a criminal approach to drug use, including the setting up of publicly funded drug treatment services and heroin clinics (that would provide legal heroin). From the 1960s on, people who used cannabis advocated for an end to cannabis prohibition. Due to their efforts, since 2018, cannabis is legally regulated in Canada. It is no longer a crime for an adult to possess 30 grams of legal cannabis. However, much to the disappointment of cannabis activists, although possibly not surprising given the Canadian governments' attachment to prohibition, the Cannabis Act consists of even more laws than before and many of these laws are quite harsh. For example, it is a criminal offence to possess more than 30 grams of cannabis and to grow more than four plants in one's home — an offence that can result in prison time.

In the early 1980s and 1990s, drug reform activists in Canada rallied to stem the tide of rising drug overdose deaths, as well as HIV/AIDS and hepatitis C infections. Without government support, activists set up services that provided education, harm reduction services and even unsanctioned safer injection sites. They also brought attention to the harms stemming from drug prohibition and called for an end to punitive laws and policies.

HARM REDUCTION

Introduced by people who use drugs, harm reduction services emerged in the 1980s in the UK and the Netherlands as a way to save lives and counter the harms stemming from drug prohibition. Allies in Canada also began to set up harm reduction services, such as needle distribution in the late 1980s and 1990s. Harm reduction is not a rejection of abstinence, but it is not the sole objective of services or drug treatment. Harm reduction advocates assert that non-judgmental and practical integrated services can reduce harms. Many of the harms linked to drugs are not actually specific to the drug; rather, they stem from criminalization and a lack of a safe supply (such as legal, unadulterated drugs), equipment and education. Drug prohibitionist policies and laws are seen as negatively contributing to and exacerbating the factors that such criminalization claims it will reduce. For example, criminalizing needle distribution negatively impacts HIV/AIDS infection rates. Criminalizing heroin and not providing a safe supply for those most affected can lead to a poisoned, unregulated, illegal heroin market and fatal drug overdoses. Harm reduction advocates see drug use and services on a continuum: for some people, abstinence-based drug treatment or twelve-step programs work best; for others, alternative options provide essential support.

The drug reform movement that emerged in Canada in the 1990s differs from past reform efforts because, for the first time, people who used drugs like heroin, cocaine or methamphetamine — people with experiential knowledge — were at the forefront of the movement. The first drug user union, Vancouver Area Network of Drug Users (VANDU), emerged in Vancouver BC in 1997. VANDU continues to advocate for an end to drug prohibition and provides outreach, harm reduction services and education, while also seeking to protect the human rights of people who use drugs. Since the 1990s, many other "unions" have been established across Canada, such as the Western Aboriginal Harm Reduction Society (WAHRS), Alberta Alliance Who Educate and Advocate Responsibly (AAWEAR), L'Association Québécoise pour la promotion de la santé des personnes utilisatrices de drogues (AQPSUD), the Cape Breton Association of People Empowering Drug Users (CAPED), and the BC/Yukon Association of Drug War Survivors (BCYADWS). In 2010, a national association representing regional groups emerged to push for drug reform at the federal level: the Canadian Association of People Who Use Drugs (CAPUD). Along with their allies, these groups and others have set up harm reduction services and strive to end the war on drugs, to end criminalization. These groups also argue that access to safe, legal drugs, including legal access to heroin, will curb preventable illegal overdose deaths across Canada. These drug user unions have ruptured long-held stereotypes about who the heroin user is. To be clear, people who use heroin in Canada most often consume other opioids, both legal and illegal, when heroin is unavailable or too costly.

In the 1955 film, *The Man with the Golden Arm*, heroin withdraw is depicted as so horrendous that people will kill to escape it. (Reprinted with permission from Photofest.)

DEPICTIONS OF HEROIN AND HEROIN USERS

Due to the efforts of drug user unions and allies, conventional ideas about people who use heroin have been challenged. This work is essential because for over a century conceptions and perceptions of heroin have been foundational to drug policy. Heroin has been depicted as addictive and dangerous, as have the people who use the drug. Fictional movies, including old classics such as *Narcotic* (1934), *The Man with the Golden Arm* (1955) and *The Panic in Needle Park* (1971), depict heroin as instantly compelling and addictive, withdrawal as horrific and degradation, criminal activity and overdose death as inevitable. In one of the first major Hollywood films to depict heroin use, *The Man with the Golden Arm* depicted heroin users as cheats and liars who are willing to kill for a "fix." Heroin withdrawal is shown as so horrific that people who use the drug need to be locked up.

In the 1971 film, *The Panic in Needle Park*, degradation is depicted as inevitable following heroin use. (Reprinted with permission from Photofest.)

In drug films, fields of opium poppies (from which heroin is derived) are depicted as the domain of ruthless foreign and racialized traffickers. Many contemporary films adopt similar themes. People who use illegal heroin are othered. They are depicted in both popular culture and in some academic theories as pathological and criminal. In many ways, we fear criminalized drugs and the people who are suspected of using them. Sensationalized drug imagery also frames some drugs as desirable, giving them almost magical qualities to uplift and then destroy people.

FROM IMMORAL TO DISEASE, BUT ALWAYS CRIMINAL

Stories and research about people who use heroin and addiction over the last century most often include similar storylines: from a law-abiding patient to a weak-willed, immoral, criminal and pathological person. These ideas have informed approaches to heroin use in Canada and other nations. For quite some time, however, critical drug researchers have challenged assumptions about illegal drugs, including heroin, and the label "addiction."[8] Our ideas about addiction, drugs and the people who use them are central to prohibition because they influence drug policy (including drug services) and law.

"The Tree of emperance." This 1872 lithograph depicts temperance — an abstinent life — as leading to, amongst other positive outcomes, health, success, love and virtue. (Coloured lithograph by Currier and Ives, reprinted with permission from Wellcome Library, London.)

In the mid-nineteenth century, using alcohol was not just depicted by moral reformers as immoral but as leading to death. (Photo from Molson Portrait Collection, Molson Archives, Montreal, Quebec, 1855–1891, reprinted with permission from Library and Archives Canada.)

SOBRIETY AND PUNISHMENT

Prior to industrialization, people who were thought to consume opium or alcohol too often (even though ideas about consumption shift over historical eras), were not demonized in the West. For example, prior to industrialization, beer and wine were an integral component of social life for Western men — it was consumed at breakfast, lunch, dinner and in the workplace. Beer was considered to be nutritious and was used as a medicine and a tonic to prevent disease (alcohol is, in fact, one of our oldest drugs). Opium, from the poppy plant, was considered to be an essential plant medicine since the Egyptian, Greek and Roman empires. Opium was used for pain management, intestinal ailments and respiratory conditions and infections and consumed in teas, elixirs and tinctures, and sometimes smoked. Opium and opium-based medicines were also part of the social fabric of many cultures, including those in Western nations.

As we will explore in more depth in the following pages, societal and legal responses to plants and substances constantly change. The temperance movements and anti-opium movements in the 1800s championed "sobriety" and Christian religious (Protestant) dedication as the template of white moral respectability; those who did not comply were constructed as weak-willed, immoral and, for non-Christians, heathen. The temperance movement and anti-opium movements purported that white Christian morality, self-control and abstinence was the solution to many social problems, including poverty, violence and immorality. The consumption of drugs like alcohol or opium (in smoking form), especially by racialized people, came to be seen through a white-supremist, Christian lens. However, white people were not prohibited from or punished for consuming drugs, or for drug possession or sale. A person might be arrested for intoxication or being a public nuisance, but it was legal to buy and consume many plant-based, mood-altering substances, including heroin.

MEDICAL AND NON-MEDICAL DRUG USE

The categorization of "medical" or "non-medical" use of drugs is a fairly new idea. Ideas about punishment and abstinence as cures to drug use began to emerge more forcefully in the Indian Act of 1876 and in the early 1900s. Sobriety and punishment were advanced as the solutions to what increasingly came to be defined as the problem of drug use. Proponents of drug prohibition linked immorality and social ills to racialized people, who were depicted as foreigners to and debasers of the moral, white Christian nation. Thus, in the early 1900s narcotic legislation was enacted in Canada and other Western nations to punish racialized people for using opium (in smoking form) and other narcotics for non-medical purposes. Canada's first narcotic legislation was enacted in 1908, establishing a criminal justice approach to drugs, rather than a social or health model. Policing and punishment became the bedrock of Canada's approach, and law enforcement became the dominant knowledge producers about all activities related to drug use and "addiction."

A NEW CONCEPT

In the West, prior to early drug laws, there was not yet a dominant school of thought about drug use, nor a specific profession that saw drug use as their domain. In 1928, the foundational text, *The Opium Problem*, by Charles Terry and Mildred Pellens, was published in the US. It was the most comprehensive work to be published at that time on the "drug problem." The authors focused mainly on opiates — such as heroin, morphine, opium, and codeine — and provided comprehensive reviews of the medical and scientific literature of the time about "chronic use," treatment, tolerance and withdrawal. Significantly, Terry and Pellens also discussed the legal control of opiates in the US, such as the establishment and closure of legal "narcotic clinics" following drug prohibition. The authors also note that diverse terms were employed by writers to describe drug use, such as referring to people as having a habit, a craving, an appetite, a mania, an addiction and/or an addiction-problem. The authors of *The Opium Problem* preferred the term "chronic opium intoxication" to other terms.[9] Their important text reveals how narcotic use moved from the social sphere into the domain of medicine and, similar to today, how dogmatic, arbitrary, biased and ungrounded "evidence" shape our ideas about heroin and other drugs, "addiction" and treatment.

CANADIAN STEREOTYPES

In Canada, unlike western nations like the UK, the concept of the "criminal addict" was advanced in the 1930s to explain the nature of illegal drug use and to justify punitive drug laws in the first half of the twentieth century. People labelled criminal addict were seen as criminals first and foremost, and their use of heroin (or other drugs) was considered secondary. Thus, it was believed that even if poor and working-class people stopped using heroin or other illegal drugs, they would remain a menace to society due to their criminal nature. Stemming from these misinformed ideas, publicly funded drug treatment was not set up in Canada until the late 1950s and 1960s and recommendations by reformers to establish heroin clinics were rejected by law enforcement, moral reformers and law and order politicians. However, in the 1950s and 1960s a shift emerged in Canada when the disease concept of addiction was popularized and the study of "drug addiction" flourished. Poor and working-class people who used illegal drugs like heroin continued to be labelled criminal addicts, yet they were increasingly seen by social workers, medical professionals and prison authorities as both criminal and pathological.

ADDICTION AS A DISEASE

Sociologist Craig Reinarman argues that the disease concept of addiction "was not a scientific discovery and, as a concept, has been 'continuously redefined'."[10] The disease model of addiction came into prominence in the mid-twentieth century, although tenets of it have existed in temperance writing since the 1700s.[11] Drug dependency, the disease model purports, lies in the biological and neurological processes of the body and brain, rather than as a moral failing of the individual found in early models of habitual drug use. Its proponents advance that addiction is a progressive and permanent disease. The goal of treatment of this disease is sobriety, however, relapse is seen as part of recovery. The majority of the drug services and treatments in Canada draw from this model — sobriety is required or seen as the end goal. Yet, there

Alcoholics Anonymous (AA) emerged in the 1930s. It is a volunteer organization that now has chapters around the world. Today alcoholism is understood by AA advocates as a disease rather than a moral failing and the cure is abstinence for life for those afflicted. AA also adopted Christian morality as the bedrock to sobriety. The twelve steps of Alcoholics Anonymous lay out a roadmap for recovery. Giving one's will and life to God, sobriety, attendance at voluntary support meetings and following the twelve steps are seen as integral to remaining alcohol-free. Later, twelve-step programs were integrated into drug treatment programs and Narcotics Anonymous. The adage "one day at a time" is integral to AA/NA philosophy. Less emphasis is placed on the evils of the drug (alcohol or heroin) or on alcohol as the root of evil, and instead the individual is understood to have a lifelong disease.

The Disease Concept of Alcoholism, written by E.M. Jellinek in 1960, advocated the twelve-step principle and the disease model of addiction. Jellinek expands on the concept of disease originating with Benjamin Rush in the late 1700s and AA advocates since the 1930s. He argues that "alcoholism" stems from a recognizable physical disorder, not a flaw of character. Jellinek was a prominent alcohol expert from the 1940s on and his book was adopted for a national campaign to convince doctors that alcoholism is a disease — one that is biological, progressive and permanent. Since then, although critics maintain that Jellinek's claims are not supported by research or scientific evidence, the disease model remains the core of conventional drug treatment and popular belief in North America.

are contradictions in this approach to drug treatment, as even Alcoholics Anonymous (AA) and Narcotic Anonymous (NA) members do not discontinue all drug use. Interestingly tobacco, coffee and tea are not banned, although they are mood-altering drugs.

The contemporary concept of addiction as a disease has changed over time. Even though addiction is purported to be a disease, scientists have not been able to discover a fixed answer to the "nature of addiction." Nor has recent neuroscientific research.[12] Alternative frameworks of drug consumption are not a rejection of abstinence or sobriety; rather, these frameworks explore more fully social and cultural factors, including religion, that shape drug use in a specific historical era. In Canada today, addiction continues to be seen as a disease *and* as a criminal matter. Critics ask how punishment can be effective if addiction is a disease — over the years our ideas and policies about drugs are often contradictory.

OPIOID USE DISORDER AND THE DSM

In the twenty-first century, despite the advent of harm reduction philosophy and services in the 1990s, people who are labelled addicted or dependent on illegal heroin and other opioids continue to be seen as deviant, criminal and/or pathological. It has been assumed that framing daily or regular illegal heroin use as a disease or pathology, rather than as criminal and deviant behaviour, reduces stigmatization. How-

The earliest known photograph (May 20, 1851) of a meeting of the Association of Medical Superintendents of American Institutions for the Insane, the founders of the American Psychiatric Association and the *Diagnostic and Statistical Manual of Mental Disorders*, regarded by Western nations as the leading text on diagnoses and treatment of those labelled disordered, including those suffering from chronic alcohol and drug use. (Photo from APA Archives, reprinted with permission.)

ever, that has not been the case.[13] Critical researcher Suzanne Fraser and her colleagues note, "the reality of addiction is brought into being in research labs, clinical encounters, health policy meetings, legal schedules and texts such as the DSM [*Diagnostic and Statistical Manual of Mental Disorders*, authored by the American Psychiatric Association]. Addiction is produced in these contexts through the assemblage of certain elements and the exclusion of others."[14]

Conventional narratives of illegal drug use and those identified as dependent on or addicted to heroin include: experiences of increased use; loss of control; immoral and criminal activity; drug treatment failure; and, for some, control through abstinence or participation in a drug-substitution program such as methadone maintenance treatment.[15] Alternative narratives are most often excluded from the "addiction" trajectory.

Redefined concepts of addiction and dependence over time are evident in the different classifications and the list of criteria in the *Diagnostic and Statistical Manual of Mental Disorders* (DSM) since its inception in 1952. The DSM is regarded as the primary mental health diagnosis manual in Western nations.[16] DSM-I framed drug addiction as primarily a symptom of a personality disorder. In contrast, the DSM-5 (the most recent edition, revised in 2013) includes a growing number of new specific substance use disorders (SUDs), such as Opioid Use Disorder (OUD), Alcohol Use Disorder and Cannabis Use Disorder. The DSM-5 criteria for OUD includes these symptoms: "problems fulfilling obligations at work, school or home"; "giving up or reducing activities because of opioid use"; and "recurrent opioid use in situations in which it is physically hazardous."[17] The DSM-5 OUD criteria is based on a list of symptoms thought to be associated with extended use of opioids. The problem with this is that many of these "symptoms" are tied to social status, such as experiencing structural vulnerability, poverty, lack of private space and opioid substitution programs, homelessness and being the target of punitive drug policies and laws.[18]

In Canada, methadone maintenance is recommended for people labelled OUD; however, opioid users must meet the DSM-5 criteria for severe OUD in order to receive heroin-assisted treatment and/or injectable hydromorphone drug substitution treatment.[19] It is thought that being diagnosed with a disorder — a pathology — rather than being viewed as a criminal will reduce stigma. However, in Canada, that has not necessarily been the case. Canada's drug laws continue to criminalize those people labelled as having OUD.

The front cover of American Psychiatric Association's *Diagnostic and Statistical Manual of Mental Disorders*, first published in 1952. The APA framed addiction as primarily a symptom of a personality disorder. (Photo from APA Archives, reprinted with permission.)

IS ADDICTION A DISEASE?

Rather than understanding some drug use as a permanent lifelong disease. Others argue that there are other avenues in and out — and within — drug use,[20] and people's diverse experiences with heroin and other drugs cannot be divorced from historical, political, legal, social, cultural and biological contexts.[21] As made clear earlier, much of the harms we attribute to heroin use since criminalization (such as a higher risk of overdose and infection) actually stem from prohibition (such as overdose death due to toxic and adulterated heroin bought on the illegal market). Researchers also assert that repeated and regular drug use does not need to be understood as a fixed pathological identity or a "neurobiological condition." Alternatively, addiction could be understood instead as a habit.[22] Researchers Suzanne Fraser, David Moore and Helen Keane examine the concept of habit. They define it as: "a settled or regular tendency or practice, especially one that is hard to give up ... [such as,] he has an annoying habit of interrupting me [and/or] good eating habits." So, they say, "habit is neither good nor bad."[23] Yet, people who use illegal drugs such as heroin continue to be seen and treated as abnormal, disordered and criminal.

Conventional theories about addiction and drug policies ignore how the experiences and outcomes of drug use are influenced by one's social status (race, class, gender, sexuality) and one's cultural, legal and social environment. Nor do conventional theories take into account people's expectations of a drug, or the context of drug use. For example, in the late 1960s, Norman Zinberg, a US psychiatrist, visited the UK and observed their heroin maintenance practices, where some people were prescribed maintenance doses of heroin by a doctor. Zinberg noted that, unlike people in the US who used illegal heroin and were labelled criminal, in the UK, recipients of legal heroin lived "normal lives" — non-criminal lives. Zinberg attributed the difference between the US and UK heroin users as stemming from their different social settings (that is, their different social and legal perspectives on heroin).[24]

In the 1960s and 1970s there was a heroin panic attributed to soldiers coming home to the US from Vietnam who were introduced to heroin smoking while overseas. In contrast to conventional beliefs about addiction and heroin at that time, follow-up research on 900 US soldiers concluded that the majority of the veterans discontinued using heroin altogether and only about 7 percent were deemed "dependent" after their return home. In a three-year follow-up study of the soldiers, it was found that 12 percent used heroin again at some point in those three years, challenging the popular belief, "once a junkie, always a junkie."[25] Many soldiers used heroin occasionally in Vietnam without ever becoming dependent and the majority of those who claimed to be dependent on heroin while in Vietnam stopped using on their return home — the majority of whom stopped without drug treatment. The conventional idea that dependence on heroin is easily acquired and near impossible to break was dispelled by the research findings. The soldiers' heroin use in Vietnam was attributed to the terrible war conditions that they were subject to there.[26]

As Zinberg and other researchers assert, it is not solely a drug's pharmacology that shapes individual experience. A person's relationship, attitude and expectations about a specific drug, the physical, cultural and social environment where the drug is consumed and sanctions and prohibitionist laws and policies also shape drug use. People who use illegal heroin or other criminalized drugs in Canada continue to be subject to discriminatory and punitive legal, social and medical policies. Moreover, poor and racialized people are more likely to be severely criminalized and punished and to have less access to equitable health care service. The social consequences of illegal drug use are not equal.

Abandoning conventional ideas about drug use and treatment does not mean abandoning sobriety, or that the pain and suffering people experience related to their drug consumption or attempts to maintain sobriety should be dismissed. Nor does it mean that the suffering some people experience related to heroin (or any other drug) use or withdrawal should be ignored. Nor should we discount the pleasure or relief experienced by many people when sober, or conversely the similar feeling experienced after consuming a drug. In fact, alternative conceptualizations of drug use are relevant to everyone: those who wish to curtail or stop using a specific drug and those people who continue to use some drugs. More diverse understandings of drug use are necessary. More diverse services are also necessary.

DRUG USER UNIONS

Canada's first drug user union, the Vancouver Area Network of Drug Users (VANDU), emerged partially in response to the failure of all levels of government to take action to save lives during the first overdose death crisis in Vancouver's DTES in the 1990s. VANDU also ruptured conventional stereotypes about people who use criminalized drugs such as heroin. Until the emergence of drug user unions in Canada, including the SALOME/NAOMI Association of Patients (SNAP), and harm reduction advocates, the voices of people who used heroin regularly (who did not fit conventional abstinence discourses) were mostly ignored by politicians and policymakers (including the criminal justice system and the medical profession).[27] Rather than view illegal drug use as solely destructive, criminal or pathological, their members emphasize that some forms of drug use are positive and enhances their health and wellbeing.

Today, drug user unions and their allies are again at the forefront of activism to stem the current illegal overdose death epidemic in Canada by setting up alternative services, proposing alternative drug policies and honouring the memory of those people who have died due to government inaction.[28]

The harms and benefits of drug use can be compounded, and in some cases wholly created, by drug policy. Heroin, the drug, is neither good nor bad. As we will see, the pharmacology of any drug, including heroin, is really only a small part of its story.

Heroin is a potent drug and like most drugs there is a potential for harm. However, illegal heroin has many more harms associated with it due to its unknown quality and quantity. This has become even more evident with the current illegal drug overdose crisis, heightened by a poisoned illegal drug supply. Unlike legally produced heroin, the illegal market is unregulated — there is no cost, quality, or dose control.

For the Loved Ones We Have Lost (2019). A mural in the dtes by Trey Helten and Shawn "Heph." (Reprinted with their permission.)

The harms associated with heroin are also disputed when longtime regular users of the drug are provided legal daily doses in heroin-assisted treatment programs. Heroin has never been a widely used or popular drug, like cannabis or alcohol. Yet, pundits throughout the decades have continued to stoke drug scares about "heroin epidemics" sweeping across the nation and enticing moral, white youth and adults into a life of degradation.

The following chapters introduce the events that influenced heroin policy and the illegal overdose crisis. Although I refer to events across Canada, I focus mostly on international controls, federal policies, the city of Vancouver and the province of British Columbia. Vancouver has long been the epicentre of illegal drug use, drug regulation and heroin regulation in Canada. Events in Vancouver and BC continue to shape local and federal drug policies, however, I've included other events outside of BC that are important to this history, such as the setting up of harm reduction services, the closure of life-saving services and resistance to closures.

END NOTES

1. BC Coroners Service, 2022, p. 3
2. Gomes, et al., 2021; Health, Government of Alberta, 2020
3. BC Coroners Service, 2021a
4. For those readers who are interested in the sources cited in this book or the methodology and theoretical perspectives, please see Appendix I
5. Hall, 1997, p. 258 (italics in original)
6. Green, 2013
7. Rolles, et al., 2021, p. 4
8. See Alexander, 2008; Campbell, 2007; Fraser, 2017; Fraser, Moore and Keane, 2014; Hart, 2017; Keane, 2002; Levine, 2015; Pienaar and Dilkes-Frayne, 2017; Reinarman, 2005; Reinarman and Granfield, 2015; see Appendix 1 for a discussion about critical theory and methodology
9. Terry and Pellens, 1970 [1928], p. xx
10. Reinarman, 2005, p. 307
11. Musto, 2002
12. Campbell, 2007; Hart, 2017
13. See Fraser, 2017; Pienaar and Dilkes-Frayne, 2017; Reinarman & Granfield, 2015
14. Fraser, Moore, & Keane, 2014, p. 26
15. Boyd, 2008; Fraser and Valentine, 2008; Pienaar and Dilkes-Frayne, 2017
16. Blashfield, et al., 2014; Fraser et al., 2014; Robinson and Adinoff, 2016
17. APA, 2013, p. 541
18. Boyd, Ivsins and Murray, 2020
19. Health Canada, 2019
20. Reinarman and Granfield, 2015, p. 16
21. Fraser, 2017
22. Fraser, Moore and Keane, 2014; Keane, 2002
23. Fraser, Moore and Keane, 2014, p. 22
24. Zinberg, 1984
25. Robins et al., 2010, p. 206
26. Robins, Davis and Goodwin, 1974
27. Boyd, MacPherson and VANDU, 2019; Boyd, Murray, SNAP and MacPherson, 2017; Boyd, MacPherson and Osborn, 2009
28. BCYADWS, 2019; Thomson et al., 2019

2

Drugs, Colonialism and Criminalization

Pre-1900s

Worldwide, until the nineteenth century, medicines were derived from plants. Remedies were made from plant leaves, roots, bark, seeds, fruit, flowers and sap to treat illness, reduce pain and maintain health. Remedies made from medicinal plants were available and used based on knowledge and traditions. As they do today, individuals also used plant drugs for pleasure and for cultural and spiritual use. For thousands of years and in many societies there was no distinction between medical and non-medical use of plant drugs. People cultivated plants and made remedies for their families' use, or bought them from healers, apothecaries, herbalists or doctors. Throughout history, depending on the region, plant medicines such as white willow, cinchona bark, turmeric, valerian, opium poppy, cannabis and coca were harvested for use. These plant medicines can be taken orally, in elixirs, tinctures and teas, or applied to the skin or chewed. Some can also be smoked. It is also important to remember that for Canada, prior to universal healthcare in twentieth century, access to doctors was expensive and in many rural areas, doctors were few and far between. Plant medicines and remedies for healing and the maintenance of health were important for individuals and families until quite recently.[1]

Diverse Indigenous peoples living on lands that are referred to now as Canada used plant medicines native to this land, and local botanical

Eastern hemlock and Balsam fir were used by Indigenous peoples in what is now called Canada as medicines. (Image from Treaty of trees and shrubs that are grown in France, by Pierre-Joseph Redouté and Henri-Louis Duhamel du Monceau, reprinted with permission from Creative Commons, public domain.)

Common Yarrow, another plant medicine commonly used by Indigenous peoples. (Image from Kohler's *Medizinal-Pflanzen*, 1887, reprinted with permission from Creative Commons, public domain.)

knowledge was built up over many centuries. Many edible plants have medicinal qualities — about four hundred plants used by Indigenous peoples in Canada have medicinal properties. For example, different parts of the Balsam fir tree were used by Indigenous peoples in eastern Canada to treat a range of ailments such as burns, wounds, infections, coughs and tuberculosis.

From the 1500s onwards, European traders, missionaries and settlers arrived in what is now Canada. Colonization was a violent process — which continues to the present — of dispossessing land that was already inhabited by diverse Indigenous nations with their own governance, political, social, cultural and healing traditions. Yet, Indigenous knowledge and plant medicines were also introduced to white settlers. French and British trading posts, missionaries and settlements were established on the homelands of Indigenous nations. White settlers brought with them plant medicines commonly used in France and Britain (such as opium-based medicines), as well as alcohol, which was

A female apothecary mixing up a prescription for a child. (Etching by G. Greux, 1870–1879, from Q.G. van Brekelenkam 1620–1668, reprinted with permission from Wellcome Library, London.)

consumed for pleasure and as a food, medicine and tonic.

Plant medicines are still popular and used around the world today. However, with the advent of the modern pharmaceutical industry in the 1800s, and the rise of the medical and pharmacy professions in many Western nations, including Canada, plant medicines were depicted as inferior and dangerous in comparison to new drugs produced by chemists. Calls for the regulation of plant medicines later accompanied colonialism, the rise of the pharmaceutical industry and drug prohibition.

FRENCH AND ENGLISH PHARMACOPEIA AND OPIUM

Whereas early white settlers were introduced to diverse Indigenous medicines, they also drew from English and French pharmacopeia.

Early Western pharmacopeias, such as *The English Family Physician*

An apothecary in his laboratory concocting a mixture. (Wood engraving by Henry S. Marks around 1876, reprinted with permission from Wellcome Library, London.)

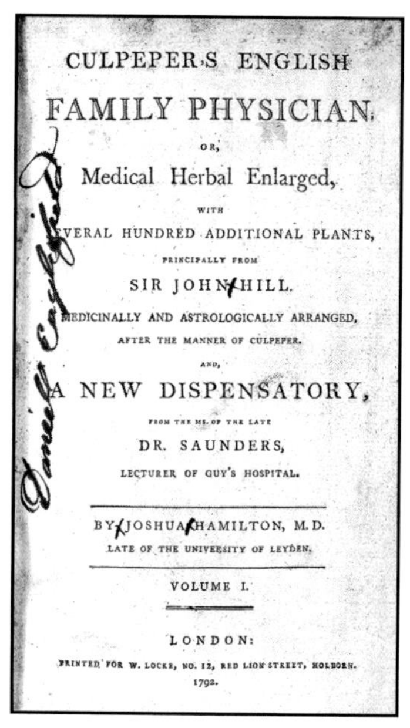

CULPEPER'S ENGLISH
FAMILY PHYSICIAN;
OR,
Medical Herbal Enlarged,
WITH
SEVERAL HUNDRED ADDITIONAL PLANTS,
PRINCIPALLY FROM
SIR JOHN HILL.
MEDICINALLY AND ASTROLOGICALLY ARRANGED,
AFTER THE MANNER OF CULPEPER.
AND,
A NEW DISPENSATORY,
FROM THE MS. OF THE LATE
DR. SAUNDERS,
LECTURER OF GUY'S HOSPITAL.
BY JOSHUA HAMILTON, M.D.
LATE OF THE UNIVERSITY OF LEYDEN.
VOLUME I.
LONDON:
PRINTED FOR W. LOCKE, NO. 12, RED LION STREET, HOLBORN.
1792.

Culpeper's *The English Family Physician* provides essential information about plant medicines and the aliments that they can be used for, directions for making syrups, oils, plasters and ointments, and how to plant, gather, dry and preserve plants — including the flower, roots, seeds, and bark. (Reprinted with permission from Wellcome Library, London.)

by Nicholas Culpeper, first published in 1652, included beautiful illustrations of medical plants and remedies and instructions for their use in maintaining health, treating illness and reducing pain. The opium poppy was heralded as a widely used medicinal plant. In a later edition of *The English Family Physician*, a few poppy plant recipes are recommended: "The black seed boiled in wine, and drank, is said also to stay the flux of the belly, and women's courses. The empty shells, or poppy heads, are usually boiled in water, and given to procure rest and sleep."[2]

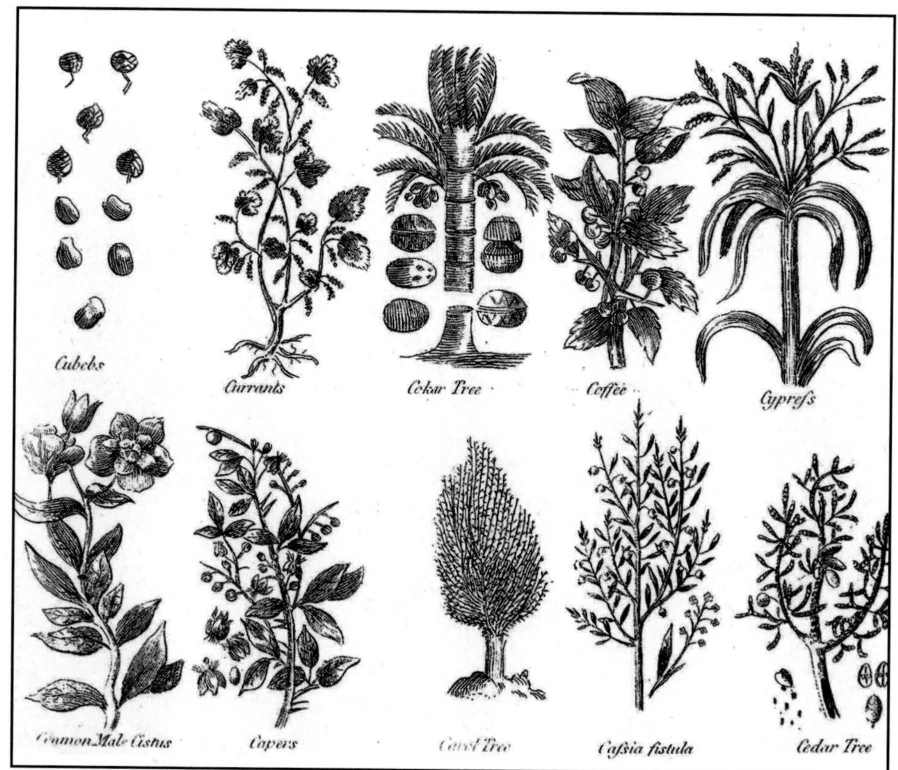

Engravings from Nicholas Culpeper's *The English Family Physician* (1789). (Reprinted with permission from Wellcome Library, London.)

Opium poppy (*Papaver somniferum*) is the source of heroin and has been a medicinal plant for centuries. (Photo by Sue Snell, reprinted with permission from Wellcome Library, London.)

THE OPIUM POPPY

What is referred to as heroin today – diacetylmorphine – was not discovered until 1874; however, its origin is tied to the opium poppy (*Papaver somniferum*). Without this variety of opium poppy, morphine and then heroin would not have been discovered. Opium is one of the oldest and best-known plant medicines. In fact, it is thought that the use of opium goes so far back in history that its origins are lost. It was used and traded in the Middle East, Mediterranean, Asia Minor and Western Europe.[3] The opium poppy has long been an essential medicine, cultivated for its sap, which is collected and dried to produce raw opium. Opium is also a natural drug, or plant medicine. It is one of many plants that have psychoactive properties. Opium is classified today as a narcotic and is commonly used for the treatment of pain and intestinal and respiratory problems.

The Arctic poppy (*Papaver radicatum*) grows in Nunavut. Different species of poppy plants grow around the world and have different potencies. (Photo by photographer John Olsen, reprinted with permission from him and Library and Archives Canada.)

THE OPIUM TRADE AND COLONIALISM

There are about fifty species of the poppy plant, such as the Arctic poppy that grows in Nunavut and other species that grow across Canada, the US and other countries. Some species of poppy plants grow wild, and others are planted in gardens for their attractive flowers. These poppy plants are usually less potent than *Papaver somniferum*, which is legally cultivated to make medicines (and illegally cultivated and sold on the illegal market). Today, the legal cultivation of opium poppies is under international drug control. India and China are currently the two main sources of legal opium poppies for the production of raw opium used for global medical and scientific purposes. Hungary, Spain, Turkey and Australia also cultivate legal opium poppies.[4] Today, opium cultivation is regulated and restricted by international and national drug conventions, such as the International Narcotics Control Board. Opium is also sold around the world illegally.

However, opium has long been a traded commodity. Internationally, it was "exported" from India to China, and sold by Portuguese, Dutch and then British traders. Starting in the late 1500s the British East India Company's colonial and imperialist domination shaped how opium fit into international trade and relations. The British brought opium from India and forced it onto China (where importation was prohibited), "trading" it for tea and other products. These actions led to two wars, often referred to as the Opium Wars (fought from 1839 to 1842 and 1856 to 1860), in order to force the Chinese government to allow the opium trade to continue. From 1560 to 1874, the British East India Company was not just a "trading company" but rather became an aggressive colonial power, a corrupt and violent private international corporation located in one building in London, with vast stolen lands, looted goods and offices in India, China and other nations in what would be referred to as the "British Empire." The British East India Company's

Indian men carrying a white European officer in a palanquin. The British East India Company hired its own private army to impose trade in India. (Gouache by an unknown Indian artist in the 1800s, reprinted with permission from Wellcome Library, London.)

A massive drying room in the opium factory at Patna, India. (Lithograph by W.S. Sherwill, 1850, reprinted with permission from Wellcome Library, London.)

An equally massive stacking room in the opium factory at Patna, India. (Lithograph by W.S. Sherwill, 1850, reprinted with permission from Wellcome Library, London.)

"My Mamma," circa 1880–1889. One of a series of twenty-two cards (one a year for twenty-two years) for Dr. Jayne's Expectorant, which contained opium, advertised as curing a wide range of aliments. (Reprinted with permission from Wellcome Library, London.)

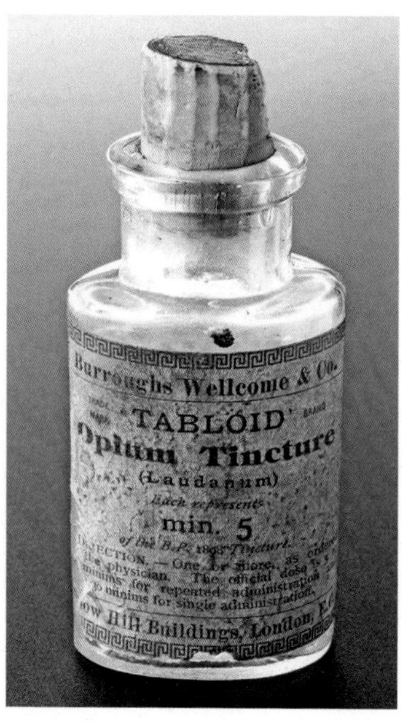

Bottle of opium tincture, London, England, 1880–1940. Science Museum, London. (Reprinted with permission from Wellcome Library, London.)

founding charter authorized it to wage war. To do so it employed its own army in a violent quest for global domination. With the backing and partnership of the British Parliament, the British East India Company monopolized the opium trade and was a key force advancing imperialism and racialized colonization.[5]

Although there were opium trade agreements between nations, until narcotic prohibition in the early 1900s, anyone could buy opium or opium-based remedies in Canada. In the late 1800s and early 1900s, crude opium was imported from India to Canada. During this era, these drugs, along with a variety of other plant medicines, were available in general stores and pharmacies and by mail order. In Canada, opium manufacturing was open and fairly widespread, with a number of operations in Vancouver, Victoria and New Westminster, BC. It was boiled into powdered opium, then made into tonics, elixirs and patent medicines. Some factories produced opium for smoking. Each year crude opium was imported into Canada and other nations because it was deemed an important medicine.[6] In 1919, for example, 34,000 pounds of crude opium were imported into Canada.[7]

MORPHINE

While opium was commonly used in Western nations, chemists sought to discover other narcotics and drugs that were more potent. The opium poppy, like all plants, is made up of many compounds. However, it was not until 1803 that a chemist isolated morphine (an organic compound) in opium, the first compound to be isolated from a plant. The discovery of morphine is a predecessor to the modern pharmaceutical industry. Morphine is more potent than opium, and also less bulky and easier to transport.

Medicine containing morphine, issued by the Dr. Seth Arnold Medical Co., in the 1880s. (Reprinted with permission from Wellcome Library, London.)

Gardner's Iron Pills/ Female Pills for "female ailments" and "afflictions of the weaker sex": menstrual and menopausal disorders, weakness, nervous troubles, wan complexion and vomiting! (Wood engraving by John Henry Walker, 1850–1885, reprinted with permission from McCord Museum.)

Clear glass bottle for liquid morphine, United States. Science Museum, London. (Reprinted with permission from Wellcome Library, London.)

Of course, opium-based drugs were not the only plant medicines available to Canadian consumers in the 1800s and early 1900s. An array of heroin and cocaine-and cannabis-based remedies were also available alongside opium and other herbal remedies. Many patent medicines and remedies also contained alcohol. They were sold by mail order and available in apothecaries and pharmacies across Canada.

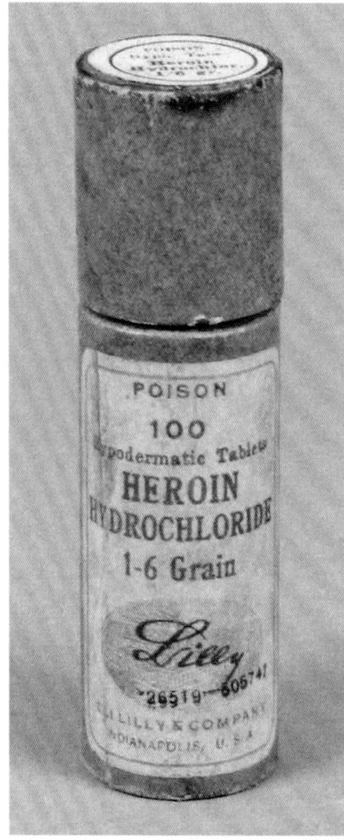

An old heroin bottle manufactured by Eli Lilly & Company, which could be purchased at chemists and drug stores. (Reprinted with permission from National Museum of American History.)

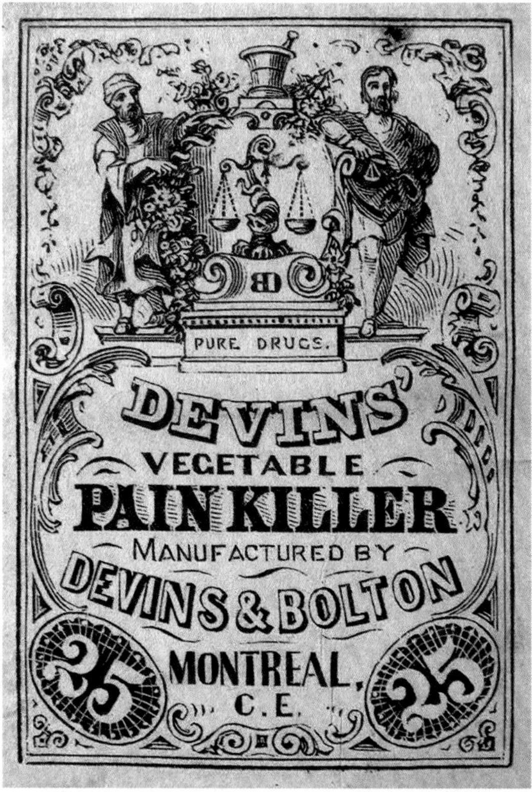

Devins' Vegetable Pain Killer — made of opium or morphine tincture plus various plant extracts and often used for calming children and getting them to sleep — was popular in Quebec and across Canada. (Wood engraving by John Henry Walker, 1850–1885, reprinted with permission from McCord Museum.)

BY APPOINTMENT,
Chemist and Apothecary to His Excellency the Governor General.
GEORGE MORTIMER,
Pharmaceutical Chemist and Druggist,
29 SUSSEX STREET, OTTAWA, ONT.
Proprietor of the Canadian Cough Emulsion and Celebrated
CHOLERA MIXTURE.
Look for 29 Sussex Street, and the Royal Arms in the Window.

George Mortimer Pharmaceutical Chemist and Druggist in Ottawa, 1875. Heroin products were sold at local drug stores in Canada. (Reprinted with permission from Library and Archives Canada.)

Ayer's cherry pectoral, which contained heroin, 1870. James Cook Ayer became fabulously wealthy manufacturing this medicine that claimed to cure dreaded childhood afflictions such as whooping cough, influenza, consumption, as well as all diseases of the lungs and throat. (Reprinted with permission from Wellcome Library, London.)

COLONIALISM, ALCOHOL AND OPIATES IN CANADA

Although it may not be evident how colonialism shaped ideas about people who use drugs, the following sections explore just that. European imperialism and the quest for new resources led to the colonization of what is now called Canada. Eminent scholar Sunera Thobani explains, "The European 'discovery' of what the Christians defined as the 'New World' led to the extension of their control across the Americas through the genocide and enslavements of the Indigenous peoples, racialized as 'savage' and without 'religion' and the brutal trans-Atlantic slave trade."[8] Colonizers also brought "Europe's religio-racial and class hierarchies" alongside of gender inequality and gendered violence.[9] Additionally, colonization informed early drug laws.

Early white colonizers and traders in what is now Canada consumed alcohol and opiate-based medicines. Indigenous peoples, prior to colonization, did not. White settlers and traders introduced alcohol to Indigenous peoples and then later condemned and criminalized them for using alcohol and opiates. The early history of alcohol and other drugs in Canada is intimately tied up with colonization imposing on Indigenous peoples Christian religions, Western values and laws, diseases and alcohol.

White missionaries and Christian temperance reformers sought to ban the sale and trade of alcohol to Indigenous peoples and did so through legislation. For example, on advice from Jesuit missionaries in New France in the 1600s, the King of France, Louis XIV, prohibited the sale and trade of "intoxicating liquors" to Indigenous peoples. Jesuits at that time asked, "Is it permitted to a Christian to sell to a Savage what makes him like a beast, changes him into a Lion, and prevents him from receiving the Faith of Jesus Christ?" White missionaries claimed that alcohol consumption by Indigenous peoples impeded their conversion to Christianity. Alcohol control was seen as one method among many to subjugate, convert and control Indigenous peoples. Christian white supremacy prevailed, as one Jesuit wrote about Indigenous peoples, "It is good to bring them gradually under the control of

Hudson's Bay Company and North West Company Forts at Île-à-la-Crosse, February 28, 1820. (Watercolour by George Back, reprinted with permission from Library and Archives Canada.)

those whom God has chosen to command them."[10]

The intent to colonize Canada began with missionaries and the fur trade. To challenge French trading with Indigenous peoples, the Hudson's Bay Company (HBC), a London-based company incorporated in 1670, became a key colonial power in what is now Canada. From the 1770s to early 1800s, HBC became the key competitor to the Montreal-based North West Company, initially run by Scottish immigrants who hired experienced French-Canadian fur traders. The HBC was not just a fur-trading company, but was in fact an English colonial agency that was granted immense power, financial support and land. Trading posts were set up on stolen Indigenous lands, and in many areas the HBC executed colonial government on white settlers and Indigenous peoples. The HBC was an active agent of colonialism and white supremacy, along with missionaries and settlers.

Following the conquest of New France, and prior to confederation, the British colonial government formed the Indian Department to counter French and Indigenous alliances. However, by the early 1800s, their focus shifted more directly to dispossession and assimilation (or racialized state violence). Following Confederation in 1867, the so-called responsibility for Indigenous peoples was handed over from the

British Crown to the Canadian government. Although the Department of the Interior included an "Indian Branch," the Department of Indian Affairs was also established in 1880.

Colonial systems to attempt control of Indigenous peoples and dispossess them of their land travelled through many British and then Canadian government institutions. The HBC and Indian agents (who existed from 1830 to the 1960s, first for the British Crown and then for the Canadian government under the Indian Act and the Department of Indian Affairs) acted for the British and the Canadians. Canada created the Northwest Mounted Police in 1873 (who became the Royal Northwest Mounted Police in 1904), and the Royal Canadian Mounted Police (RCMP) in 1920 (a result of the merger of the RNWMP and the Dominion Police, founded in 1868) for the explicit purpose of clearing the land

Fort Pitt, an HBC post on the North Saskatchewan River, 1884. Left to right: Thomas Trueman Quinn, Indian Agent; Inspector Francis Jeffries Dickens, nwmp; James Keith Simpson, son of Sir George Simpson, the Governor of the hbc; Frederick Stanley Simpson, HBC clerk; and Angus McKay, HBC Post Manager. (Reprinted with permission from Library and Archives Canada.)

Coqualeetza Residential School in Sardis, BC, opened in 1886 and closed in 1940. (Reprinted with permission from UBC Museum of Anthropology, Jean Telfer fonds, Archives Image.)

of Indigenous peoples. All aspects of Indigenous life, including use of alcohol and other drugs (the use, sale or trade of which Indigenous peoples were solely criminalized), were subject to deep surveillance by these various colonial forces.

One of the most insidious and violent systems was the residential school system. Established as early as the 1600s, it was not until 1883 that the federal government formally authorized Indian residential schools. Indigenous children were forcibly taken from their families and sent to government-funded, mostly Christian-run, residential schools across Canada until 1996. Depending on the era, the region and the administration and staff, Indigenous experiences of residential schools are diverse. However, at these schools thousands of children died, were neglected and starved, were physically and sexually abused, and were experimented on. They were denied their families and the freedom to speak their own language or practice their cultural and spiritual beliefs. Christian morality was enforced at the schools, where white supremacy, Christianity, Western morality and sobriety were oftentimes violently enforced, an institutionalized, racialized template for citizenship for Indigenous peoples.

THE INDIAN ACT

Throughout the early colonization period, Indigenous peoples continued their plant medicine practices, but white colonizers would seek to suppress Indigenous knowledge and criminalize healers. Colonization included laws and policies that stole traditional lands and resources and banned Indigenous self-governance, languages and knowledge. Early colonial laws that applied to "Indians" (for example, Nova Scotia prohibited the sale of alcohol to "Indians" in 1829) were consolidated in the Indian Act of 1876. The Act applied to the provinces (then Ontario, Quebec and the Maritimes), the Northwest Territories (now Manitoba, Saskatchewan, Alberta, Nunvut and Yukon) and the Territory of Keewatin (now eastern Manitoba and northwest Ontario, also created by Canadian law in 1876) and all "status" Indians. All members of First Nations that signed a treaty with the Crown are referred to as "status Indians" and members of those nations that have not signed a treaty with the Crown are labelled "non-status" by the Act. The Act granted the federal government of Canada the power to regulate all aspects of status Indians, including but not limited to land, governance, identity, spiritual and cultural practices and education. The Act also regulated what plant drugs, including alcohol, that status Indians consumed. As we will see, the prohibition of alcohol and opiates intersect with one another, not only in relation to the banning of these substances, but in relation to ideas about white supremacy, Christianity, intoxication, sobriety, morality, punishment and citizenship.

The Indian Act was amended in 1880 by the government of Canada to prohibit and to criminalize Indigenous healers and healing ceremonies, including the use of medicinal plants (whether consumed orally or topically or burned). Therefore, not only were healers criminalized, but people receiving Indigenous medicine were also subject to prison time. For example, ceremonies such as the sun dance and the potlatch were criminalized under the Indian Act. The importance and centrality of potlatch among Indigenous peoples of the northwest coast is described by Gitksan and Wet'suwet'en Chiefs, as "one and the same time political, legal, economic, social, spiritual, ceremonial and educational."[11]

Prior to colonization, as noted above, alcohol was not part of the lives of Indigenous peoples — they did not produce or consume alcohol recreationally. Traders, missionaries, the military and white settlers introduced Indigenous peoples to alcohol and opiate-based medicines. Yet, colonizers not only banned Indigenous healing practices, but they also enacted legislation to ban Indigenous peoples from consuming, selling and trading alcohol (outside of medicinal use). Canada's first federal drug law was imposed for over a century on status Indians, while those labelled non-status and people who were non-Indigenous were exempt.

There is evidence that some Indigenous nations supported alcohol prohibition. For example, 1876 Treaty No. 6 between the Queen and the "Plain and Wood Cree Indians and other tribes of Indians," includes a provision stating that "within the boundaries of Indian reserves … no intoxicating liquor shall be allowed to be introduced or sold, and all laws now in force, or hereafter to be enacted to preserve Her Indian subjects inhabiting the reserves … from the evil influence of the use of intoxicating liquors, shall be strictly enforced."[12] However, official support by Indigenous nations for alcohol prohibition can also be understood within the larger context of colonial violence, including loss of land and sovereignty, the extermination of animals, small pox epidemics, the trade in ammunition and arms by non-Indigenous people to Indigenous peoples, the negative impact of the fur trade and governance granted to the HBC and North West Company by colonizers and language and translation barriers. Treaty No. 6, possibly inadvertently, supports provisions banning alcohol set out in the Indian Act of 1876. The consequences of the Act, including harsh penalties, would not yet be fully realized. As well, the Indian Act banned opium and opium-based preparations and imposed severe penalties on those who used them.

BANNING OPIATES

Earlier colonial laws banning the trade and sale of alcohol to Indigenous peoples labelled status Indian were consolidated into the Indian Act in 1876 under Prime Minister John A. Macdonald, Canada's first prime minister. Whereas earlier legislation banned only alcohol, the Indian Act included other intoxicants, such as opium. Significantly, the Act also banned "intoxication," making it "lawful for any constable, without process of law, to arrest an Indian or non-treaty Indian whom he may find in a state of intoxication" to be locked up until sober and then brought before a judge to be sentenced.[13] Keep in mind that at this time opium and alcohol were legally and readily available to and consumed by white settlers. As the Indian Act of 1876 stated the matter:

> The term "intoxicants" means and includes all spirits, strong waters, spirituous liquors, wines, or fermented or compounded liquors or intoxicating drink of any kind whatsoever, and any intoxicating liquor or fluid, as also opium and any preparation thereof, whether liquid or solid, and any other intoxicating drug or substance, and tobacco or tea mixed or compounded or impregnated with opium or with other intoxicating drugs, spirits or substances, and whether the same or any of them be liquid or solid.[14]

Penalties were harsh for any status Indian making, selling or in possession of any intoxicant for non-medical use. Under the Indian Act, if a status Indian was discovered intoxicated or in possession of an intoxicant, a fine or jail term was also imposed if the person refused to confess from whom they bought or traded the intoxicant. Indian agents and informers were rewarded for surveilling infractions of the Act — they received half of the imposed fine. The Indian Act is a repressive colonial tool that continues to assert control over the lives of Indigenous peoples and nations in Canada. For over a century, this race-based colonial policy related to alleged intoxication led to the social control, arrest and imprisonment of thousands of Indigenous people.

Notice of the Indian Act's Intoxicating Fluid law posted on telegraph pole in Bella Coola, BC. (Photo by Harlan I. Smith, 1923, reprinted with permission from Canadian Museum of History.)

A DIFFERENT DRUG POLICY FOR WHITE SETTLERS

To be clear, alcohol (beer and distilled beverages such as rum and brandy) was popular as a food, beverage and medicine for white traders and settlers in pre-industrial colonial Canada. It was also an important trade commodity. In New France and later British North America, alcohol was brewed and consumed in homes, as well as in workplaces and later in taverns. In pre-industrialized New France and British North America, alcohol was provided daily to workers and soldiers, while settlements established public taverns for both locals and travelers. Although women went to taverns once they were established, it was predominantly a male space. The public tavern also became an important social and political space.

White settlers drank heavily in relation to contemporary standards, but there was no federal legislation in the eighteenth or early nineteenth centuries prohibiting the possession, production or sale of alcohol, nor of alcohol or opium intoxication. Although HBC workers might be fined or even imprisoned for disorderly or criminal conduct while inebriated, there was little public condemnation. There were few legal impediments to drinking or using opiates in Canada. Yet political, cultural, economic and social changes took place as Canada and other Western nations industrialized that were accompanied by changed norms around alcohol and opiate consumption.

By the 1820s, more organized campaigns to drink moderately or to abstain altogether began to emerge in North America. At first, only distilled alcohol was disapproved of, but eventually, beer, cider and wine were portrayed as evil. Alcohol was banned from the workplace by the late 1800s and sobriety was espoused by local Christian organizations and later larger organizations, such as the Daughters of Temperance and later the Canadian Temperance League (1889). White women were prominent in the temperance movement (although not in its leadership), seeing alcohol consumption as evil and sobriety as a moral im-

A temperance movement cartoon from the BC *Saturday Sunset* newspaper. Partial alcohol prohibition came into effect in BC on October 1, 1917, and was in place until 1921. (Reprinted with permission from Royal BC Museum.)

perative for white Christian citizenship. From the mid-1800s on, alcohol would no longer be deemed as integral to Canadian life. So, alcohol production, sales and consumption were regulated and increasingly took place in taverns and licensed venues. Newly appointed police forces were established in towns and cities, and laws were enacted to ban public drunkenness and disorderly conduct. However, legal prohibition of alcohol was not considered plausible for white settlers in the 1800s. In contrast, informed by Christian white supremacist, racial colonial and eugenics ideology, only Indigenous peoples, who were negatively depicted as uncivilized heathens by the colonial government, would be subject to federal law prohibiting alcohol sale, trade and consumption and opiate consumption and intoxication. Sobriety was federally enforced upon Indigenous peoples labelled status Indians. It was not until 1908 that opium for non-medical use was criminalized for non-Indigenous people, and not until World War I that federal alcohol prohibition would be enacted for all people. But, only for a brief time.

White supremacy, Christianity, racial violence and the criminalization of alcohol and non-medical opiates for status Indians, as well as the suppression of local Indigenous knowledge and plant medicines, were integral to colonialism. In Canada, Indigenous knowledge never disappeared, but it was negatively impacted. In the later part of the twentieth century, many repressive colonial laws and policies related to language and healing practices were repealed. Diverse Indigenous nations continue to build on medicinal knowledge and healing practices and recognize traditional healers. The First Nations Health Authority in BC makes clear that Indigenous cultural knowledge and traditional health practices and medicines continue to be essential to Indigenous wellbeing.

Yet, as we will see, white supremacy and colonialism are ongoing, and remain reflected in contemporary drug policy in Canada. Where there had once been no distinction between medical and non-medical use of plant drugs, the Indian Act banning status Indians from consuming alcohol and non-medical opiates initiated a framework of racialized categories between moral and immoral people, good and bad drugs, legal and illegal drug use. These notions, along with the adoption of criminal justice and punishment and fear of the other, was established to achieve and maintain white supremacy and citizenship, Christianity, sobriety and morality. These ideas, central to colonial power, were about to be directed at another group of people, framed as foreign outsiders to the white Christian nation.

END NOTES

1. See Turner, 2014; Whitlock, 2020
2. Culpeper, 1824, p. 229
3. Hodgson, 1999, p. 13
4. International Narcotics Control Board, 2020
5. See Dalrymple, 2019
6. Department of Pensions and National Health, 1936, p. 126; Department of National Health and Welfare, 1956, p. 37
7. Department of Pensions and National Health, 1936, p. 126
8. Thobani, 2021, 83
9. Thobani, 2021, 83; Million, 2013
10. Simons, 1986, p. vi
11. Delgamuukw v. BC, [1991] 3 W.W.R. 97 (BCSC.C.)
12. Government of Canada, 2021b
13. Venne and Hunge, 1981, ch. 18
14. Venne and Hunge, 1981, ch. 18

3

The Racialized Other and the Opium Act

The Early 1900s

Heroin would not exist without the poppy plant and opium. Following the isolation of morphine from opium, in 1874 Charles Alder Wright synthesized diacetylmorphine. As mentioned earlier, diacetylmorphine is a semisynthetic drug derived from the compound morphine with the addition of acetic acid.[1] In 1898 Frederick Bayer and Company marketed diacetylmorphine and branded it as "heroin." Heroin was successfully promoted as a pain reliever and cough suppressant, superior to morphine because a smaller dose was needed for the same effect. Bayer placed advertisements for heroin in prestigious medical journals and retail mail-order catalogues distributed in Canada by Eaton's and Simpson.[2] Heroin was never as popular as opi-

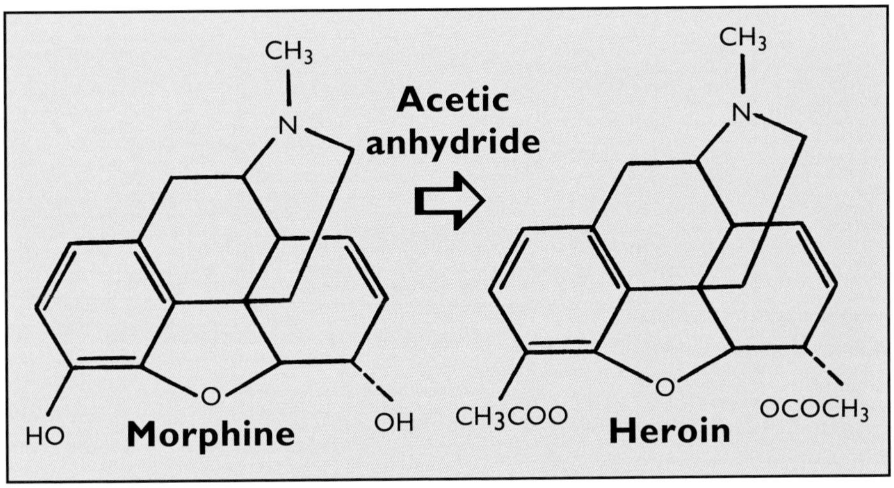

Synthesis of heroin from morphine.

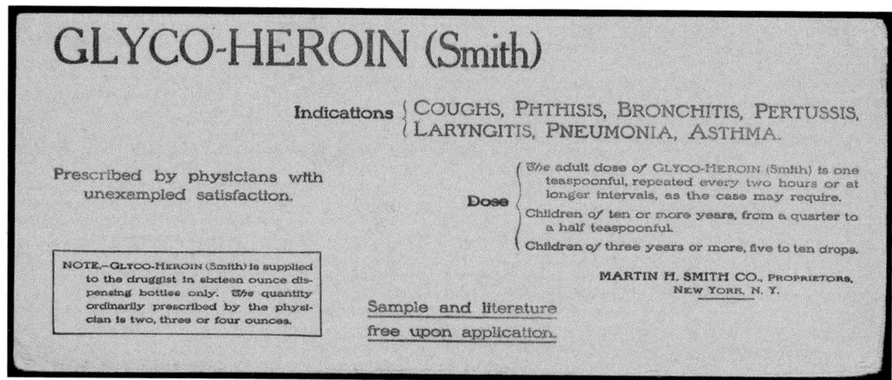

A heroin product for children and adults manufactured and sold by the Martin H. Smith Company as remedy for coughs, phthisis, bronchitis, pertussis, laryngitis, pneumonia and asthma, 1905–1915. (Reprinted with permission from Wellcome Library, London.)

um-based medicines or morphine, possibly because in the early 1900s it was most often advertised for respiratory problems rather than wider applications like opium and opium-based medicines.

Uses of opium, morphine and heroin were rarely associated with deviant or criminal activities prior to criminalization.[3] Although it was recognized early on that some people developed a "habit" after continuous use of a narcotic, most people did not. The benefits of opium-based remedies outweighed their drawbacks, and they became an essential medicine for most families due to poverty, unsanitary housing and work environments and a lack of healthcare. However, ideas about plant medicines and drug use began to change due to shifts in social and political thought and as new drugs were discovered by chemists and made more available to consumers.

People who used opium were not stigmatized, discriminated against nor criminalized. Rather, people from all walks of life used opium and written accounts are diverse. Contrary to popular thought today, a habit was not seen as lifelong; rather it was seen as situational and, more often than not, time specific. However, some early theories in the 1700s and 1800s about drug use were rooted in ideas about morally weak-willed people tempted or compelled by a drug.

Following the discovery of morphine, another innovation changed the way people consumed drugs. The syringe was invented in the mid-

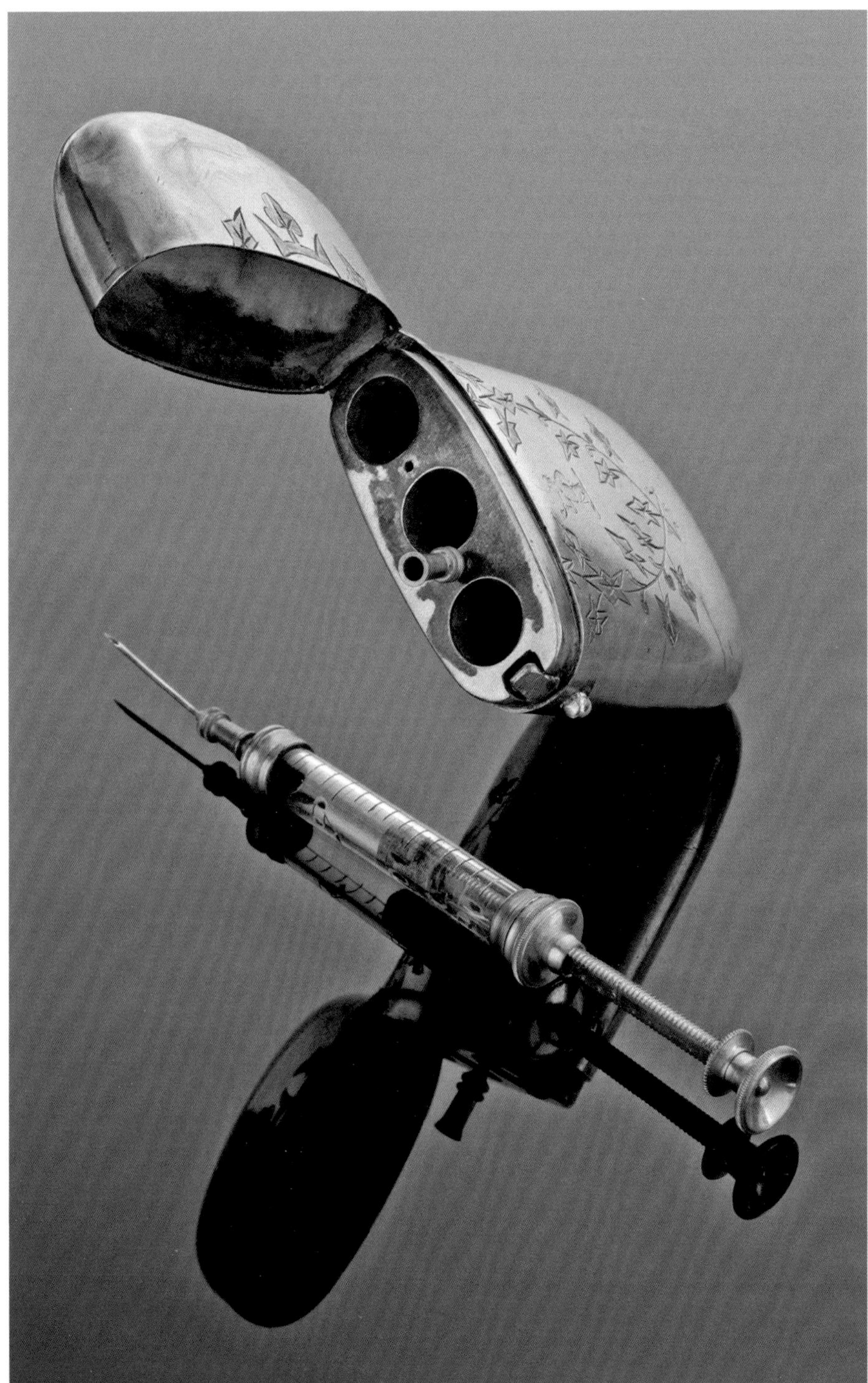

Hypodermic syringe with spare needle and decorated metal case, circa mid-1800s.
(Science Museum, London, reprinted with permission from Wellcome Library.)

1800s. Now refined drugs such as morphine could be injected rather than consumed orally. When drugs are injected, their effect is felt more quickly than when a drug is consumed orally. Whereas raw opium cannot be injected, refined drugs like morphine, heroin and cocaine can. The syringe is now an important and familiar medical tool. However, where, by whom and for what reason the syringe is employed determines whether it is seen as health affirming (good) or destructive (bad). For example, a syringe in a medical setting held by a nurse or doctor is almost always viewed as health affirming. In contrast, a person in lay clothing injecting themselves is viewed as deviant and destructive; add the backdrop of a dirty alleyway and that person is viewed as a public menace.

After Canada's first narcotics laws came into effect in the early 1900s — resulting in the closure of opium dens and less access to legal sources of opium — morphine and heroin, much easier and less bulky to smuggle, began to replace opium on the newly generated illegal market. The syringe, rather than the opium pipe, was employed now by some people consuming these drugs. Over time, outside of a medical setting, the syringe came to symbolize illegal heroin use and a life of degradation.

GOOD DRUGS OR BAD?

Opium, tobacco and alcohol were part of the social fabric of Western nations in the 1800s and early 1900s. However, whether a drug is considered good or bad is determined by social, cultural and political ideas and context in a particular historical era. Colonial power, Christian moral reformers, fear about "new drugs," who is thought to be using a drug and panic about a drug being sold cheaply and thus being more accessible can inform the negative construction of a drug. Distilled alcohol in the 1700s and crack cocaine in the 1980s were considered bad for some or all of these reasons. All of these social and cultural factors inform which drugs are constructed as good or which as bad in a specific era. This is all despite and outside the actual properties and popularity of a drug. Some mood-altering drugs have never been universally accepted, even when popular and widely consumed. For centuries in Western nations, alcohol was used as a medicine and a tonic, and beer was considered nutritious and safer than (contaminated) water in some places. Alcohol consumption was also seen as pleasurable. Yet, some Christian Western nations criminalized alcohol and some Muslim-led nations continue to have bans on alcohol today. Even in nations that historically accepted alcohol use, Christian temperance reformers in the 1700s and onward sought to ban some forms of alcohol, especially hard liquor (distilled alcohol).

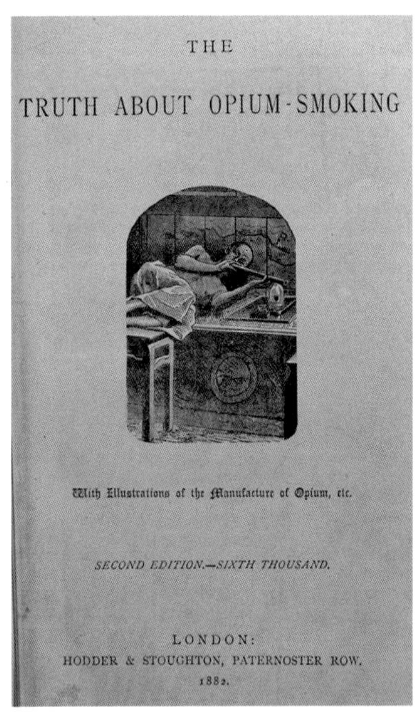

Published in 1882, *The Truth About Opium Smoking*, 2nd edition, sought to convince the public that smoking opium was bad. (Reprinted with permission from Wellcome Library, London.)

Colonization was accompanied by white missionaries from Western nations who set out in the late 1700s to "civilize" and convert non-Christian people throughout China and the British Empire, including what is now known as Canada. The adoption of the protestant ethic of sobriety and self-control as the template of white Christian middle-class

Anti-opium pills used in 1904–1905. In the late 1700s, leading US temperance advocate and physician Benjamin Rush listed opium preparations as a substitute for consuming distilled alcohol (such as brandy or gin) for some ailments.[5] (Reprinted with permission from Wellcome Library, London.)

respectability and the Christian missionary movement's dedication to temperance coalesced in the mid-1800s, advancing the idea that opium, especially in smoking form, was evil. Even moderate use was considered impossible. The anti-opiate movement, together with members of the temperance movement, sought the prohibition of smoking opium and did not call for a ban of opium-based patent medicines and remedies that were popular at the time.[4] Numerous publications were printed by moral reformers weighing in on the pros and cons of the opium trade and opium smoking.

CONFESSIONS

OF AN

ENGLISH OPIUM-EATER.

To weep afresh a long since cancell'd woe,
And moan the expense of many a vanish'd sight.
SHAKSPEARE'S *Sonnets*.

SECOND EDITION.

LONDON:
PRINTED FOR TAYLOR AND HESSEY, FLEET STREET.
1823.

Confessions of an *English Opium-Eater*, 2nd edition (1823) by Thomas De Quincy. De Quincy does not represent the majority of opium users at that time; rather, his book details his excessive and regular use over time. (Reprinted with permission from British Library, public domain.)

Notions about heroin use today draw from early temperance and anti-opium doctrine that demonized some drugs and advocated for sobriety and self-control as the template of white Christian moral citizenship. However, societal views about specific drugs are not static and, in fact, often change. Similarly, assumptions or ideas about drug use can change. Drug consumption is a highly contested arena. Claims about what entails problematic drug use are disputed, as are solutions to what is deemed problematic use. In the 1700s and 1800s, people who used drugs habitually or were thought to consume drugs too often were oftentimes deemed morally weak or, at the least, as having a "habit." However, in the mid-1800s, the field of "addiction" came into being and doctors constructed drug addiction, or narcotic addiction, as their domain. Doctors set about reporting symptoms of addiction and attempted to distinguish and define non-medical and medical use of drugs. Opium eating was popularized by authors such as Thomas De Quincy in his book *Confessions of an English Opium-Eater*, published serially in 1821, which documents his excessive use of the drug, and periods when he abstained or used moderately. Later editions of De Quincy's book included much more sensationalist book covers than the original. However, in Canada and other Western nations, heroin and other opioids used in pill and liquid forms were not constituted as a social problem as they are today.

CANADA AND NARCOTIC PROHIBITION

As discussed in Chapter Two, in 1876 a provision in the Indian Act prohibited "intoxication" for those labeled status Indians, as well the consumption, possession, sale, trade or production of alcohol or opium for non-medical use. They were also prohibited from being "intoxicated." Although it appears that most arrests under this provision in the Act were related to alcohol, non-medical use of opium was also prohibited. It took another fifty-six years for the non-medical use of opium to be prohibited in Canada for non-Indigenous people.

Joined by Christian temperance advocates, the anti-opiate movement and other moral reformers, a push for the global regulation of opium grew. In the early 1900s, moral reformers expanded their surveillance of Chinese men in Canada, increasingly depicting them as foreign culprits who took jobs away from white workers and who smoked and sold opium to moral white men and woman, leading them into a life of degradation.[6] Canada was imagined as a white Christian nation by settlers. Indigenous peoples and other racialized people were constructed as others, outsiders to the nation. Disenfranchised and subject to systemic discrimination and legal and social barriers, Chinese Canadians were not granted the same rights as white Canadians. For Chinese Canadians who had worked and died on the national railway, further discriminatory legislation was enacted. For example, a head tax was applied to people from China immigrating to Canada, they were denied the vote and restrictions were put in place on where they could live and work after the completion of the national railway in 1885. To be clear, Indigenous, Japanese and other racialized people were also discriminated against at this time, yet only Chinese immigrants were subject to the head tax and Chinese men were soon to be depicted by white Christian colonizers as evil opium smokers.

Chinese workers on the Canadian Pacific Railway, 1884. (Reprinted with permission from Royal BC Museum.)

Chinese workers laying track on the Canadian Pacific Railway, between 1880 and 1885. (Reprinted with permission from Royal BC Museum.)

Following an economic slump in BC, racist tropes and white supremacist propaganda surged as workers and politicians wrongly blamed Chinese Canadians for taking jobs away from white people. News coverage from the late 1800s to the early 1900s called for a white BC, including white supremacist ideology and imagery alongside anti-immigrant discourse and imagery about vilified racialized people. In 1907, two weeks after a political illustration was printed in the newly formed Vancouver-based, *BC Saturday Sunset* newspaper, the Canadian Anti-Asiatic Exclusion League in Vancouver, with help from local white politicians and labour unions, organized a parade and rally in downtown Vancouver.

"Keep Orientals out." *BC Saturday Sunset* newspaper, August 24, 1907. (*BC Saturday Sunset*)

On September 7, 1907, the anti-Asian rally turned into a riot. Chinese and Japanese people were physically threatened, and homes and businesses were destroyed by white rally-goers. Following the anti-Asian race riot calling for a "white only" BC and Canada, Mackenzie King (deputy minister of the Department of Labour at that time and later prime minister), came to Vancouver to assess damages. At that time King also met with three members of the Anti-Opium League who sought to suppress the "evil opium." It is well reported that a few days after meeting with the representative of the Anti-Opium League, King declared that he was intent on banning opium production in the Dominion, stating: "We will get some good out of this riot yet." King became the architect of Canada's first drug law (outside of the Indian Act), recommending to Parliament in his 1908 report, "The Need for the Suppression of the Opium Traffic in Canada," that drug control be enacted to stem the "evil opium" to preserve the morality of the white

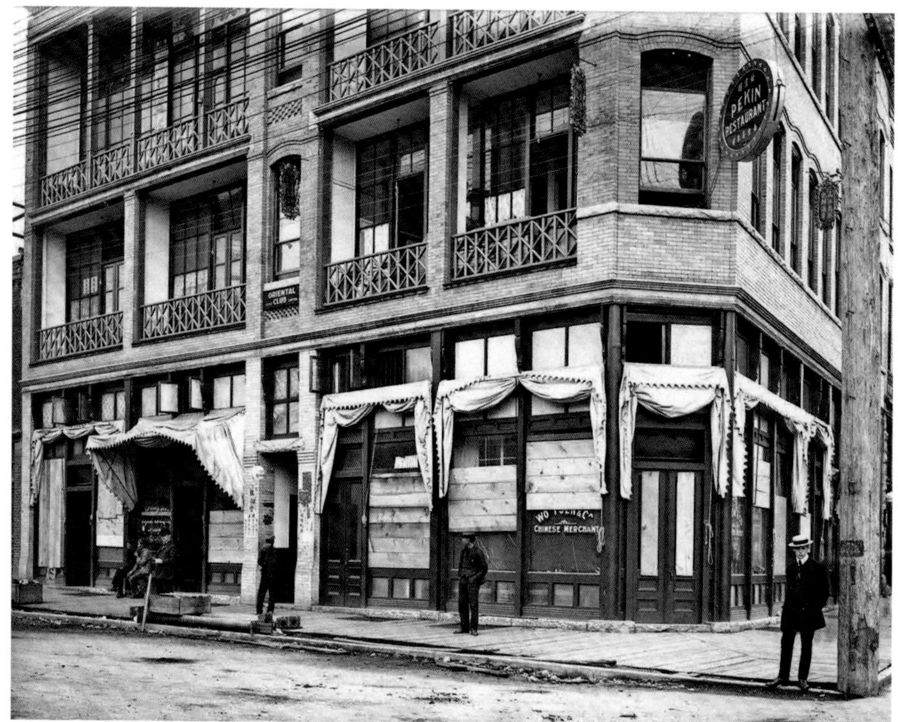

Damage by white supremacist rioters to Chinese businesses and homes on September 7, 1907, in Chinatown, Vancouver, BC. (Reprinted with permission from Vancouver Public Library.)

Christian nation. The short report includes only nine pages to lay out the issue and the evidence supporting prohibition.

King argued for the criminalization of smoking opium by drawing on a letter by the Chinese Anti-Opium League, anecdotal narratives by individuals and the media and a short, biased history of steps taken by other nations to stop the use of opium and trafficking. King failed to note in his report that Chinese people in Canada smoked opium for medicinal purposes, for pain relief and to relax. There are no official statistics, however, given that most Chinese men in the Vancouver area worked long grueling hours at low-paying jobs as labourers, servants and cooks, it is likely that most of those men who smoked opium did so in moderation. Ignoring these factors, King framed smoking opium and opium dens as evil.

Prime Minister Mackenzie King outside his house, no date. (Reprinted with permission from Library and Archives Canada.)

Drawing from a Vancouver news article that chronicled the down-

Awful Effects of Opium Habit
Vancouver Daily Province, June 1908

In the police court this morning, while Vancouver lay in the beauty and brightness of early sunshine, there emerged into the light, ugly and horrible evidence of the dire influence which the opium traffic is exercising among the ranks of British Columbia womanhood. May Edwards, pretty and young, has been found in a Chinese den ... Much the sadder of the cases, however, was that of Belle Walker. A terrible record of the effects of indulgence in opium was written upon her appearance this morning. She was found by the police in an opium den. She had been there for three weeks. Magistrate Williams sent her to prison for six months.[8]

fall of white "womanhood" in opium dens, King used the supposed degradation of moral white women at the hands of Chinese men to support anti-opium legislation.[7]

King was determined to "wholly eradicate this evil and its baneful effects." To do so, he included stories about opium-intoxicated Chinese Canadians, the corruption of white women and the threat to the white moral Christian nation.[9] King claimed:

> I was told by one of the leading physicians of Vancouver that he has been shocked at the number of cases of women addicted to the habit which have come to his notice in the regular course of his practice during the past year. As for the Chinese, the casual visitor to their quarter of the city may see them in numbers at any hour of the night or day indulging in and under the influence of this drug.[10]

King's report contributed to racialized and gendered ideas about smoking opium, opium dens and the people who use, produce and sell opium. White supremacy, racial stereotyping of Chinese Canadians, defending the moral "manhood of a nation" against demonized foreigners and the evils of smoking opium were central themes in King's report advocating for drug control. Canada's first federal narcotic law, the 1908 Opium Act, was passed with little debate in Parliament. It prohibited the importation, sale and manufacture of crude and powder opium for non-medical purposes. It did not prohibit non-medical possession or opium intoxication as the Indian Act did.

During this era, patent medicines were popular in Canada and other Western nations. Doctors were expensive and not available in many rural areas of Canada, so many people relied on home remedies and patent medicines to care for their health. However, due to fears generated by emerging Canadian medical and pharmaceutical associations about patent medicines (also driven by their fear of lost revenue), in the same year that the Opium Act was passed, the Proprietary or Patent Medicine Act was enacted. Patent medicines often sensationalized the healing qualities of its medicines. Some claims were even fraudulent, such as advertising that a product cured baldness. Some patent medicines included alcohol, opiates and/or herbs, although consumers were not always aware of the contents or the potency of the medicines that they bought. The 1908 Proprietary or Patent Medicine Act required that all medicines be registered and include a list and quantity of each ingredient. The Act banned the use of cocaine and large quantities of alcohol as ingredients. Heroin was not banned as long as the patent medicine was registered and the drug was included as an ingredient on the label. To be clear, there is no indication that Canadians used heroin extensively in any form (whether prescribed by a doctor or in a patent medicine) at that time. Violation of the Opium Act included steep fines of up to $1,000 and up to three years prison time. Violations of the Proprietary or Patent Medicine Act were more lenient, with fines for infractions from $50 to $100. White Canadians were much more likely to use patent medicines that contained opium than to smoke opium. And whereas opium factories and opium dens were closed down, patient medicine producers were able to continue selling their products.[11] It was not until 1919 that opium or its derivatives were prohibited in patent medicines. Yet, interestingly, heroin was not banned then and continued to be included as a legal ingredient in the 1927 Proprietary or Patent Medicine Act.

International events also influenced domestic drug control. In 1909, the US-led International Opium Commission met in Shanghai, China, and later in The Hague in 1912 to stem the opium trade in non-Western nations.[12] Right from its inception, international and domestic drug policy has been shaped by white supremacy and racial colonialism. Mackenzie King took an active role in promoting a punitive drug control system domestically and internationally in order to free people "from a bondage which is worse than slavery."[13] King claimed Canada was invited to the International Opium Commission in 1909 (the first step to international drug control) due to the passing of the Opium Act in 1908, which he had recommended.[14] He also boasted that the US acknowledged Canada's lead on narcotic control and sought to emulate it in their drug legislation.[15] In 1912, the first international drug control treaty was crafted in The Hague, with representatives from many nations, including the US, Germany, the UK, Canada and China. The delegates focused on, among other concerns, consideration of the prohibition of opium smoking, the regulation of raw opium and a ban on non-medical/scientific trade in opium. It took about ten years for the treaty to be ratified by member states. The treaty is recognized today as the framework for centralized international drug control, taken up by the League of Nations and later the United Nations.

Historians have shown that Canada's first narcotic laws were race-based, directed at Chinese Canadians and fuelled by class and gender tensions.[16] White supremacist discourse shaped ideas about plant-based drugs and the people associated with them. A media-fueled cocaine drug scare contributed to the enactment of the 1911 Opium and Drug Act (an expansion of the earlier Act) criminalizing non-medical and non-scientific use of substances in the opiate and cocaine families, including morphine and its salts and compounds. Significantly, the offence of possession was added to the Act and doctors were legally

Broken Blossoms (1919) depicted white moral women being corrupted by foreign, evil racialized men. (Reprinted with permission from Photofest.)

banned from prescribing drugs for non-medical purposes, such as prescribing maintenance doses to known "addicts."

The "Red Scare" following the Russian Revolution in 1917 and the Winnipeg General Strike in 1919 fueled many repressive laws and police action in Canada. The lead-up to World War I (1914 to 1918) and the War Measures Act contributed to mounting fears about foreigners, many of whom, such as labour activists, strikers and narcotic users, were labelled enemy aliens. Illegal narcotic use was linked to outsiders that threatened the nation.

During WWI, narcotic convictions rose from 684 in 1913 to 1,044 in 1914 and 1,375 in 1915. Overwhelmingly, most convictions were for men of Chinese heritage. A number of fictional films also began to depict dangerous aliens threatening the white nation, especially Chinese and Black men enticing white women and men into opium dens and a life of degradation.

CONVICTIONS FOR DRUG OFFENCES IN CANADA

1912 - **342**	1918 - **915**	1924 - **997**
1913 - **684**	1919 - **1195**	1925 - **835**
1914 - **1044**	1920 - **1797**	1926 - **743**
1915 - **1375**	1921 - **1864**	1927 - **491**
1916 - **1165**	1922 - **1858**	1928 - **608**
1917 - **790**	1923 - **1297**	1929 - **616**

Drug categories and offences are different today than they were in the early 1900s. Given the racialized origins of our early narcotic laws, law enforcement profiled Chinese Canadians and opium smoking. Most convictions under the narcotic laws were for opium smoking-related offences: possession of opium, smoking opium, frequenting opium dens and possession of pipes and paraphernalia. Only a small percentage of drug convictions were for selling and distributing or importing drugs. For example, in British Columbia in 1929 there were a total of 295 drug convictions; of those, only thirty were for selling and

Royal North West Mounted Police recruits on parade, Regina, SK, 1904–1925. (Photo by Albertype Company, reprinted with permission from Library and Archives Canada.)

distributing and one was for importing. Although law enforcement and politicians claim that harsher drug laws and bigger budgets are necessary to catch major traffickers, this has never been the case. From the start, most drug offences in Canada have been for possession.

The national Royal North West Mounted Police was established in 1873 as a semi-military force that advanced colonial and economic interests of the government, including white settlement and the social

Oakalla Prison Farm, 1914. (Reprinted with permission from Heritage Burnaby.)

control of Indigenous peoples. It was not until 1920 that the federal RCMP replaced the Royal North West Mounted Police. The RCMP reorganized and became the enforcers of federal statutes across the country, including drug control, the Indian Act, the Immigration Act and national security. In 1921, the Opium and Narcotic Drugs Branch (renamed the Narcotic Division in 1925) centralized drug control in Canada. Local police also contributed to drug control, setting up special narcotic divisions that profiled Chinese and Black men. In Burnaby, BC, the Oakalla Prison Farm opened its doors in 1912. It was soon to become infamous for its large prison population of people who used illegal heroin and, later, for its experimental mandatory drug treatment units established in the 1950s.

> The Oakalla Prison Farm opened in 1912 and was hailed as the most modern facility of its kind. Initially designed to hold 150 men and fifty women, by the 1950s the population was well over one thousand. A working farm, the prison had its own dairy, vegetable gardens and livestock. From the beginning, the location of Oakalla on 185 acres of scenic land next to Burnaby's Deer Lake was the source of contention, with residents petitioning the government to relocate the prison. By 1979 it was decided to close the farm and sixty-four acres of land were transferred to Burnaby for inclusion on the Deer Lake Park. In 1991, Oakalla closed forever, and the buildings were demolished to make way for a new residential housing development and an expansion of the park.[17]

Early narcotic laws worked to criminalize racialized people. Punishment was advanced as the tool to curtail drug use. Soon, drug control and police surveillance expanded to encompass poor and working-class people who used heroin or other narcotics.

END NOTES

1. Sneader, 1998
2. Boyd, 2017
3. Terry and Pellens, 1970 [1928]; Ministry of Health, 1926
4. Boyd, 2017
5. Musto, 2002, p. 36
6. King, 1908; Murphy, 1922c
7. King, 1908, pp. 6, 8
8. King, 1908, pp. 7–8
9. King, 1908, p. 5
10. King, 1908, p. 8
11. see Green, 1986
12. Bewley-Taylor and Jelsma, 2012
13. King, 1908, p. 9
14. *Hansard*, 1920, p. 559
15. *Globe and Mail*, 1909; *Hansard*, 1920, Vol. 1, p. 559
16. N. Boyd, 1984; Boyd, 2017; Comack, 1986; Giffin, Endicott and Lambert, 1991
17. Heritage Burnaby, 2022

4
Heroin Criminalization

The 1920s and 30s

EMILY MURPHY AND THE DRUG SCARE

In the 1920s, most Canadians had little knowledge about non-medical drug use, such as the recreational use of heroin. Moral reformer and white supremacist Emily Murphy sought to educate Canadians in a 1920 four-article series in the widely read national *Maclean's Magazine,* and in her 1922 book, *The Black Candle*. Murphy was from a prominent upper-class family in Ontario. She was a renowned journalist and the first female magistrate in Canada and the British Empire.[1] She was also a celebrated fiction writer under the pseudonym Janey Canuck. Murphy became a temperance leader, eugenics supporter, suffragist and legal reformer. Her racist and white supremacist stances are especially evident in her writing about drug control.

In her book and articles about drugs, Murphy drew mostly on anecdotal stories from law enforcement and criminal justice professionals in the US and, to a lesser degree, Canada. Murphy linked opium, heroin, cocaine and cannabis use to sexual immorality, broken homes and a rapid descent into addiction, insanity, criminality and murder. Murphy associated the "drug menace" to the "lowest classes" of Chinese and Black men, whom she depicted as preying on innocent white women and men. She was especially fearful of women's descent into sexual immorality, abandonment of the home and the "mixing of the races." Similar to Mackenzie King's 1908 report, "The Need for the

Photo from Emily Murphy's *The Black Candle* (1922).

Suppression of the Opium Traffic in Canada," the destruction of the white Christian nation was a prominent theme in her articles and her book.[2]

Emily Murphy argued for more drugs to be added to the drug schedule and warned about the perils of opium, morphine, heroin, cocaine and cannabis use. Murphy conflated supposed harms stemming from the use of any drugs; therefore, the supposed harms that she assigned to smoking opium were attributed to heroin, morphine, and cannabis too. Murphy feared that white women and men would be in close proximity to racialized men in opium dens. She argued that women's impending downfall was swift, stating: "When she acquires the habit, she does not know what lies before her; later she does not care."[3] Murphy and other moral reformers continued to racialize and sexualize drug use and sought to alert people to the seemingly destructive and compelling addictive nature of opium, heroin, cocaine and cannabis. In her book, she claimed that heroin is a "hell-dust" and "the powder of destruction," and that "heroin orgies" are "frequent because the drug gives ... a 'thrill' sooner than opium."[4]

In order to support drug prohibition, Murphy and law enforcement also reinforced the idea of the dope fiend and evil foreign drug deal-

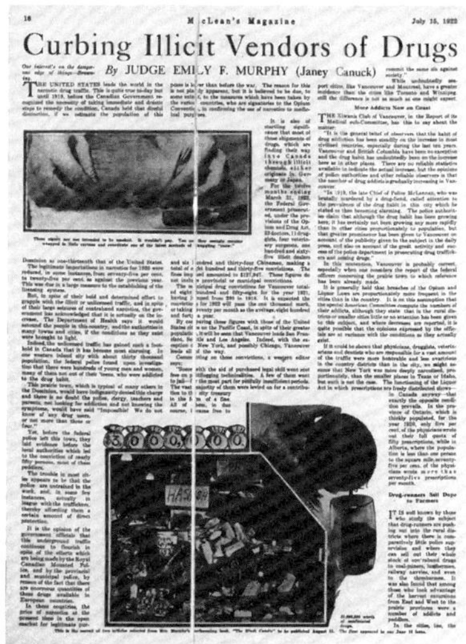

Maclean's Magazine July 15, 1922

Curbing Illicit Vendors of Drugs

By JUDGE EMILY F. MURPHY (Janey Canuck)

The first of the four-part series on the evils of drug use by Emily Murphy, "'Joy Shots' that Lead to Hell," published June 1922 in *Maclean's Magazine.*

ers as new and dangerous enemies. Although, foreign-run opium dens and drug traffickers were demonized following the enactment of the 1908 Opium Act, in the 1920s, Emily Murphy, law enforcement and the media further cemented the idea of non-Christian racialized men and foreign traffickers as a threat to the white nation. In her writing, she claimed that Chinatowns in Canada control drug trafficking and that Montreal and Vancouver are home to the largest drug rings, working with "yellow men and black men" and the lowest of white men and women.[5] To stem the destruction of white Christian Canada, Murphy recommended more police powers, deportation and harsher sentences.

Murphy also rejected setting up narcotic clinics where legal doses of narcotics are provided to people thought to be "addicted." Instead, she argued that in order to cure the "addict," they must abstain from drugs and be subject to the "most rigid regulations" in government institutions. She suggested that institutions could be located on islands to prevent patients from leaving and to ensure no drugs are brought in. Murphy further warned that "drug addicts" have an aversion to fresh air, so treatment in rural environments could present some problems.[6]

JUNE 15th, 1922

MACLEAN'S

J. VERNON McKENZIE, Editor J. L. RUTLEDGE, Associate Editor

"Joy Shots" That Lead to Hell

Menace of Opium, Morphine and Other Narcotics Not Yet Checked in Canada.

By JUDGE EMILY F. MURPHY

One of the four-part series by Emily Murphy published in *Maclean's Magazine*, "Curbing Illicit Vendors of Drugs," July 1922.

POPULAR CULTURE

News media and popular culture contribute to our ideas about heroin and other narcotics, race, addiction and criminal justice solutions. Filmmakers, especially in the US, produced a number of cautionary films in the 1920s and 1930s that contributed to ideas about drugs and the people who used and sold them. Canada had little participation in the film industry in the 1920s and 30s. At that time, outside of French-Canadian films, audiences relied on US and British films for entertainment. Narcotic control was championed in many US films, which is not surprising given that the US led efforts for punitive drug control at home and internationally. In these early films, white, moral women were often depicted as being lured into drug use by unscrupulous racialized dealers. Degradation and the abandonment of family and

Human Wreckage (1923), an early US propagandist film about the dangers of narcotics and addiction in which white, moral women were framed as being lured into drug use. (Reprinted with permission from Photofest.)

home were central themes. The US film, *Human Wreckage*, produced in 1923, depicts the dangers of narcotics. Outside of moral reformers like Emily Murphy, the Narcotic Division and the RCMP, Canadians learned about dangerous dealers, illegal drugs and the people who used them through film and other media.

THE NARCOTIC DRUGS BRANCH

Because heroin is in the opiate family, it was essentially covered in the 1911 Opium and Drug Act. However, it was not until 1923 that heroin (a brand name), codeine and cannabis were added to the Canadian Drug Schedule. As well, in 1929, heroin was finally categorized separately from other drugs in the annual report *Statistics of Criminal and Other Offences*, previously included in the category "drugs not specified." Furthermore, in 1932 the word "heroin" was replaced by the term diacetylmorphine in the Schedule. To better enforce the new drug laws, the principle of "innocent until proven guilty" was abandoned in the 1920s and the onus of proof was on the accused (reverse onus). Individuals charged with possession of heroin (or opium or cocaine) would have to prove that they were innocent. At that time, the provision of reverse onus was usually applied only to serious crimes like treason.

In Canada, the federal Opium and Narcotic Drugs Branch was set up in 1921, followed by the Narcotic Division in 1925, centralizing punitive drug control. The RCMP was given the task of enforcing the new federal laws across the country. Interestingly, this mandate saved the RCMP from being disbanded for violence and corruption.[7] Local (municipal and provincial) police and specialized narcotic squads within the RCMP worked with the Narcotic Division, which in turn worked with the US Bureau of Narcotics, to coordinate narcotic control between Canada and the US.[8] The RCMP took up the enforcement of narcotic control with zeal, publishing public annual reports about the menace of illegal drugs threatening the nation, the force's successes and the need for harsher laws. The RCMP's first report, released in 1922, states:

> An immense amount of work has been entailed by the inception of a vigorous attempt to check the illicit traffic in narcotic drugs, conducted in close relations with the Department of Health. It is over a dozen years since the Opium and Narcotic Drug Act of 1908 was passed; since then international conventions have rendered the work of suppression mandatory. I regret to be obliged to state that despite the efforts put forth, the use of these pernicious drugs is increasing instead of diminishing.[9]

Rather than consider that criminalization was a flawed policy that may have contributed to increased illegal drug use and, unsurprisingly, given that drug enforcement saved the RCMP from being disbanded, the RCMP recommended doubling down: harsher laws, more police powers, bigger budgets and increased surveillance.

1921, Canada, Opium and Narcotic Drug Act
Total Convictions: 1,864

1923, Canada, Opium and Narcotic Drug Act
Total Convictions: 1,297 (73 percent for possession)[10]

Report of the Royal Canadian Mounted Police, 1922

Our investigators have uncovered a volume of addiction which seriously threatens our national life, and apart from the aspect of public policy, numerous most distressing and lamentable cases have come to our notice. The dreadful suffering endured by those addicted to the drugs, the ruin of lives which should be useful, do not constitute the whole of the evil, for the ills spread to their families. Children rob their parents, husbands and fathers plunge their families into misery, wives ruin their husbands. In one case which came to our knowledge, a man discovered that his wife had been an addict for months, that she had disposed of much of his property and had sold his clothes to procure the poison. To show the personal degradation suffered by many of our fellow-citizens, a young white girl recently was discovered in a Chinese resort so destitute as to be all but naked, her body pitted with the marks of the hypodermic needle. These are but single instances which could be multiplied from our records.[11]

CRIMINAL ADDICTS

In Canada, as noted, drug control was constructed to be primarily a criminal justice issue. Over the decades, more drugs were added to the drug schedule, and police powers and budgets expanded. From the 1920s on, the concept of the "criminal addict" was employed by law enforcement, the Division of Narcotics, some health professionals and Canadian policymakers to justify punitive regulation.[12] No publicly funded drug treatment services or narcotic clinics were set up (similar to clinics set up in some regions of the US following prohibition), and doctors were banned from providing maintenance doses of narcotics to their patients. Although the 1911 Opium and Drugs Act had already prohibited the non-medical prescribing of narcotics, the 1929 Opium and Narcotic Drug Act strengthened and clarified the offence to read: "physicians forbidden to prescribe narcotic drugs to addicts." In Canada, the Narcotic Division Chief (along with the RCMP and special prosecutors) rallied for tougher laws and new offences, including stronger laws to restrict which drugs could be prescribed by doctors and to whom.

Early drug criminalization targeted Chinese-Canadian men, opium smoking and dens, as evidenced by convictions. 60 percent of all drug convictions in 1922 were of Chinese Canadians. The criminalization and deportations of Chinese Canadians continued in the following years. Drug offence categories included: possession, transportation, sale or distribution of drugs; importing drugs without a license; smoking opium; frequenting an opium den; possession of an opium pipe or other paraphernalia; and obtaining drugs from more than one physician.

In the late 1920s, the Narcotic Division Chief, Colonel Sharman, also strove to prohibit legal heroin from being produced and prescribed for medical purposes in and outside Canada, a US-led effort that he supported. The stereotype of the "dope fiend" was taken up by US prohibitionists to support both domestic and international drug control. It was purported that heroin was stronger than morphine (a known fact), and that people who used heroin were brutal recidivist criminals with no moral conscious. They were successful in their efforts and in 1924 heroin was banned in the US for medical use.

At the international level, US delegates continued to press for global prohibition of heroin for medical use. Other nations were not aligned, however, because they believed that heroin had distinct advantages over other opiates for some medical conditions. Unable at that time to criminalize medical use of heroin in Canada, the Narcotic Division called for harsher penalties for illegal use. Yet, in 1929, there were only twelve heroin possession charges recorded and the following year only eight. Despite this, there was tremendous effort by the Narcotic Division to stamp out these "criminal addicts." Although records of drug charges can only provide a partial picture, it appears that the illegal heroin user in Canada was blown out of proportion along with other people categorized as "criminal addicts."

Deporting Chinese Drug Users
Government of Canada, Annual Report, 1931

During ... [1929] 69 aliens, convicted of narcotic offences, involving six months imprisonment or more, were deported, 59 were Chinese. This brings the total of deportations, since the inauguration of the present policy in 1922, to 731, of whom 578 were Chinese.[13]

CRIMINAL ADDICTS ARE INTRODUCED AGAIN

In 1930, the Canadian federal Department of Pensions and National Health clarified different categories of "addicts." Three class-biased categories of drug users were constructed: 1) "criminal addicts," an underworld type "who spends a considerable time of his life in jail"; 2) "medical addicts," who were classified as people who became "addicted" while receiving medical treatment, some of whom were terminally ill; and 3) "professional addicts," who were classified as members of the medical profession (doctors, nurses, and others) who obtained and used narcotics through their work.[14] The Narcotic Division was sympathetic to middle- and upper-class medical and professional "addicts," stating, "In such instances there can be nothing but sympathy for the persons concerned."[15]

Labelling people "criminal addicts" implied that poor and working-class people addicted to illegal drugs were criminals first and "addicts" second. The criminal addict was depicted as the "most dangerous menace to society."[16] It was claimed that (people labelled) criminal addicts would continue to be criminals even if they had some kind of treatment, such as abstinence-based residential treatment or narcotic clinics (what we now refer to as heroin-assisted treatment or drug substitution programs). At this time, publicly funded drug treatment was not set up in Canada, nor were drug substitution programs. It was well understood by politicians and law enforcement that those labelled criminal addicts would spend most of their life in jail or prison for narcotic or other related charges. Even the expanding illegal market (which flourished after prohibition), selling over-priced drugs, did not deter staunch prohibitionists. In fact, the federal government argued in 1930, that "the price of opium has increased three hundred percent in the past three years on the Pacific coast, which is in itself a good indication of the progress made."[17]

Government of Canada, Annual Report, 1931

The criminal addict, who spends a considerable proportion of his life in jail, either on narcotic charges or for other crimes usually committed in an endeavor to maintain a supply of the drug of addiction at the high prices now obtaining.[18]

Although the illegal narcotic situation was thought to be markedly improved by 1934, in 1936 the federal government's Department of Pensions and National Health records showed that most of the convictions were essentially for using drugs (possession, smoking opium, frequenting opium dens). Moreover, BC was an outlier; over half of drug convictions nationally were in BC.[19] By 1935, a total of 1,173 people had been deported following their prison time for a drug conviction. The vast majority — 82 percent — were Chinese Canadians (961 people).[20]

Critical scholars have long explored how racism and white supremacy are embedded in ideologies, texts, government documents and popular culture. These ideas are often made concrete by policy and legislation, such as the Indian Act and drug law and policy. Canada, particularly the province of BC, was envisioned as "white" by settlers. All other people were disenfranchised and seen as inferior, lawless and a threat to the white nation. The violence of colonization and white supremacy is oftentimes invisible. On the surface, the intersection of race and law, including drug laws, was often not well known. During the early drug criminalization periods, drug scares in Canada (and the US) linked specific drugs to racialized groups, but also included "white" outsiders such as the poor and the working class.

By the late 1930s, following deportations, arrests and convictions of Chinese men and the closure of most opium dens, law enforcement shifted their focus to also include poor and working-class white people. For example, 1935 was the first time since federal narcotic control was enacted that more white people were convicted of a drug offence

TABLE 1C—CONVICTIONS—YEARS ENDED SEPTEMBER 30, 1925—1944. NATURE OF OFFENCE

Year	Possession of Drugs	Selling Distributing or Offering	Importing Without a Licence	Transporting Drugs Without a Licence	Cultivating, Gathering or Producing Opium Poppies	Smoking Opium	Frequenting Opium Den	Possession of Pipes, etc.	Section 13 Sending Drugs by Mail	Obtaining Drugs from More Than One Physician	Professional Cases Under Sections 5, 6 and 9 of the Act and Section 8 of Regulations	Not Defined	Total
1925	381	55	...	...	...	139	208	...	...	...	...	52	(a)835
1926	302	33	...	...	...	149	180	...	...	...	...	79	(b)743
1927	163	37	...	...	...	85	81	...	...	...	...	124	(c)490
1928	183	52	...	...	...	69	69	28	...	...	...	29	430
1929	150	38	1	...	...	103	223	47	...	1	4	...	567
1930	166	32	2	...	...	47	155	46	...	5	5	...	458
1931	173	45	3	...	...	42	39	24	...	...	7	...	333
1932	138	45	4	2	...	71	51	25	...	3	1	...	340
1933	111	39	5	...	...	17	42	24	...	1	1	...	240
1934	101	29	4	...	...	8	44	26	...	10	4	...	226
1935	91	18	5	3	...	11	18	13	...	2	2	...	163
1936	113	16	2	...	...	9	14	11	...	1	2	...	168
1937	123	26	...	...	...	...	5	5	...	1	1	...	161
1938	127	21	1	2	...	1	3	4	...	1	2	...	162
1939	148	26	...	3	...	1	1	1	...	1	2	...	183
1940	137	28	...	3	4*	...	1	2	...	6	1	...	182
1941	139	9	...	2	...	...	2	...	1	4	8	...	165
1942	73	9	...	1	...	...	...	1	...	1	13	...	98
1943	87	7	1	1	...	3	...	...	...	1	4	...	104
1944	140	9	...	...	...	...	...	12	...	1	3	...	165

* These 4 convictions were the first obtained for this charge under the legislation which became effective August 1, 1938. There were other previous and subsequent convictions involving Poppy Heads or Poppy Head Brew obtained under charges of possession, selling and transporting as follows, which are included in the foregoing figures under such classifications.—

DEPARTMENT OF NATIONAL HEALTH AND WELFARE

Convictions under the Opium and Narcotic Drug Act for 1925 to 1935 were essentially for various forms of using drugs. However, convictions for smoking opium and frequenting an opium den decreased greatly from the mid-1930s on. (Table IC, p. 125. Ottawa: Dept. of Pensions and National Health, 1936.)

TABLE 1A—DETAILS OF CONVICTIONS UNDER THE OPIUM AND NARCOTIC DRUG ACT FOR THE JUDICIAL YEAR ENDED SEPTEMBER 30, 1935

Province	Nature of Offence									Total
	Possession of drugs	Selling or distributing	Importing without a licence	Transporting drugs	Smoking Opium	Frequenting Opium den	Possession of pipes, etc.	Obtaining drugs from more than one physician	Professional cases under Secs. 5, 6 and 9	
Prince Edward Island										
Nova Scotia										
New Brunswick										
Quebec	10	10	1	2		2	1			26
Ontario	13	1				2	1		1	18
Manitoba	11	3								14
Saskatchewan	1			1						2
Alberta	16	2							1	19
British Columbia	40	2	4		11	14	11	2		84
Total	91	18	5	3	11	18	13	2	2	163

Most of the convictions under the Opium and Narcotic Drug Act were in BC. (Table IA, p. 124. Ottawa: Department of Pensions and National Health, 1936).

than Chinese Canadians (of a total of 165 convictions, 98 people were categorized by the RCMP as white and 64 people as Chinese).[21]

Convictions for frequenting an opium den and smoking opium decreased greatly from the mid-1930s to 1940s. Rather than opium smoking, heroin was now the new menace. Discourse about the evils of smoking opium was easily and conveniently applied to illegal heroin, heroin users and traffickers. As early as the 1920s, Emily Murphy and other moral reformers who championed drug control condemned racialized others, and conflated drugs such as opium, cocaine, heroin and cannabis as interchangeable menaces that threatened white Canada.[22] By the 1930s, poor, white, illegal-narcotics users were increasingly othered and deemed to be a danger to the nation.

POPULAR CULTURE AND DRUGS

The 1934 US film *Narcotic* depicted the shift from opium to heroin use. In the film, heroin is linked to moral degradation, addiction, criminality and death — familiar representations in contemporary films that fetishize heroin and depict heroin users as degraded "junkies."[23]

These films sought to "educate" US and Canadian movie goers about the dangers of drug use. They also championed criminal justice control as a means to stop the drug menace from spreading.

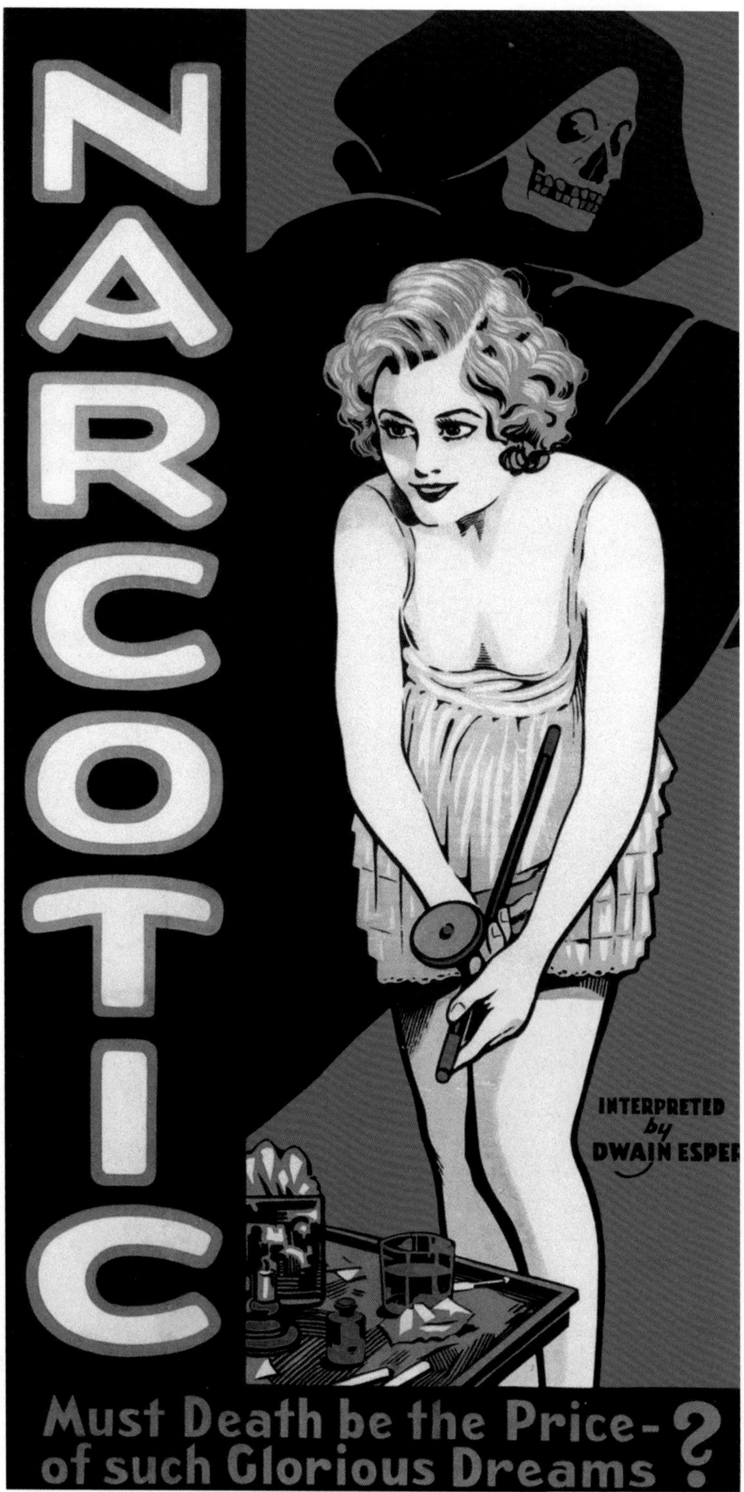

In the 1934 film, *Narcotic,* drug users were flirting with death, the inevitable outcome of using heroin. (Reprinted with permission from Photofest.)

WHO FRAMES DRUG CONTROL?

Colonel Charles Henry Ludovic Sharman was to become one of the most influential framers of the criminal addict and of punitive Canadian and international drug control policy. He held the position of Division Chief of the Narcotic Division in Canada from 1927 to 1946. He was also a member of the UN Advisory Committee on Traffic in Opium and Other Dangerous Drugs from 1934 to 1954. His punitive framework of drug control dominated for decades to come. Constituting the illegal heroin user as the other resulted in the enactment of harsh drug laws and policing of heroin users in Canada. Between 1930 and 1946, 73 percent of all drug convictions under the Narcotic Act led to imprisonment.[24]

Canada's early drug laws were race-based, targeting first Indigenous peoples (alcohol and opium prohibition) and then Chinese and Black men (narcotic prohibition). White supremacy, the social basis of these laws, draws from several influences, including Christian patriarchal social and political theories, eugenics, law and popular culture, to construct some groups of people as non-human and inferior. However, representation of and ideas about race are neither fixed nor stable, and not all white people are equal. Specific hierarchies exist in specific historical times and, in some of those times, some "white" people — such as women, the poor and those labelled non-heteronormative (LGBTQ+), insane, disabled or criminal — have also been constructed as inferior or subhuman. While racial colonialism and systemic racism are not the same as the subjection of these other vilified groups, white supremacy is fluid even as it is hierarchal. Through social and political theory, law, representation and popular culture, various groups of people are depicted as other in specific historical eras. In Canada, poor, white, illegal heroin users have been othered and represented as "criminal addicts." Yet, racism and white supremacy are central to Canada's drug prohibition history. The trope of foreign (that is, non-white) traffickers and producers threatening the white moral nation would become equally central to punitive drug policy in the coming decades.

Reefer Madness (1936), a morality film that depicts white, moral youth transformed into crazed and murderous fiends after smoking cannabis. (Reprinted with permission from Photofest.)

END NOTES

1. Jackel, 2008
2. Murphy, 1920, 1922c
3. Murphy, 1922c, p. 30
4. Murphy, 1922c, pp. 359, 360
5. Murphy, 1922c, p. 170
6. Murphy, 1922c, pp. 375–376
7. Hewitt, 2006
8. Josie, 1947, p. 31
9. RCMP, 1922, p. 13
10. Giffen, Endicott and Lambert, 1991, pp. 593, 599
11. RCMP, 1922, pp. 13,14
12. CBC, 1960; Price, 1946; Stevenson, 1955
13. Canada, 1931, pp. 72–73
14. Canada, 1931, p. 70; MacLeod, 1963; Stevenson et al., 1956, p. 375
15. Canada, 1931, p. 69
16. Canada, 1931, p. 70
17. Canada, 1931, p. 77
18. Canada, 1931, p. 70.
19. Department of Pensions and National Health, 1936
20. Department of Pensions and National Health, 1936, p. 129, Table 5
21. Dominion Bureau of Statistics, 1936, p. xvi
22. Murphy, 1922c
23. Boyd, 2008
24. Josie, 1947, p. 27

5

Curing the Heroin User with Jail

The 1940s and 50s

DRUG LAW ENFORCEMENT IN THE 1940S AND 50S

In the 1940s, drugs sold on the illegal market were adulterated and purity had decreased substantially. Although overdose is always a risk when buying on the illegal market, there was not an overdose crisis at the time. Law enforcement, however, reported that "criminal narcotic addicts" were buying less on the illegal market and were increasingly going to doctors, and more than one doctor at a time, to obtain legal prescriptions. Drugs like heroin, morphine and cocaine could still be prescribed by doctors for therapeutic use and prescriptions were filled at pharmacies; however, legal supplies of codeine and heroin were rationed during the war years.

Canada was dependent on legally imported drugs for domestic medical use. The federal Department of National Health and Welfare provided annual records of all narcotics imported for legal sale (as required by international drug treaties). Raw opium and its preparations, morphine, heroin and other drugs were imported and distributed through a licensing system regulated by the Narcotic Control Division and the Department of National Health and Welfare. The Division kept a record of all narcotic sales and the RCMP inspected the records of pharmacies across Canada. Narcotic supplies in hospitals were also audited. Any person suspected of using narcotics illegally was inter-

TABLE 24
(Narcotic Control Division)

ESTIMATED CONSUMPTION OF THE MAIN NARCOTICS
For period 1940–1949 Inclusive

Unit of Weight—Ounce, Pure Drug

Year	Raw Opium	Medicinal Opium and Preparations	Morphine	Heroin	Cocaine	Ethylmorphine	Dilaudide	Papaverine	Codeine	Demerol
1940	6,173	5,538	3,527	882	1,446	498	13	168	18,143	....
1941	2,363	10,123	3,527	1,023	1,376	528	14	56	19,964	....
1942	3,562	8,219	3,704	917	1,517	615	14	138	21,983	....
1943	3,704	5,645	4,445	811	1,623	739	12	171	21,630	....
1944	3,810	7,090	3,633	740	1,480	1,458	14	280	22,241	1,042
1945	3,175	6,314	3,351	670	1,305	691	12	381	22,809	1,102
1946	3,422	4,797	3,492	1,058	1,552	1,110	22	455	36,191	2,045
1947	3,932	4,734	3,090	881	1,390	1,107	15	715	36,484	5,894
1948	2,090	6,026	3,074	995	1,407	1,032	22	1,416	39,672	5,642
1949	2,010	3,606	2,718	898	1,197	949	16	1,359	44,443	6,852

This table shows that legal drug imports, including heroin, were necessary trade items for the health needs of people in Canada. (Department of National Health and Welfare, 1950.)

TABLE 24
(Narcotic Control Division)

ESTIMATED CONSUMPTION OF THE MAIN NARCOTICS
For period 1940–1949 Inclusive

Unit of Weight—Ounce, Pure Drug

Year	Raw Opium	Medicinal Opium and Preparations	Morphine	Heroin	Cocaine	Ethylmorphine	Dilaudide	Papaverine	Codeine	Demerol
1940	6,173	5,538	3,527	882	1,446	498	13	168	18,143	....
1941	2,363	10,123	3,527	1,023	1,376	528	14	56	19,964	....
1942	3,562	8,219	3,704	917	1,517	615	14	138	21,983	....
1943	3,704	5,645	4,445	811	1,623	739	12	171	21,630	....
1944	3,810	7,090	3,633	740	1,480	1,458	14	280	22,241	1,042
1945	3,175	6,314	3,351	670	1,305	691	12	381	22,809	1,102
1946	3,422	4,797	3,492	1,058	1,552	1,110	22	455	36,191	2,045
1947	3,932	4,734	3,090	881	1,390	1,107	15	715	36,484	5,894
1948	2,090	6,026	3,074	995	1,407	1,032	22	1,416	39,672	5,642
1949	2,010	3,606	2,718	898	1,197	949	16	1,359	44,443	6,852

In the 1940s, opium, morphine, heroin, codeine and cocaine remained essential medicines prescribed to and consumed by Canadians. (Department of National Health and Welfare, 1950.)

viewed and placed under surveillance, and a file was opened on them and maintained by the Narcotic Control Division.

Although drugs were imported into Canada for legitimate medical use, the Narcotic Control Division also continued its tight surveillance on illegal importation and use. With the introduction of the War Measures Act in 1939, the sale and consumption of codeine or any other narcotic without a prescription was expected to decrease. However, the outbreak of World War II (1939 to 1945) did not put an end to narcotic convictions. In 1940 there were 182 narcotic convictions; the largest category was for heroin, followed by opium and morphine. Narcotic convictions decreased in 1942 and 1943 (136 convictions in each year),[1] however, there was a shift in who was being convicted for drug offences. By the 1940s, Chinese Canadians no longer made up the majority of narcotic convictions; rather, white Canadians did.

Prison time for a narcotic conviction prevailed. Of the 165 narcotic convictions in 1944, 92 percent received a jail term (under two years) or penitentiary sentence (over two years), even though the majority of convictions were for possession.[2] By 1944 the Division estimated that about four thousand people across Canada had used illegal drugs — quite a small number given the population of Canada at that time. The Division also stated that morphine cases surpassed heroin cases in 1944, possibly due to the disruption of both legal and illegal sources. As was the case then and remains the case today, there are many factors that influence annual official crime statistics, including laws, resources and priorities of law enforcement, enforcement practices, police profiling of racialized and poor people and judicial sentencing. Yet, examining official statistics over time provides important information in relation to policing priorities and those criminalized.

It was during World War II that a marked shift occurred as people who used illegal drugs sought to obtain legally prescribed drugs from more than one doctor at a time (which was illegal) and, to a lesser degree, to steal narcotics from legal sources (such as a pharmacy). The RCMP, which continued to be the primary knowledge producer in Canada about heroin, continued to firmly reject narcotic or drug substitution clinics. A 1946 RCMP annual report included an article by Constable H.F. Price, titled "The Criminal Addict." Price interviewed fifty-two "addicts" who were all under arrest. He reported that the "most popular" view advanced by the people he interviewed "was of the establishment of Government operated Clinics that would provide proven addicts with their daily requirement of narcotics." The interviewees also asserted that setting up clinics would eliminate drug trafficking and, for some, petty crime to support their habit. Constable Price rejected the setting up of narcotic clinics and a medical approach and instead advocated for an "automatic life sentence" for criminal addict recidivists.[3] The idea of establishing narcotic clinics in Canada was not new, yet the Narcotic Division and the RCMP remained strongly opposed to them in the 1940s.

The Narcotic Division and law enforcement stepped up their efforts after WWII leading to 355 convictions under the Opium and Narcotic Drug Act in 1949. Of the total convictions, 94 percent were for possession. Of those, heroin made up 84 percent. 40 percent of all convictions were in BC, followed by 36 percent in Ontario.[4] [5] A year later, in 1950, 356 people were convicted of a drug offence. 95 percent of the convictions were for drug possession, and 84 percent of these were possession convictions for heroin.[6] Drug conviction data in 1949 and 1950 are not an anomaly; drug possession charges have historically made up the majority of drug convictions in Canada.

In 1954, the Department of National Health and Welfare claimed in their annual report, "As before, illicitly imported heroin is the chief, almost the only, drug of addiction in Canada. Over 90 per cent of cases involved this drug."[7] In 1954, of the 340 total drug convictions, 87 percent were for possession. Of the total drug convictions, 95 percent were for heroin convictions, and of those heroin convictions, 91 percent were for possession.[8] Heroin possession convictions continued to make up the majority of drug convictions in Canada. As well, 56 percent of all drug convictions were in BC, and 98 percent of these were for possession. Keeping in mind that most convictions in 1954 were for possession, prison sentencing was harsh. Of the total 340 convictions, 338 people convicted of a drug crime received prison time; 328 of these were for heroin. Only two cases received a fine.[9]

Responding to fears about narcotic trafficking and use, the 1955 Senate Special Committee on the Traffic in Narcotic Drugs was established. The Senate claimed that in 1955 there were a total of 3,212 "addicts" in Canada — 515 medical addicts, 333 professional addicts and 2,364 criminal addicts. The Senate report also claimed that more than half of Canada's "criminal addicts" were residing in BC.[10] Yet, given the small number of supposed "criminal addicts," it is incredulous that such an extraordinary amount of tax dollars was spent to finance the Narcotic Division, RCMP and police drug squads, bigger budgets, court proceedings and prisons in the surveillance and punishment of this small group of criminalized people.

Drug offence data at that time suggest that there was not, in fact, a heroin epidemic in Canada in the 1940s and 1950s, even though law enforcement, some politicians and the media acted as if the drug was a national menace spreading across the country. Concern about young white men being introduced to heroin contributed to fears about addiction and contagion threatening the moral white nation.[11] This had an impact: the small group of individuals, well-known to law enforcement, who used illegal heroin and other opioids, with no access to legal heroin or even publicly funded drug treatment, were subject to police profiling, and prison time was common.

OAKALLA PRISON FARM

At Oakalla Prison Farm in BC and other prisons and jails, drug withdrawal in a prison cell without support was not uncommon, given that public services were not available. If drug withdrawal was deemed serious when admitted to Oakalla, sometimes oxygen and intravenous saline and glucose were administered. In 1954, the Inspector of Gaols in BC claimed that the "percentage of drug addicts and number of inmates is still increasing," thus making the policy of segregation at Oakalla impossible.[12] Volunteer groups such as Alcoholics Anony-

BC Report of Inspector of Gaols, 1953

The Oakalla [Prison Farm] Women's Alcoholics Anonymous group holds a meeting every Sunday evening. These meetings are usually attended by over two-thirds of the girls, and it is felt that not only the alcoholics but many of the drug addicts have benefited from the philosophy of the Alcoholics Anonymous and from the personalities of the members who come out.[14]

Oakalla Women's Residence in the 1950s. (Reprinted with permission from Heritage Burnaby.)

mous (AA) visited the prison and held weekly meetings there. The AA meetings were popular in the women's unit.[13] However, change was on the horizon. Oakalla Prison Farm was soon to become the site of an experimental prison drug-treatment program.

DRUG ADDICTS IN DOCUMENTARIES AND POPULAR CULTURE

In many ways the media and popular culture also contributed to the moral panic about the heroin menace in Canada. In 1948 the National Film Board of Canada produced its first "illegal drug" film with the RCMP. *Drug Addict* was intended to "educate" professionals and the public. The realist black and white voice-over drama introduced viewers to law enforcement and psychiatric discourses about the "problem" of illegal drugs (especially heroin), racialized traffickers and addiction and proposed solutions to the "problem." The documentary was filmed in Montreal and included people who used drugs to enact scenes in the city, including injecting drugs. The film begins with scenes about opium smuggling and use. Foreign Asian men are depicted smuggling opium into Canada and smoking it.

Racialized drug traffickers checking out their illegal imports in the 1948 Canadian film *Drug Addict.* (Reprinted with permission from National Film Board of Canada.)

Smoking opium in the 1948 Canadian film *Drug Addict.* (Reprinted with permission from National Film Board of Canada.)

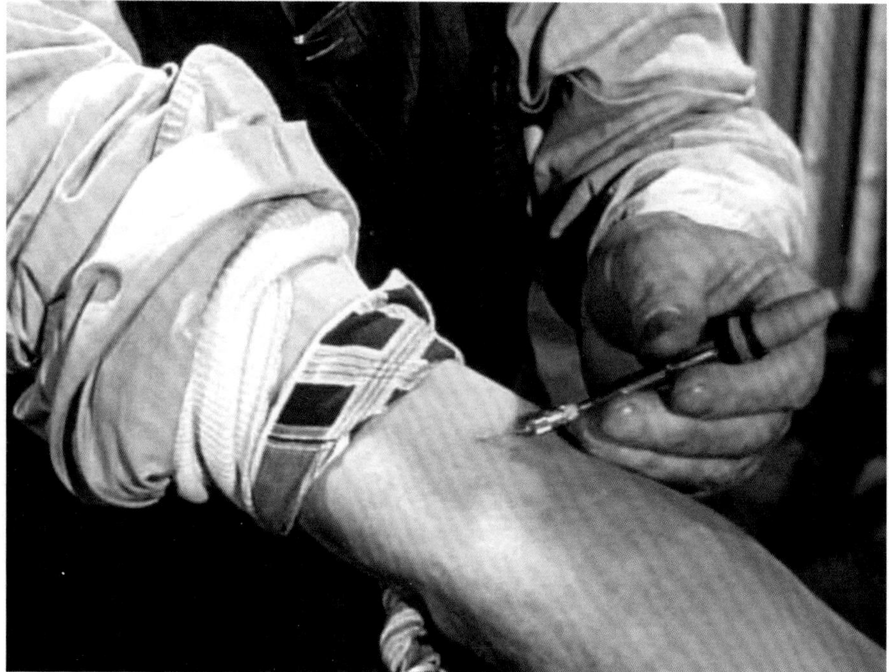

An iconic fixing scene using a homemade syringe in the 1948 Canadian film *Drug Addict*. (Reprinted with permission from National Film Board of Canada.)

The film then turns to the menace of heroin and other narcotics. It depicts a familiar close-up image of injecting with a homemade needle.

Keep in mind that publicly funded drug treatment was still not available to Canadians at this time. Nor was there publicly funded healthcare for Canadians. Private treatment was provided in some asylums, and by the mid-1950s the provinces of BC and Ontario set up compulsory abstinence-based (not drug maintenance) treatments in some prisons. The narrator of the film claims that narcotic clinics "spread addiction." Viewers were then told that psychiatry working with criminal justice can provide a solution to those new to heroin: abstinence in compulsory psychiatric units in prisons.[15]

One scene in the film shows the door to possibly a fictive Mental Health Division. Inside sits a white male doctor who speaks directly to the camera, telling the viewer that "some addicts want treatment" and others want to go on using narcotics. The scene then shifts to an older white man, who also speaks directly to the camera. He says,

> If I could procure them [drugs] at a clinic at cost price for a dollar and a half a week instead of paying $150 to $200 a week, I could get a job and avoid dodging the police and spending half my life in jail.

The camera then cuts back to the doctor who quickly discounts the elderly man's statement by claiming that narcotic clinics "spread addiction which is dangerously contagious." The doctor then notes that instead of feeding their "appetite for drugs," new psychiatric knowledge offers more promise. This body of knowledge can address the fact that "addicts" suffer from a "weakness in personality that can be corrected" and the "solution to addiction to drugs is curing the addict." The narrator states that "curing the addict" is almost impossible without professional help. That help, of course, could be easily and best provided through the introduction of compulsory treatment in prisons. As there are no such facilities in Canada, the narrator suggests that new prison wards for compulsory treatment be set up to cure the addict in the future. Thus, the film's narrative firmly rejects publicly funded drug treatment outside of prison and narcotic clinics or drug maintenance programs in Canada. The narrator then underscores his point by explaining that it is an "offence to supply habitual users drugs." The narrator is referring to the fact that in Canada it was still illegal for doctors to prescribe narcotics for maintenance purposes to any person identified as an "addict." Abstinence and sobriety were advanced as the only cure. *Drug Addict* concludes that law enforcement will always have to play a dominant role in drug control. However, contrary to drug stereotypes at that time, the documentary does claim that "very seldom" does a person who uses narcotics commit a violent crime; rather, petty crime and prison time are their fate.

A 1948 *Maclean's Magazine* article, "The Hopheads Are Ahead," played no small role in the ongoing demonization of people labelled heroin addicts. A former head of the RCMP Drug Squad in Toronto, T. Greenfield, described to reporter Frank Hamilton what needs to be done to stem narcotic addiction in Canada. In the article, Greenfield asserts that prison sentences must be harsher, and that "addicts"

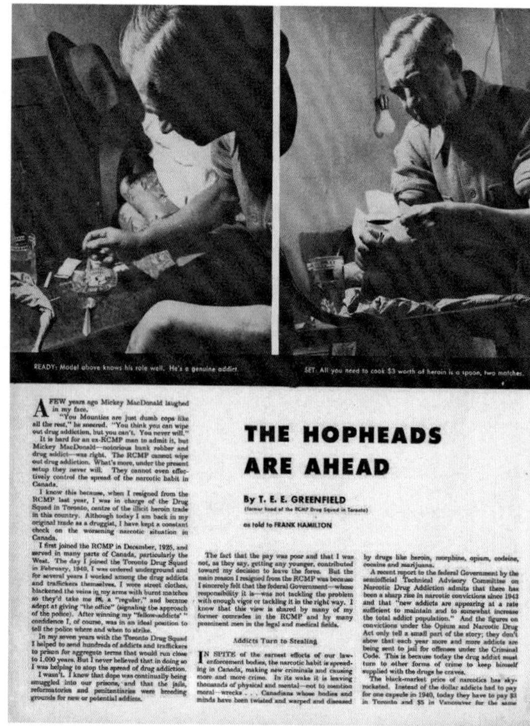

READY: Model above knows his role well. He's a genuine addict.

SET. All you need to cook $3 worth of heroin is a spoon, two matches.

THE HOPHEADS ARE AHEAD

By T. E. E. GREENFIELD
(former head of the RCMP Drug Squad in Toronto)

as told to FRANK HAMILTON

A FEW years ago Mickey MacDonald laughed in my face.

"You Mounties are just dumb cops like all the rest," he sneered. "You think you can wipe out drug addiction, but you can't. You never will."

It is hard for an ex-RCMP man to admit it, but Mickey MacDonald—notorious bank robber and drug addict—was right. The RCMP cannot wipe out drug addiction. What's more, under the present setup they never will. They cannot even effectively control the spread of the narcotic habit in Canada.

I know this because, when I resigned from the RCMP last year, I was in charge of the Drug Squad in Toronto, centre of the illicit heroin trade in this country. Although today I am back in my original trade as a druggist, I have kept a constant check on the worsening narcotic situation in Canada.

I first joined the RCMP in December, 1925, and served in many parts of Canada, particularly the West. The day I joined the Toronto Drug Squad in February, 1940, I was ordered underground and for several years I worked among the drug addicts and traffickers themselves. I wore street clothes, blackened the veins in my arms with burnt matches so they'd take me for a "regular," and became adept at giving "the office" (signaling the approach of the police). After winning my "fellow-addicts'" confidence I, of course, was in an ideal position to tell the police where and when to strike.

In my seven years with the Toronto Drug Squad I helped to send hundreds of addicts and traffickers to prison for aggregate terms that would run close to 1,000 years. But I never believed that in doing so I was helping to stop the spread of drug addiction.

I wasn't. I know that dope was continually being smuggled into our prisons, and that the jails, reformatories and penitentiaries were breeding grounds for new or potential addicts.

The fact that the pay was poor and that I was not, as they say, getting any younger, contributed toward my decision to leave the force. But the main reason I resigned from the RCMP was because I sincerely felt that the federal Government—whose responsibility it is—was not tackling the problem with enough vigor or tackling it in the right way. I know that this view is shared by many of my former comrades in the RCMP and by many prominent men in the legal and medical fields.

Addicts Turn to Stealing

IN SPITE of the earnest efforts of our law-enforcement bodies, the narcotic habit is spreading in Canada, making new criminals and causing more and more crime. In its wake it is leaving thousands of physical and mental—not to mention moral—wrecks . . . Canadians whose bodies and minds have been twisted and warped and diseased by drugs like heroin, morphine, opium, codeine, cocaine and marijuana.

A recent report to the federal Government by the semiofficial Technical Advisory Committee on Narcotic Drug Addiction admits that there has been a sharp rise in narcotic convictions since 1943 and that "new addicts are appearing at a rate sufficient to maintain and to somewhat increase the total addict population." And the figures on convictions under the Opium and Narcotic Drug Act only tell a small part of the story; they don't show that each year more and more addicts are being sent to jail for offenses under the Criminal Code. This is because today the drug addict must turn to other forms of crime to keep himself supplied with the drugs he craves.

The black-market price of narcotics has skyrocketed. Instead of the dollar addicts had to pay for one capsule in 1940, today they have to pay $3 in Toronto and $5 in Vancouver for the same

1948 *Maclean's Magazine* article, "The Hopheads Are Ahead."

and traffickers should serve their sentence "in an isolated institution (like the former Northern Ontario concentration camp in Monteith), reserved exclusively for addicts and traffickers." He goes on to state:

> Discipline in the prison would be rigidly enforced at all times and the inmates kept under strict surveillance. The prison would be of the work-camp type and two years of hard labor without one single shot of dope would, I am sure, sweat the narcotics out of their systems ... One letter a month would be allowed ... No presents or parcels of any kind would be allowed ... I think that a "no-visitors" rule would be necessary.[16]

Similarly, a 1949 news headline in the BC *Province Magazine*, "Killer of Men and Morals,"[17] made it clear the "drug addicts" were a scourge. The headline is accompanied by a drawing of a syringe and a hooded skull, exemplifying depictions of heroin during this era.

Popular books and films continued to warn Canadians of the degradation and menace of heroin use. Under the pen name William Lee, US writer William Burroughs wrote the semi-autobiographical 1953 novel, *Junkie,* which popularized the myth: "once a junkie always a junkie."

Nelson Algren's 1949 novel, *The Man with the Golden Arm,* also popularized very negative ideas about heroin use. The novel was made into a Hollywood film in 1955. Set in post-WWII Chicago, starring Frank Sinatra and Daren Mc-

Drug addicts are "killers" says Jack Stepler (*Province Magazine,* February 26, 1949).

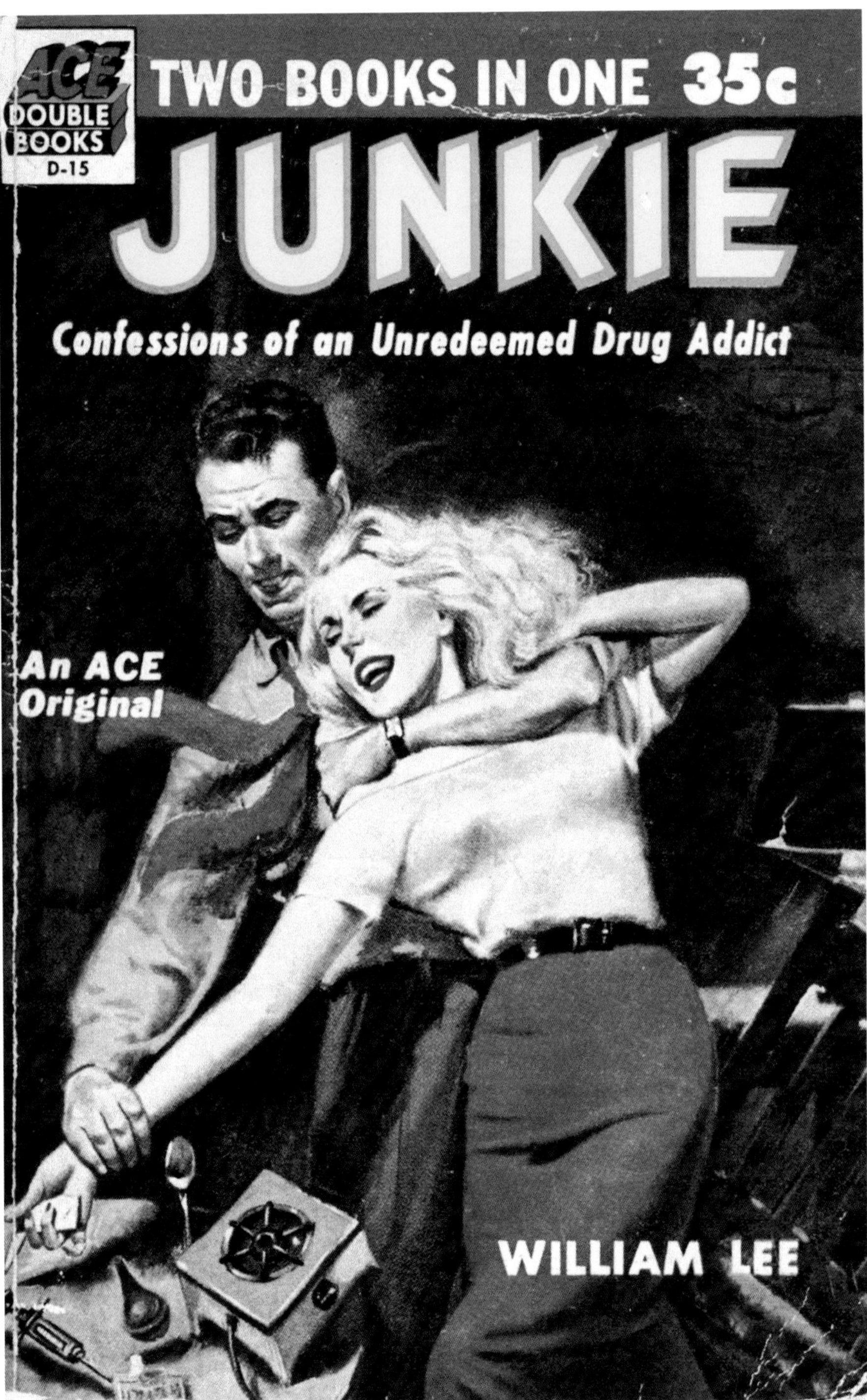

Junkie, William Burroughs' semi-autobiographical novel, paints a searing picture of heroin use. (Reprinted with permission from Photofest.)

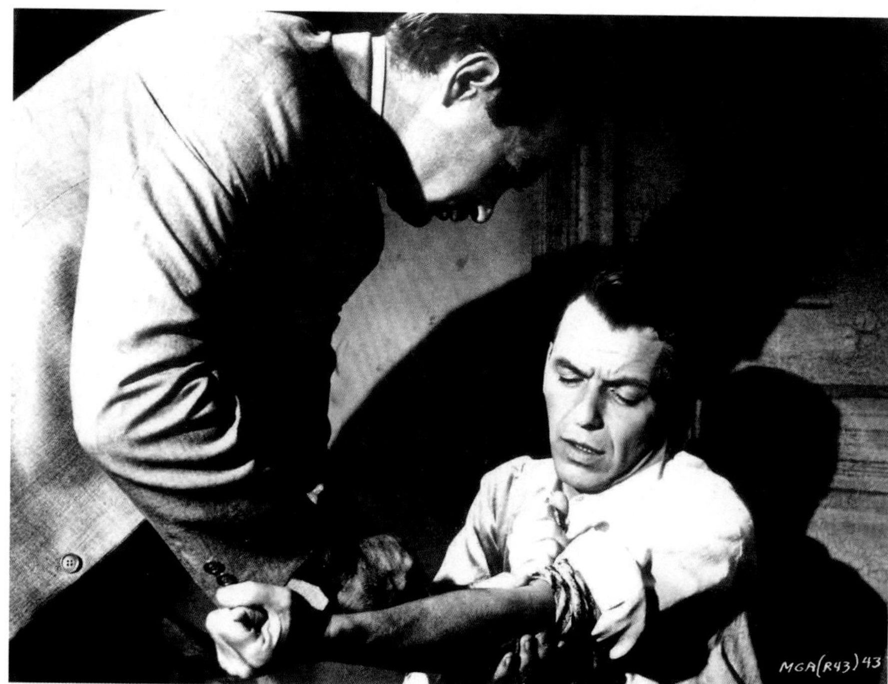

Actors Darren McGavin and Frank Sinatra ("Frankie Machine") in *The Man with the Golden Arm* (Reprinted with permission from Photofest.)

Gavin, it was directed by Otto Preminger (all of whom were movie celebrities of the era). The main character in the book, nicknamed Frankie Machine, is followed as he becomes hooked on heroin. Both the book and the film depict heroin as instantly compelling and addictive, drug withdrawal as horrific and degradation and criminal activity as inevitable. People who use heroin are depicted as cheats and liars who are willing to kill for a fix. Yet, Frankie Machine is also presented as a sympathetic character, and by the end of the film he embraces sobriety and middle-class values.

While *Junkie* and *The Man with the Golden Arm* were both produced in the US, Canadians read the books and watched the film (this was an era where Canadian popular culture had almost no English Canadian-produced fictive films). Canada's national magazine, *Maclean's*, followed in lockstep, depicting Vancouver as the "dope capital" of Canada. It's interesting to see a 1955 *Maclean's* article titled, "The Dope Craze That's Terrorizing Vancouver," accompanied by a full-page advertisement for

Captain Morgan Rum. Alongside the article's black and white photos of police, suspected drug traffickers and heroin users is a colourful ad urging readers to drink rum, a legal drug that has caused more deaths and health-related harms than heroin. Yet, the irony of the juxtaposition of the article and ad was almost certainly lost on the magazine's editors.

Captain Morgan Rum advertisement in a 1955 issue of *Maclean's Magazine*.

In the "Dope Craze" article, author McKenzie Porter claims that drug trafficking is growing in Vancouver. Referring to the "growth of the narcotic menace" in the city, he also states that the "addict" population is growing too. In large font, the heading states: "Any treatment that lets dope addicts use drugs just results in more crime." The drug used most often, the author claims, is heroin. The article ends with a quote about drug traffickers by two eminent religious men who claim: "the punishment for this offense should be death."[18]

BANNING HEROIN, REJECTING TREATMENT

Canada's drug policy on heroin from this era differs from other Western nations, including the UK where doctors retained the right to prescribe heroin to those labelled addicted. As mentioned earlier, Canadian doctors were not allowed to provide prescriptions for drug maintenance, which was considered a non-medical purpose, to people known to be "addicts." The federal Narcotic Division also kept detailed files from the 1920s to the 1970s on individuals deemed to be "addicts."[19] The files contained prosecutors' notes, drug arrests and convictions, news articles and copies of letters sent to known addicts and professionals (such as doctors, pharmacists, prosecutors). The heightened surveillance of illegal drug users led to lengthy prison sentences, especially for those

The opening of the second session of the UN Commission on Narcotic Drugs in 1947. Former Chief of the Division of Narcotic Control, Colonel C.H.L Sharman of Canada, was the Commission Chairman. (Reprinted with permission from United Nations, UN7536846.)

who were poor, working class and labelled criminal addicts.

Even though Canadian doctors could not prescribe heroin to known "addicts," they continued to prescribe heroin for therapeutic use up until the 1950s. Pharmacist records in the early 1950s show that heroin, opium and morphine were prescribed to patients.[20] However, this practice was about to end. Internationally, the World Health Organization (WHO), an agency of the United Nations, recommended in 1953 that all countries who were members of the United Nations prohibit legal importation of heroin. The WHO requested that the importation and production of diacetylmorphine (heroin) cease and that doctors and governments campaign against prescribing the drug. The WHO experts were convinced that banning legal heroin production and importation would help facilitate their quest to end illegal drug use. Canada complied on January 1, 1955. On that date, an administrative ban was put in place on the importation of heroin for medical/scientific use.[21] Canada did not produce heroin; however, licenses permitting heroin to be imported into Canada ceased to be issued, resulting in legal sources no longer being available by prescription as supplies ran out. The ban did not eliminate the illegal sale of heroin as WHO experts assumed. Following the ban in Canada, heroin could only be purchased on the illegal market at inflated prices, and the quality of the drug was unknown. In order to better control illegal heroin, an amendment to the Opium and Narcotic Drug Act was created to include trafficking in drugs and possession for the purpose of trafficking, with a maximum penalty of fourteen years for either offence. In addition, the drug schedule expanded to include new pharmaceutical preparations, including synthetic drugs that are not plant derivatives but created in a laboratory (such as methadone). Colonel Sharman, in his capacity as chairman of the United Nations' Commission on Narcotic Drugs from 1946 to 1948, pushed forward his agenda to include synthetic drugs under international drug control.

In 1948, newly criminalized synthetic narcotic drugs were brought under international control. Previous conventions covered only the natural narcotics, such as opium, morphine and cocaine, and their derivatives, such as heroin.

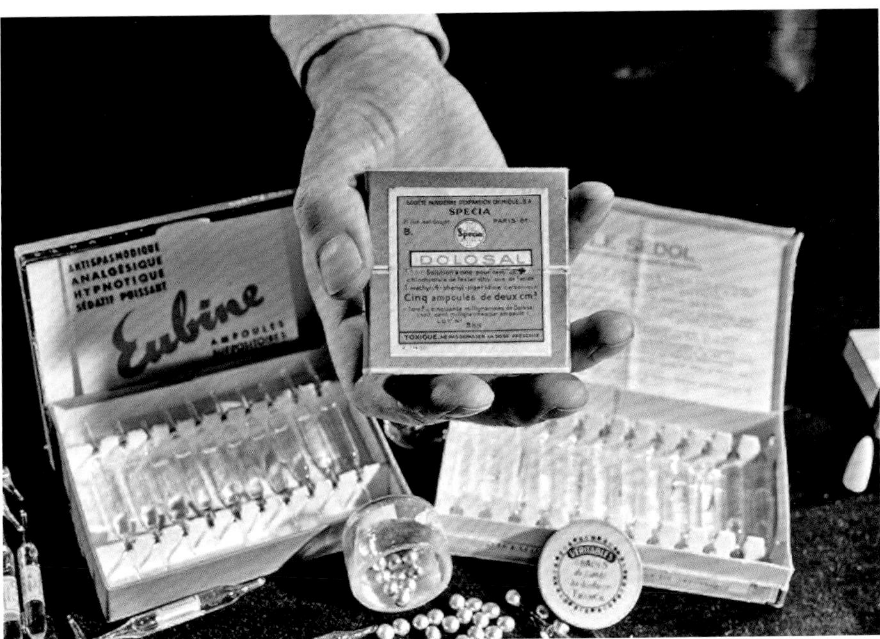

Newly criminalized synthetic narcotic drugs brought under international control in 1948. (Reprinted with permission from United Nations, UN7694352.)

FOR AND AGAINST IMPRISONING "ADDICTS"

In contrast to demands in the 1950s for increased drug control espoused by Colonel Sharman and his successor, K.C. Hossick (a former RCMP officer), in and outside of Canada, the city of Vancouver sought to change punitive drug policy, especially in relation to heroin use, due to the number of people being sent to prison for a drug possession conviction. A drug treatment movement emerged in Vancouver that included professionals such as BC MLA Ernest E. Winch. From the late 1940s on, Winch called for an end to penalties for drug possession and an end to imprisonment for drug possession charges. As well, from the late 1940s to the mid-1950s, Winch conducted research on international health and justice policies on addiction and the imprisonment of people for drug offences in BC prisons. Contrary to "criminal addict" discourse, Winch argued that most heroin users in prison did not have criminal records prior to using illegal heroin. He called for the establishment of narcotic maintenance clinics, and in 1955 he and others argued before the Senate Proceedings of the Special Committee on the Traffic of Narcotic Drugs.[22] However, Dr. George Stevenson, a vocal prohibitionist, opposed drug substitution for heroin users and advanced the criminal version of the addict to the Senate.[23] In contrast to Stevenson's unsubstantiated claims about criminal addicts, research conducted by the Canadian Department of National Health and Welfare in 1947 also concluded that people who used illegal heroin were not criminal addicts. Rather, low-level, non-violent criminal activity was directly associated with finding funds to pay for the drug on the illegal market.[24]

Vancouver's Special Committee on Narcotics also emerged in the 1950s. The diverse committee of professionals (including Ernest E. Winch) examined policies related to heroin and addiction in and outside of Canada. The committee released a report in 1952 calling for an approach to heroin use based on health rather than criminal justice. The report, *Drug Addiction in Canada: The Problem and its Solution,* is often referred to as the Ranta report after its committee chairperson, Dr. Lawrence Ranta. The Ranta report recommended that individuals convicted of narcotic possession no longer be sent to prison and that the federal government permit the provinces in Canada to set up publicly funded narcotic clinics.[25]

However, the federal government ignored all reports and calls for drug reform and the establishment of narcotic clinics.[26] The Senate Committee also ignored the contributions of 150 "addicts" imprisoned in BC's Oakalla Prison Farm who unanimously "advocated for the legalized provision of drugs."[27] Instead of listening to the voices of people imprisoned and the research, the federal government, law enforcers and moral reformers continued to perpetuate the concept of the criminal addict, vilifying people who used illegal heroin, condemning legal heroin clinics and supporting harsh drug laws and prison time as a solution rather than publicly funded drug services in the community for people using heroin.[28] The BC Inspector of Gaols repeatedly reported that the provincial prisons for both men and women were overcrowded, an "old story now"[29] he said, while the "percentage of drug addicts and the number of inmates is still increasing steadily."[30] Yet, recommendations for alternatives outside prison were ignored. Instead, prison authorities attempted to segregate "addicts" from "non-addicts" due to fears of contagion.[31]

Dr. Lawrence Ranta of the Faculty of Medicine at UBC was the chair of Vancouver's Special Committee on Narcotics. (Reprinted with permission from UBC Archives.)

In 1955 when Canada's population was just over 15 million, the now renamed Division of Narcotic Control estimated a total of 2,300 criminal addicts across the nation, most living in the Vancouver area.[32] The Division of Narcotic Control and law enforcement brutally targeted this small group of criminalized people and for those living in BC, most were sentenced to Oakalla Prison Farm. With no access to publicly funded treatment or to a legal source of heroin, a woman who used illegal heroin described life in Vancouver in the 1950s: "the addict is haunted day in, day out by the law, where the price of illegal drugs skyrockets with his need and prison is as sure as tomorrow."[33]

After the Vancouver Ranta report was released, recommending a health rather than a criminal approach and advocating the setting up of narcotic clinics, Vancouver's Special Committee on Narcotics disbanded. Another committee, the Standing Committee on the Prevention of Narcotic Addiction headed by A.R. Lord, was quickly organized to implement the recommendations of the Ranta report. A number of the contributors to the Ranta report joined the new committee. Meetings were held in Vancouver in 1952 with the new committee members, including representatives of the Minister of National Health and Welfare, the Chief of the Narcotic Control Division, the Director of the Mental Health Division and others. Establishing a pilot drug treatment and rehabilitation centre was discussed at the meetings. However, it was decided that a research project to further study narcotic use and addiction should be the first step taken. The Committee then met with representatives of the University of British Columbia (UBC) about a research project. After UBC researchers agreed to work on the project and federal funding was put in place, in 1953 the Narcotic Research Team officially began its work. The team was headed by Dr. George Stevenson (psychiatrist) and assisted by Pat Fogarty (psychiatric social worker) and Mr. Lingley (psychologist), as well as other UBC faculty and staff. Oakalla Prison Farm would become the site to conduct the research.

Dr. George H. Stevenson, Faculty of Medicine at UBC, in 1953. (Reprinted with permission from UBC Archives.)

One important caveat: the Standing Committee on the Prevention of Narcotic Addiction agreed to set aside the recommendation in the Ranta report to establish pilot narcotic clinics, in response to Dr. Stevenson's offer to first do a comprehensive study on the pros and cons of the issue to better advise the committee.[34] This would be a serious mistake and one that Canadians would pay for. In 1955, Stevenson produced a biased paper for the committee, titled "Arguments for and Against the Legal Sale of Narcotics." In it he argues that abstinence is the only cure. He discusses opium smoking in China in the 1800s and concludes that the narcotic clinics set up in the US following criminalization in the early 1900s failed. Stevenson criticizes the legal prescribing of heroin (and other narcotics) to people identified as "addicts." He claims this is "a serious debasing of the concept of 'medical treatment,' as it is the duty of physicians to treat patients in the hope of ameliorating or curing the pathological conditions."[35]

However, this simplistic view was disputed. In fact, narcotic clinics, such as the one in Shreveport, Louisiana that operated from 1919 to 1923, demonstrated that narcotic maintenance can work.[36] Doctors in the UK and at the Shreveport clinic had the evidence to support the care they advocated; these doctors understood their duty as physicians was to prevent or alleviate suffering. For the doctor who ran the Shreveport clinic, the clinic (which prescribed morphine) not only alleviated suffering, but it was helpful to other physicians and pharmacists because it prevented duplication of care. It also benefited society because it limited drug dealing, reduced harms stemming from law enforcement control and prevented overdose and "pauperizing" people (and their families) who would be forced to buy narcotics on the illegal market.[37] The Shreveport city authorities and the local police supported the clinic, but in keeping with their law enforcement efforts, the federal US Narcotic Division shut it and other clinics down. Similar to Canada, drug maintenance was not tolerated in the US and, following criminalization, doctors were prosecuted for prescribing narcotics to people thought to be "addicts."

Unlike the approach taken by the doctors at the Shreveport clinic, one of Stevenson's main arguments opposing narcotic clinics is that the clinics did not "cure addicts." He became a vocal opponent of narcotic clinics and any other type of drug substitution program. Stevenson's views and his 1955 paper for the Standing Committee on the Prevention of Narcotic Addiction were instrumental in stopping legal narcotic clinics in Canada.

END NOTES

1. Department of Pensions and National Health, 1941, 1945
2. Department of National Health and Welfare, 1945
3. Price, 1946
4. Department of National Health and Welfare,1950, Table 25, p. 137
5. Government of Canada, 1949, pp. 71, 12
6. Government of Canada, 1950, pp. 80–81, 13
7. Department of National Health and Welfare, 1954, p. 62
8. Department of National Health and Welfare, 1955, p. 34–36
9. Department of National Health and Welfare, 1955, p. 34–36
10. Canada, 1955
11. Boyd, 2008, 2013
12. Province of BC, Attorney-General, 1954a, p. 14
13. Province of BC, Attorney General, 1953; 1954a
14. Province of BC, Attorney-General, 1954a, p. 13
15. Boyd, 2013; National Film Board, 1948
16. Greenfield and Hamilton, 1948, pp. 61, 22
17. Stepler, 1949
18. Porter, 1955, p. 12.
19. Boyd, 2017; Carstairs, 2006; Giffen, Endicott and Lambert, 1991; Letter in addict file, Library and Archives Canada
20. City of Vancouver Archives, 1937; Department of National Health and Welfare, 1955, p. 34
21. *Hansard*, 1954, p. 5313
22. Winch, 1953
23. Canada, 1955
24. Josie, 1947
25. Ranta, 1952, p. 2
26. Josie, 1947; Ranta, 1952; Canada, 1955
27. Canada, 1955, Appendix C, p. 344
28. Stevenson, 1955; Stevenson et al., 1956, CBC, 1960; Price, 1946
29. Province of BC, Attorney-General, 1953, p. 9
30. Province of BC, Attorney-General, 1953, p. 11
31. Province of BC, Attorney-General, 1953; 1954a
32. Stevenson et al., 1956, p. 420
33. Porter and Earl, 1963, p. 1
34. Stevenson et al., 1956, p. 6
35. Stevenson, 1955, p. 181
36. See Courtwright, 2001; Musto, 1987; Tallaksen, 2017; Terry and Pellens, 1970 [1928]; Waldorf, Orlick and Reinarman, 1974
37. Terry and Pellens, 1970 [1928], p. 869

6

Jail for Heroin Users Ramps Up

The 1950s

OAKALLA PRISON FARM AND THE NARCOTIC RESEARCH TEAM

Through the 1950s, the "criminal addict" continued to be targeted by law enforcement and imprisoned. People who used heroin were stigmatized and discriminated against by the RCMP and police, and by the health, social service and criminal justice professions. Drug paraphernalia was criminalized, too, so it was illegal to possess a needle unless for medical purposes. In 1959, 441 improvised syringes, hypodermic needles and spoons were seized by law enforcement. In 1959, of the total number of convictions (565 convictions) under the Opium and Narcotic Drug Act, 470 of these were for possession of heroin. The province of BC made up 311 of these total heroin possession convictions, with 308 taking place in the city of Vancouver.[2] In the 1950s, some people convicted of a crime and sentenced to Oakalla Prison Farm in BC or Mimico Reformatory in Ontario were soon to be "treated" for their alleged addiction in prison.

Opium and Narcotic Drug Act:	1958/59	1959/60
Arrests	715	760
Convictions	585	671[1]

Oakalla Prison Farm was located right outside of Vancouver, in the city of Burnaby. The provincial prison farm opened in 1912 and consisted of 185 acres. People from all over the province were sentenced to serve time at Oakalla, and by the early 1950s, the number of people sentenced to Oakalla for a drug crime was steadily increasing. Due to fears about contagion, attempts were made by the prison administration to segregate "non-addicts" from "addicts." It was thought that older, more experienced "addicts" were luring young prisoners into a

Oakalla Prison Farm jail cell in the 1940s. (Reprinted with permission from photographer Jack Lindsay and City of Vancouver Archives.)

Oakalla's East Wing in the 1950s. (Reprinted with permission from Heritage Burnaby.)

life of drug use, degradation and crime. As well, some people admitted to prison were segregated for three days to withdraw from heroin. Responding to these conditions, Dr. Stevenson's Narcotic Research Team began its work at Oakalla Prison Farm in 1953. The prison warden of Oakalla and the BC Inspector of Gaols expressed hope that the research team would provide guidance as to how to work with "narcotic addicts" who were sentenced to Oakalla. Weekly meetings and discussion periods were set up at the prison, allowing experts in the field of drug addiction to speak at Oakalla.

By 1956 the research project at Oakalla Prison Farm was completed. The report, *Drug Addiction in British Columbia* (the Stevenson Report), is primarily a psychological study that examined people who used illegal heroin in BC. A sample of 100 people identified as heroin "addicts" incarcerated in Oakalla Prison Farm formed the main study, along with other sub-studies (a former user sample). The researchers also travelled to cities in Canada and the US to learn how other jurisdictions were dealing with drug addiction. They did not go to the UK, where heroin was prescribed by doctors to people labelled addicted. Most of the research subjects were white, though the researchers also decided to include "samplings of Orientals, native Indians, negroes, and other racial groups" if available. Also, about two-thirds of research subjects were men.[3] Unfortunately, aside from comparing men and women to a certain degree, the number of Indigenous people and people of colour in the study is not provided. Stevenson's report challenged some ideas about heroin and drug control, recommending that mandatory prison sentences for people convicted of possession of heroin be eliminated and that abstinence-based treatment facilities be set up. But it also maintained enduring negative stereotypes of users and again rejected the establishment of heroin clinics, claiming they would increase addiction.[4]

Stevenson, a psychiatrist and lead author of the report, continued to be a vocal moral reformer who perpetuated discourse about "criminal addicts" in his published articles, to the federal government and medical associations and at media events. He continued to vehemently oppose drug maintenance programs and advocated for abstinence-only treatment facilities. Stevenson claimed that people who use illegal drugs are "delinquent and poorly adjusted before starting drugs." He argued that the "addict" would remain a criminal and a threat to society even if they ceased using drugs. He asserted that "supplying the addict with free or low-cost narcotics cannot be expected to change him into a mature, socially well-adjusted citizen."[5]

The Stevenson report is flawed. Not only does it perpetuate negative claims about narcotic clinics and criminal addicts, but it also makes gendered and negative claims about women. The report stated that women who used illegal heroin were "virtually all prostitutes." The authors also argued, "it would not be incorrect to state that all [women in the study] were immoral and sexually promiscuous before beginning to use heroin."[6] In Canada, longer prison sentences were advocated for women who used heroin in order "to meet the challenge of this social evil" and provide rehabilitation.[7] All of the heroin users interviewed in the Stevenson report were represented as "promiscuously heterosexual" and living in common-law unions.[8] Women and LGBTQ+ people who used illegal heroin were constructed as doubly criminal and pathological for transgressing conventional gender norms (homosexuality was criminal then), which had devastating effects for them. A Canadian psychiatrist and director of the narcotics section of the Alcoholism and Drug Addiction Research Foundation at that time expressed conventional medical "wisdom" about lesbians who used illegal drugs stating, "they have been blocked in their sexual development."[9]

Drug policy is shaped by race, class and sexuality. It is also gendered. For women, the regulation of sexuality, reproduction and mothering shapes their lives. For women suspected of using drugs, surveillance and control are heightened. Poor women, Indigenous women, and women of colour bear the brunt of punitive drug control policies. For poor women suspected of illegal drug use, child apprehension by the state and loss of custody has become the norm. Their suffering is often lifelong rather than confined to a specific prison sentence.[10] The lives of people suspected of illegal heroin use in the 1950s were affected not only by police profiling and prison time for drug offences, but also by child apprehension, laws criminalizing "prostitution" and "homosexuality," forced hospitalization, violent psychiatric treatment and stigma and discrimination.

The 1956 Stevenson report also characterized Vancouver as a haven for poor criminal addicts due to the availability of heroin and other drugs. It referred to a "drug addict colony" in the east end of the city, an area depicted (then, as it is today) as a distinctive class culture and criminal space, partially made up of poor and working-class adults who were raised in the neighbourhood and who resorted to theft, prostitution and dealing to support their drug use.[11] The report includes the results of a questionnaire about addiction sent to practicing BC physicians. Of the 1,114 doctors who replied, only 266 had treated a person they identified as an "addict" in the previous five years. Yet, those hundreds of other doctors who had never treated an "addict" expressed opinions that were reported and taken seriously. Asked if there was a better way to treat addiction, physicians suggested "severe penalties for traffickers, even life imprisonment, or the death penalty," better abstinence-based treatment facilities and just over one hundred doctors suggested "legal sale or free gift of narcotics to 'confirmed' users" (the numbers making the other two suggestions was not provided).[12] The doctors suggesting life imprisonment as a solution were soon to have their directives fulfilled.

OAKALLA PRISON FARM'S "NARCOTIC ADDICTION REHABILITATION UNITS"

The BC provincial government supported the Narcotic Research Team's recommendation to open two pilot prison pods (or units) inside of Oakalla Prison Farm. The new units would be for experimental treatment for twelve male and twelve female "narcotic addicts" and to "search for a more effective means of coping with the problems of addiction" in a prison setting.[13] The treatment teams would draw from psychiatric perspectives.[14] The Oakalla Prison Farm's Narcotic Addiction Rehabilitation Units opened in March 1956. Only those deemed suitable — that is, most likely to comply with the rules — were transferred to the units. The selection of prisoners for the Rehabilitation Units was determined by the staff rather than simply accepting a prisoner wishing to be transferred to the unit. Moreover, work and program attendance became mandatory, taking up the whole day, leaving very little unplanned free time.

The warden of Oakalla Prison Farm initiated the intensive drug treatment program, drawing from established treatment developed for working with sociopaths and people suffering from personality disorders.[15] The Rehabilitation Units were separate from the general prison population, due to what was believed to be the "contagious nature of addiction." The senior custodial officer of the units described the women as "girls" who were manipulative and aggressive addicts and narcotic offenders.[16]

The pilot program's success was elusive. Dr. Guy Richmond, the prison doctor at Oakalla Prison Farm from 1952 to 1969, stated, "I cannot recall one success from this prison treatment program." Dr. Richmond strongly opposed compulsory treatment in prison (or any institution) and enforced abstinence.[17]

Group therapy and discussion were part of the Rehabilitation Units

Women's cottages at the Oakalla Prison Farm in the 1950s. (Reprinted with permission from Heritage Burnaby.)

program at Oakalla. These treatment methods were used even though the Inspector of Gaols reported that they were a total failure because the prisoners did not want to reveal personal information about themselves in the prison setting. The men and women in the Rehabilitation Units also refused to take part in the voluntary programs offered to them, such as crafts and physical recreational activities. Therefore, by 1958, a new plan of operation was set in place.

The Inspector of Gaols lamented that treatment following release from prison was important to the success of the program. However, no funds or publicly funded facilities were available for those leaving Oakalla Prison Farm's Rehabilitation Units. He also stated that without release follow-up and treatment, the "tragic certainty" is that the "narcotic addict" will "resume their habit as night follows day." The Inspector said that prisoners told him that the reason they wanted to stop using narcotics was that they were "tired of serving time." He complained that it was difficult to convince prisoners that there should be other reasons for abstaining from drugs.[18] The Narcotic Addiction

Foundation did provide some support for prisoners released from Oakalla at that time, however, it was voluntary, which aligned with the Narcotics Addiction Foundation's ethics and treatment perspectives. In sharp contrast, Dr. Stevenson called for mandatory follow-up by placing prisoners on probation and requiring compulsory reporting.[19]

MIMICO REFORMATORY

In 1956, the same year that Oakalla Prison Farm opened its first treatment units, the recommendations of the federal Fauteux Report to set up a prison medical unit in a federal prison for "narcotic addicts" was finally acted on.[20] One segregated prison unit had already been established for men identified as "alcoholics" at the Alex G. Brown Memorial Clinic in Ontario's Mimico Reformatory in 1951. It expanded in 1956 to include "narcotic addicts." Another treatment unit was established in 1967 at Matsqui, a federal medium-security prison in Abbotsford, BC.[21] Similar to the Oakalla Rehabilitation Units, addiction was constructed as a criminal and psychological matter in the federal prison units. Even within this very individualistic frame, the supposed criminality superseded any concern related to the psychological causes of addiction.

In a Canadian Broadcasting Corporation (CBC) radio show in 1959, a man described as a "criminal addict" reveals the true nature of the prison treatment programs. He was interviewed about his thirty-year drug addiction and his time in the Mimico prison program. Asked by the CBC host if the program helped him, he replies, "I would say no, that I received no assistance that would enable me to withdraw from my addictions." He then explained what happened at Mimico:

> I was taken to Mimico Reformatory about 6:30 in the evening and I was there overnight, and the following morning I arrived in the clinic. I was given a complete change of clothes and taken in by the administrator, who explained the rules and regulations to me, and I was given a copy of these rules. And I was put on this program they have there which consists of work for two or three afternoons a week and one morning, and the

> work I might say is very much of a farce ... [due to the] sheer monotony of it — you are given a shovel and a rake and you are asked to dig up a piece of ground, and the same piece of ground is dug up week in and week out for months on end.[22]

He explained that the doctors involved in the program were sincere. However, as he explained, "I didn't think the custodial staff would be in control of me about 90 percent of the time and that it was primarily a jail and not a clinic. Although the inmate is told he is a patient he is in fact not a patient; he is an inmate the same as he would be in any other institution."[23]

Rather than setting up publicly funded drug treatment services or narcotic clinics in the community, prison time and forced abstinence-based treatment programs in secure prison units became the accepted response by the Canadian state in the 1950s and early 1960s. New knowledge advanced by psychiatrists at that time claimed that addiction to criminalized drugs was a psychiatric disorder as well as a criminal activity, so the mainly poor and working-class people who were identified as addicted to heroin and other criminalized drugs were also labelled pathological criminals.[24]

MEDIA, CRIMINAL ADDICTS AND HEROIN

Radio documentaries also told stories about heroin. The CBC produced many radio shows about heroin and "addiction." A four-part series in 1957 about drug addiction in Vancouver, hosted by Jack Webster, opens with these words: "And to begin our story, Jack Webster ... speaks to Mary, a woman without hope, a drug addict."[25] The host prewarned radio viewers that the drug and criminal history of his next guest, Chuck, should make them skeptical of his "solution" to the drug problem in Vancouver. Chuck, a 50-year-old man who had been using heroin since he was 17, said:

> If drugs were legalized and medically controlled and supervised, I am positive that 80 to 90 percent of the addicts would

go to work and earn an honest living and you would hear no more from them.

Webster adds, "But you know, all the addicts say the same thing. Just give us a free supply or a cheap supply of drugs and we'll promise to keep out of crime. But we'll go into that later with an expert."[26]

This 1957 show exemplifies the pattern in these radio documentaries about heroin addicts. Whenever a current or past user of criminalized drugs is interviewed and challenges conventional discourses about drug addiction, criminal addicts, treatment or law and punishment, their comments are dismissed and even ridiculed by the host. The audience is often told that an expert such as a social worker, medical doctor, RCMP officer or another reformed criminal addict will follow up in the show or in the next episode to contest the knowledge and solutions

Jack Webster doing an interview with a security guard at the BC Penitentiary in April, 1963. (Croton Studio, reprinted with permission from Vancouver Public Library.)

expressed by people who used heroin.

Another CBC radio show, *Assignment*, which aired in 1959, begins with this statement:

> *Assignment* has made an exhaustive survey of the drug situation in Toronto where, during the past few weeks, police have made a crackdown, rounding up drug peddlers, the human parasites who live off the misery of others. Addicts are also being rounded up and sent to institutions where modern medicine tries to cure them of a habit they cannot cure themselves.

The radio host introduces audiences to people who used heroin and other criminalized drugs as "without hope," "victims" and a "blot on society," and addiction as "one of the greatest curses of civilized society."[27]

News stories, including another 1958 *Maclean's* article titled, "The Streets of Canada: Hastings," continued to depict heroin as a demon drug and Vancouver as Canada's largest heroin market. Reporter Ray Garner noted that on Hastings Street in Vancouver:

> Twenty-one-year-old Naomi drew ten years last summer for pushing heroin, at five dollars a "cap," in a Hastings Street coffee shop. Business was so good, the magistrate noted, that addicts appeared "almost to be standing in line to get a seat alongside her to buy drugs."

Thus, the media continued to frame Vancouver as a city filled with deprived heroin users and sellers.

THE ILLOGIC OF THE PRISON PUSHERS

Dr. Guy Richmond, the prison doctor at Oakalla Prison Farm from 1952 to 1969, recalled meeting over ten thousand heroin users during his time there. At Oakalla, he witnessed prisoners being flogged, withdrawing in prison cells, being subjected to forcible body searches and being forcibly injected with apomorphine to induce vomiting if they were suspected of ingesting heroin capsules. He also recalled that rectal examinations were conducted without consent and vaginal examinations were forced upon women prisoners.[28] Rather than prison time and so-called treatment units in prison, Dr. Richmond opposed the imprisonment of heroin users and argued for a program of heroin maintenance outside of prison for people who use illegal heroin. In fact, he argued in his 1975 book, *Prison Doctor,* that for most offences, but particularly drug offences, "the use of imprisonment as a deterrent or a means of correction has proved a complete failure."[29]

The vocal Dr. George Stevenson held a different opinion than Dr. Richmond. Stevenson reiterated on a CBC show that aired in 1960 that most "addicts" are criminals:

> People think that addicts, if they could get their drug legally, would work well because they wouldn't have to spend their time out stealing ... these addicts we're talking about are really a section of the underworld of Vancouver and of British Columbia and of Canada. They really are addicted criminals ... Even without their drugs, most of these people would still be criminals ... they're addicted to crime.[30]

Stevenson claimed that "total abstention" was the only goal. Unfortunately, Stevenson's strongly stated views about heroin use, users and "criminal addicts" informed drug policies and our ideas about heroin and the people who use the drug in the 1950s and 1960s, ideas that persist today.

These ideas are integral to the conventional narratives about people identified as "dependent" or "addicted" that are still familiar. The supposed trajectory of heroin use includes experiences of increased use, loss of control, immoral and criminal activity, drug treatment failure and — for some — control (not cure) through abstinence.[31] The idea that heroin users partake in criminal activity has been purported ever since the drug was made illegal. It is a circular argument given that in order to purchase the drug, one has to buy it on the illegal market. The drug that was once legal is now illegal, so users automatically become criminals. But moral reformers moved passed this logic by arguing that poor and working-class heroin users were criminals even before and outside of using heroin.

Dr. Stevenson also became well known in Canada for advocating for abstinence-only treatment models in secure prison settings. Oddly, he and his co-authors in their 1956 final report stated the following with regard to the scientific evidence of the heroin–criminal logic:

> To our surprise, we have not been able to locate even one scientific study on the proved harmful effects of addiction. Earlier investigators had apparently assumed that the ill effects were so obvious as not to need scientific verification, or they, too, had accepted without question the traditional beliefs on the harmful effects of narcotics.[32]

Given Dr. Stevenson's vocal rhetoric about criminal addicts and abstinence as the cure, we can only assume his co-researchers overruled him so that this section stayed in the report. Clearly though, he chose to ignore it in his public pronouncements. But we should ask ourselves: Where is the harm of narcotic use derived from? The drug? Addiction? Or is it laws prohibiting heroin and other narcotics, and the rejection of alternative models of drug use and substitution programs? What we assume are the harms of drugs may simply be the harms related to prohibition.

Yet, people who used heroin resisted conventional stereotypes, and challenged the laws and treatment theories created to punish, criminalize, pathologize and deny them access to safe legal drugs. When asked in 1959 by a CBC radio interviewer if there "is any solution to the problem of drug addiction," a male user responded, "I think the only definite and positive solution is to legalize narcotics."[33] In another 1960 CBC radio show, a female user proposed, "If drugs were legalized then there would be no drugs on the street. There would be no peddlers, no connections, because it wouldn't be worth their while." She also advocated providing maintenance drugs for people who use heroin.[34] By the end of the 1950s some professionals and members of the public had challenged Canada's drug laws and the criminalization of people who used heroin. For the first time, the question arose: Which came first? The "drug problem" or the law? As Canadians moved into the 1960s, drug control would come under scrutiny as drug use patterns, arrests and state responses began to shift.

END NOTES

1. RCMP, 1960
2. Dominion Bureau of Statistics, 1959, p. 156
3. Stevenson et al., 1956, p. 9
4. Stevenson et al., 1956, pp. 8, 426
5. Canada, 1955; CBC, 1960; Stevenson, 1955; Stevenson et al., 1956
6. Stevenson et al., 1956, pp. 631, 96
7. Flint, 1964, p. 247
8. Stevenson et al., 1956, p. 630
9. CBC Radio, 1965
10. Boyd, 2018, 2015; Stevenson et al., 1956; Kenny, Barrington and Green, 2015
11. Stevenson et al., 1956, p. 426
12. Stevenson et al., 1956, p. 425
13. Coutts, 1963, p. 14
14. Province of BC Attorney-General, 1956; Province of BC Attorney-General, 1958
15. Coutts, 1963
16. Coutts, 1963
17. Richmond, 1978, p. 20
18. Province of BC Attorney-General, 1958, p. 38
19. Province of BC Attorney-General, 1959, p. 24
20. Fauteux, Common, Edmison and McCulley, 1956
21. Beech and Gregersen, 1964; Coutts, 1963; McDonald, 1971; Murphy, 1972
22. CBC Radio, 1959
23. CBC Radio, 1959
24. Acker, 2002; Stevenson et al., 1956
25. CBC Radio, 1957
26. CBC Radio, 1957
27. CBC Radio, 1959
28. Richmond, 1978; see Richmond, 1975
29. Richmond, 1975, p. 182
30. CBC Radio, 1960
31. Fraser and Valentine, 2008; Boyd, 2008; Pienaar and Dilkes-Frayne, 2017
32. Stevenson et al., 1956, p. 510
33. CBC Radio, 1959
34. CBC Radio, 1960

7
Legal Heroin

The 1950s, 1960s and 1970s

By the 1950s and early 1960s, Canada had enacted some of the most punitive drug laws of any Western nation. Maximum penalties, including life imprisonment for trafficking and/or importing criminalized drugs, life imprisonment for possession for the purpose of trafficking and seven years imprisonment for possession, distinguished the Narcotic Control Act of 1961 from many other countries. The Narcotic Control Act drug schedule was lengthy: it included fourteen groups of drugs and eighty-nine of their derivatives, preparations, salts and alkaloids. Many of these drugs were synthetic rather than made from plants. In 1953 the World Health Organization recommended that member states of the United Nations ban the importation and production of heroin. The WHO also recommended that doctors and governments campaign against prescribing heroin. Heroin was not manufactured in Canada in the 1950s; therefore, it relied on supplies of the drug exported from other nations. After years of the Division of Narcotic Control campaigning without success to criminalize heroin for therapeutic use in Canada, a new avenue was sought. In 1955, the Department of National Health and Welfare announced in their annual report that an administrative ban on importation licenses for heroin was in effect. Consequently, domestic supplies of heroin ran out shortly thereafter.[1]

DRUG LAW ENFORCEMENT IN THE ERA

Since the 1920s, the drug dealer was vilified in support of harsh sentences for conviction under Canadian drug laws. Little recognition was paid to the fact that the majority of arrests and convictions were for drug possession. As early as 1955, the Special Committee on the Traffic in Narcotic Drugs in Canada, recommend heavier prison sentences for drug traffickers to be enacted and that no distinction should be made between people who sold small amounts of drugs to support their habit and "non-addict" traffickers. In practice, drug users, rather than high-level players in the drug trade, were targeted by law enforcement.[2] For example, in 1960, there were a total of 467 drug convictions in Canada. Of that total, 413 convictions (88 percent) were for possession and 374 (91 percent) of the possession convictions were for heroin.[3]

CBC Radio Assignment on Drug Addiction, November 21, 1959

"We're going to examine the problem of drug addiction, one of the greatest curses of civilized society, first through the eyes of a drug pusher, a man who's known drugs and its victims for the better part of his life. He's known the desperate pleadings of the addict. He's felt the soul-killing pangs of conscience that told him he was a blot on society, and he's experienced the loneliness and hopelessness of jail cells as he attempted to pay for his crime."

The Division of Narcotic Control continued its surveillance of "licensed dealers" (pharmaceutical firms and retail pharmacies), criminal addicts and professional addicts. In 1960, the Division estimated that there were 2,929 known criminal addicts in Canada. The Division claimed a substantial decrease in medical addicts (people who became "addicted" while receiving medical treatment, or when terminally ill) from 515 in 1954 to 237 in 1960. The decrease was thought to be due to the Division providing information to doctors about synthetic drugs and addiction.[4] The small population of criminal addicts continued to be targeted by the Division and sent to prison, especially in BC.

In BC, Oakalla Prison Farm was the destination of many poor and working-class people who used narcotics. Of the 1,266 new admissions of women at Oakalla in 1961–1962, it was thought that most were suffering from withdrawal from narcotics or alcohol. Imprisonment for alcohol offences far outnumbered narcotic offences. 474 women were admitted to Oakalla for breaches of the provincial Government Liquor Act, while 75 women were admitted for breaches of the federal Narcotic Control Act. In 1961, 6,006 men were admitted to Oakalla for a Government Liquor Act offence (drunkenness in a public place was the most common offence), compared to 156 men admitted for a drug offence.[5] Even though law enforcement, politicians and the media were publicly demonizing criminal addicts, alcohol offences made up the vast majority for those imprisoned at Oakalla Prison Farm. Yet compared to narcotic offences, penalties for alcohol offences were much less severe. The 1962 BC prison annual report noted that in Oakalla the Old Gaol Annex had close to "200 older alcoholics accommodated" in double bunks and the east wing of Oakalla was made up of "narcotic addicts (50 percent), alcoholics (25 percent) and habitual delinquents (25 percent)." The prison was consistently overcrowded.[6]

By 1962–63, 7,504 men and women were admitted to Oakalla for breaches of the Government Liquor Act, compared to 247 men and women for breaches of the Narcotic and Drug Act. Of the total Government Liquor Act breaches, 10 percent were by women, and of the total Narcotic and Drug Act offences, 37 percent were by women.[7] Moreover, overrepresentation of Indigenous peoples also characterized the era (as it does today). Indigenous peoples made up roughly 3.8 percent

United Nations' 1961 Single Convention on Narcotic Drugs

Canada joined with other nations in the adoption of the Single Convention on Narcotic Drugs. The Single Convention replaced all existing international drug control treaties. The treaty required that all nations criminalize non-medical use of cannabis, opioids and cocaine. The World Health Organization was tasked with assessing the scientific literature about drugs in order to recommend scheduling of each drug to the United Nations Commission on Narcotic Drugs.

of the BC population, but they made up 18 percent of the prison population of Oakalla in 1961–62. Of the total admissions for all offences, Indigenous women from across the province made up roughly half of the women's 1,160 admissions in 1962–63.[8] Due to police profiling, the percent of Indigenous women imprisoned for alcohol charges was increasing under the Indian Act and provincial statues.[9]

DRUG "TREATMENT" IN PRISON

Prison was the main form of so-called treatment for drug use. By the mid-1960s, a number of new BC prisons had opened: Twin Maples Farm for women (especially for those labelled "alcoholics"); Chilliwack Forest Camps; Snowdon Forest Camp; Lakeview Forest Camp; Alouette River Unit; Haney Correctional Institution; Kamloops Regional Gaol; Vancouver Island Unit; Prince George Gaol; and New Haven Correctional Centre.

At Oakalla Prison Farm, due to changes stemming from the 1961 Narcotic Control Act, synthetic opioid methadone was introduced for the first time to treat prisoners experiencing withdrawal symptoms.[10] From February 1958 to February 1963, 107 men were admitted into the Narcotic Drug Treatment Unit at Oakalla. Women were also admitted to the Narcotic Drug Treatment Unit at Oakalla and the mandatory requirements for women prisoners in the treatment unit were quite strict. All of the women prisoners in the unit had to attend group counselling sessions from Monday to Saturday. Several medications were no longer available to the women, including aspirin, painkillers, tranquilizers, sedatives, sleeping medication and diet pills. Only if a woman had a tooth extracted or a sprained ankle, would she be allowed aspirin or 222 pills (an over-the-counter medication that included a low dosage of codeine).

A third restriction was placed on the women and their friends and family in and outside prison: unless married, women prisoners in the Narcotic Drug Treatment Unit were not allowed to write letters or visit the men's unit, nor were they allowed to spend any money they received from outside the prison. This restriction was put in place so that the women had an incentive to behave in order to obtain higher paid jobs within the prison (pay ranged from 30 cents a day to 80 cents a day). The warden thought that if the women could not spend money or receive parcels from old boyfriends and associates outside of prison, they would eventually sever their ties to them.[11]

Additionally, the women prisoners were expected to monitor their fellow prison mates' behaviour to decide whether or not they deserved "good conduct" pay. And finally, a common institutional belief was that the longer an adolescent girl or woman was incarcerated, the "greater her improvement in personality."[12] Longer sentencing for women stemmed from long-held gendered ideas about women's morality.

A seven-year follow-up study of a small sample of "criminal narcotic addicts" who had been imprisoned in Oakalla, by Dr. Stevenson and his colleagues, concluded that 20 percent of criminal addicts "recovered" without any special drug treatment. Recovery was measured by whether or not the person was arrested again after they left prison.[13]

HEROIN IS THE DRUG OF CONCERN

By 1965 the Division of Narcotic Control feared that because doctors could now legally treat people known to be "addicted" without fear of criminal prosecution, "addicts" would flock to doctors to get narcotics on the "pretext" of treatment.[14] Heroin continued to be the main drug of concern. Of the 337 convictions for drug offences under the Narcotic Control Act in 1964, 80 percent were for heroin offences. 90 percent of all drug convictions were for possession.[15]

Due to the production of semi-synthetic and synthetic drugs, new drugs were added to the drug schedule, including methadone, dilaudid and oxycodone. New over-the-counter and prescribed stimulants and barbiturates were regulated under the Food and Drug Act, a parallel act to the 1961 Narcotic Control Act. Whereas the Food and Drug Act was driven by health concerns and did not include a possession offence, the Narcotic Control Act was the vehicle for law enforcement to obtain drug possession convictions.

Breaches of the Government Liquor Act continued to make up the majority of drug offences in the province. Only one prisoner in 1966–67 was identified as a marijuana user (at New Haven).[16] While marijuana convictions rose rapidly through the 1960s, marijuana users would eventually far outstrip narcotic users in convictions in the decades to follow. From the 1950s to the mid-1960s, illegal drug use was mostly confined to heroin, cocaine and morphine. The 1965 RCMP annual report stated that "heroin was the main drug of addiction, but the abuse of marihuana gained prominence."[17]

Marijuana charges increase by 8200 percent in the 1960s, the vast majority for possession.[18]

Year	Charges
1962/63	20
1963/64	56
1964/65	78
1965/66	162
1966/67	398
1967/68	1678

The 1968 RCMP annual report noted the increase of marijuana offences across Canada (note that cannabis is the official term used today).

In their annual report, the RCMP wrote that in 1968, although "heroin continues to be one of the more serious problems, it has been confined mainly to the city of Vancouver. Of 483 offences involving heroin, 369 were detected in Vancouver, 85 in Toronto and only 24 in Montreal."[20] Even with the rise of marijuana offences, the surveillance and punishment of heroin users continued unabated.

The RCMP argued that heroin and addiction were still serious problems. They pointed to a growing number of "known addicts" between 1957 and 1967:[19]

1957 — 2792
1958 — 2958
1959 — 3004
1960 — 2929
1961 — 3048
1962 — 3136
1963 — 2963
1964 — 2947
1965 — 3180
1966 — 3182
1967 — 3335

THE PHARMACEUTICAL INDUSTRY

While the Division of Narcotic Control continued their surveillance of illegal narcotics users, pharmaceutical firms in and outside Canada were busy creating new synthetic narcotics, minor tranquilizers and other drugs to patent and sell to Canadians. While the rise of synthetic drugs began in the 1940s, by the early 1960s Canadians had only three hundred marketed prescription drugs to choose from. In contrast, in 2020, there were over 7,352 prescription pharmaceutical drugs and 2,753 over-the-counter drugs marketed in Canada.[21] The move away from plant medicines was partially motivated by profit; plants cannot be patented, whereas synthetic drugs can. Pharmaceutical firms profit from patented drugs because they can then hold a monopoly on the production, marketing and sale of the drug for many years (currently twenty years, which is up from seventeen years prior to 1993). Nevertheless, legal opium-based medicines, such as morphine, remain popular.

Drug Scheduling

The NDS [National Drug Schedules] program consists of three schedules and four categories of drugs. Schedule I drugs require a prescription for sale. Schedule II drugs require professional intervention from the pharmacist (e.g., patient assessment and patient consultation) prior to sale. Schedule III drugs must be sold in a licensed pharmacy, but can be sold from the self-selection area of the pharmacy. Unscheduled drugs can be sold without professional supervision, from any retail outlet.[22]

Unlike the days of unregulated remedies and patent medicines, all legal drugs are authorized for sale in Canada once they have successfully gone through a drug review process under Health Canada. Drugs were regulated through the Food and Drug Act and the Narcotic Control Act. Pharmaceutical drugs are often viewed as "good drugs" in contrast to criminalized drugs. Yet, drug categories are unstable; their status can change over time. As we have seen, drugs such as heroin were initially thought to have therapeutic value, but later demonized, banned and criminalized for non-medical use in Canada.

In 1959, a new synthetic drug, fentanyl, was seen as a breakthrough for pain control. Fentanyl was patented by Dr. Paul Janssen in 1959. It is thought to be one hundred times stronger than morphine and it is still used today as a pain reliever and anesthetic for medical use. However, drugs do not stay neatly in their assigned categories. Today, fentanyl is widely associated with the illegal overdose death crisis in Canada (and other countries). Yet, the overdose crisis in Canada is not due to legal therapeutic prescriptions of fentanyl; rather it stems from illegally produced fentanyl sold on the illegal market, and illegal fentanyl added to heroin, cocaine and amphetamines.

GOING TO BRITAIN FOR LEGAL HEROIN

For Canadians who used illegal heroin in the 1950s and 1960s, treatment outside of an experimental unit in prison did not exist; rather, systemic discrimination and stigma, harsh drug laws, police profiling, long prison sentences and the absence of a legal source of heroin and other opiates prevailed. In 1961 federal legislation was introduced that enabled indefinite incarceration for people identified as "addicts" (it was passed but not promulgated). In response, between 1951 and 1969, around ninety-one Canadians went to the UK to receive prescription heroin so that they could, as the majority of those interviewed in a study of the heroin emigres stated, "lead normal lives" or "non-criminal lives."[23] These heroin users explained that they emigrated because in Canada they lived in constant fear of imprisonment. They had heard that people addicted in the UK were treated better: they were offered legal heroin maintenance.[24] The perspective of these Canadians who went to the UK illustrates that state responses to heroin use matters. The UK Rolleston Committee were clear on this in the 1920s, claiming that providing care and prescription heroin maintenance through the National Health Service to people thought to be addicted allowed them to live a normal and useful life.[25]

This woman was a drug addict. Here she tells how she found

In Canada: TERROR

In Britain: HELP

LONDON

■ I came out of the beer parlor on Cordova St. that rainy afternoon with the little packet wrapped in tinfoil in my hand. Since I had just arrived back in Vancouver after a long time away, I was expecting no trouble. Not so soon.

Two men walked up to me–big men. For once I didn't panic. I could tell they weren't sure about me. Maybe I looked too well dressed.

"Would you mind walking to our car?" one asked.

Nearing it, I recognized a city policeman sitting in the car, a man from the narcotics squad. I had to get rid of the little packet fast. Suddenly I darted ahead of the two detectives, not to escape but to get a chance to swallow the evidence.

The next I knew, a detective landed on my back. I am barely five feet tall and skinny. I slid on my face on the wet sidewalk into a doorway with the detective's hands round my throat. He was trying to force up the stuff. Out of a black mist, I heard the other detective.

"She's turning blue, Mac. Let her up!"

I came to in the car. My first words were: "Did you get anything?"

A detective said: "No–lucky for you!"

The one who had jumped me saw I was suffering. My fix–injection of drugs–was long overdue.

"You'll be lots sicker by morning," he said. "I'm holding you 24 hours for investigation."

He was wrong. I didn't get sicker. In the jail I put a finger down my throat and brought up the stuff and used it. If you knew where to look, there was always an outfit to prepare and inject drugs in the old Vancouver city jail. Next day, I was released. That was one time they had nothing on me, nothing to show.

I hadn't always been so lucky. Once in Toronto, twice in Vancouver, I've been arrested on drug charges and sent to jail. Though that was my only personal experience of deliberate police brutality (the detective is no longer with the force), I have seen others treated as badly or worse and have lived in constant terror of a second dose of the same.

I am convinced, and highly respected Canadian addiction experts agree, that it is this tension caused by terror–terror of the police, of prison, of not being able to get drugs–that makes the habit nearly impossible to cure in Canada, as the law stands. The very attitude, that addiction is a crime instead of an illness, is what breeds conditions for terror.

Now I know it doesn't have to be that way. The dead-end street that life had become, through drugs–and the fear that goes with addiction at home–was why I left for England in January, 1962.

I did not know then that the kindest fate of my life would lead me to the front door of Isabella, Lady Frankau, who looks like a white-haired grandmother and actually is a specialist in psychiatric medicine and Britain's leading expert in curing drug addiction. You could say that in the past couple of years she has also become something of an expert on the Canadian addiction problem: For since the recent change in the law at home to provide indeterminate imprisonment for convicted addicts, some dozens of Canadian men and women cursed with the habit have scraped up the

Star Weekly Magazine, April 27, 1963.

In contrast to the UK, Canadian heroin users were imprisoned for possession of illegal heroin, the prescription of legal heroin was illegal and treatment was unavailable. Universal healthcare was enacted in Canada in 1957, but it was not until 1963 that methadone maintenance therapy was available in Vancouver, and 1970 when it was available in Toronto.[26] Methadone maintenance therapy (MMT) in Canada consisted of providing daily doses to eligible patients; however, MMT was confined to urban centres, was strictly regulated and was stigmatizing and punitive. The concept of the "criminal addict" in Canada meant that abstinence and prison time were advocated rather than drug substitution programs. One drug policy researcher concluded, "the availability of a legal supply of heroin [in the UK] from a physician means that criminal activity is not a *necessary* consequence of addiction."[27] Reflecting on his life in the UK, one Canadian, stabilized on prescribed heroin, with a home and a full-time job, noted to his wife, "do you realize that we pass at least a dozen cops every day of our lives now, and not one of them even knows who we are?"[28] For the majority of Canadians who went to the UK to receive legal heroin in the 1950s and early 1960s, it made all the difference.

UK policy around the prescription of heroin changed in the late 1960s and early 1970s; specialist doctors and MMT became the preferred mode of treatment for people labelled addicted to opioids.[29] However, heroin treatment was never fully abandoned and it is currently expanding due to the failure of other treatment modalities to curtail overdose deaths and arrests.[30]

One Canadian explained his weekly routine in the UK in 1963, which exemplifies the alternative patient model employed:

> Every Tuesday morning I get my weekly supply. I take my daily fixes and don't have to worry about being arrested nor do I have to worry about my next week's supply. As a result drugs have lost their importance.[31]

British doctor Lady Frankau,[32] who treated up to fifty Canadians in the 1950s and 1960s, argued that the "treatment of drug addiction is a medical problem."[33] She described her Canadian patients as suffering from "psychopathic personalities" who "will resort to almost any means — however unreasonable or dangerous — to satisfy this insistent craving."[34] This is very similar to the way heroin "addicts" were seen in Canada (pathologizing people who use heroin), though expressed more forcefully. But in Canada the "addict" was represented as *both* pathological *and* criminal, hence, there were very different results: prison in Canada and prescribed heroin maintenance and stability in the UK. In a 1960 CBC radio show, a Canadian heroin user clearly identified the consequences of the differing views on addiction treatment stating:

> I'm sure anyone will agree that the three essentials for a life of fulfillment are let's say security. First you've got to have bread and a roof over the head. Second, acceptance and approval. And then the feeling that you belong, you know. Well, the whole three are denied an addict and an ex-addict.[35]

DRUG TREATMENT IN THE ERA

The concept of the criminal addict curtailed the creation of publicly funded voluntary drug treatment and drug substitution programs in Canada.[36] Dr. Robert Halliday, Director of the Narcotic Addiction Foundation of British Columbia (NAFBC), founded in 1955, noted that the then-current methods [harsh prison sentences and abstinence] to treat "drug addicts" had all failed.[37] In response to this failure, the NAFBC opened a provincially funded community clinic in Vancouver in May 1958, with a small four-bed voluntary residential program for men withdrawing from narcotics. The clinic expanded to include a twelve-day methadone withdrawal program the following year. This was the first time that methadone (a synthetic narcotic) was prescribed for individuals withdrawing from other opioids such as heroin. It was not until 1963 that the clinic was able to provide prolonged MMT.[38] That is, rather than restricted to only withdrawal treatment, daily doses of methadone were now prescribed for long periods of time (thus, maintenance). Until the passage of the Narcotic Control Act in 1961, doctors in Canada were not allowed to prescribe methadone (or any other drug) as a substitution drug to a "known addict."

In contrast to criminal addict discourse that advocated prison, the NAFBC worked with people living in the community who used illegal heroin and/or other opioids and sought voluntary treatment. The NAFBC valued voluntary treatment in the community, supportive relationships between staff and clients and follow-up.[39] Community and health services, rather than prison, were advocated by the NAFBC. In the 1956–57 annual report for the NAFBC, Dr. Halliday points to the problem of conducting studies of "addicts" in prison in mandatory treatment units. He concludes: "It is important, at this point to underline the fact that all previous methods developed to treat drug addicts have been in agreement in only one thing, i.e., they have failed."

Not abandoning the idea of so-called treatment in prisons, Matsqui, a federal medium-security prison in Abbotsford, BC, created an experimental pilot treatment unit in 1967. The pilot project aimed to achieve behavioural changes and to measure how effective their experimental treatment was.[40] The Narcotic Drug Treatment Unit at Oakalla Prison Farm was phased out when Matsqui federal prison was set up. The opening of Matsqui was seen as the federal government's "most concerted effort to date to [study and] rehabilitate narcotic addicts."[41] The government claimed that half of the prison population at Matsqui were "addicts."

Matsqui set up separate pilot treatment units for men and women. As the pilot began, men were assigned to four-person cells. In keeping with the "experimental" nature of the unit, "incompatible" men were "forced to live together" in their cell so that they could learn how to get along.[42] A therapeutic community approach that included daily group therapy and formal schooling (to Grade 10) was required in the experimental prison unit. Treatment was also offered to other prisoners in the main Matsqui prison, however, while they were offered group therapy, they were confined to single cells and usually worked during the day in the institution instead of attending school.

Although Matsqui prison was a "drug-free" institution and prisoners were regularly subject to urine tests to detect use, illegal drugs were in fact available and used. The researchers thought that "the addict is a master in the art of manipulation."[43]

The experiment seems to have been a failure. An evaluation of the pilot treatment unit "surprisingly" found that these prisoners were less successful upon release than the general population at Matsqui in relation to illegal activity and illegal drug use. The 1971 evaluation report concluded that "compulsory treatment" for people identified as "addicts" in the Matsqui experimental treatment program was a failure.[44] However, the researchers did not know what caused the "difference in effectiveness" between the treatment group and the general prison population. Although contradictory, it was hypothesized that upon release from prison, the pilot treatment prisoner inadvertently became a "well-adjusted, well-educated" dope fiend who had more illegal earnings and used more illegal drugs than the general prison population at Matsqui.[45]

The 1972 federal evaluation of Matsqui's experimental prison treatment unit challenged some conventional ideas about addiction and criminal addicts, arguing that people engage in petty crime "only when it is difficult for addicts to obtain supplies of satisfactory opiates easily and cheaply." Thus, they did not fit the "criminal addict" framework. The report recommended experimenting with the prescription of morphine, heroin, smoking opium and methadone to "addicts" to determine if use would stabilize or decline.[46] The report also argued that people who use opiates can maintain occasional use and engage in legal work (rather than solely criminal activities) to maintain their drug use. Additionally, the report challenged ideas about addiction and the criminal addict:

> Opiates have no demonic powers although their use in conjunction with certain other social and legal factors leads to some undesirable results ... The urge to increase the dose of opiates seems ... to be both overrated and more complex than generally acknowledged. The few old time addicts with whom I have spoken, who were able to get cheap legal supplies of morphine many years ago, report that they maintained stable dosages for years even though a week's supply cost but a few cents and was readily available ... I have on file monthly records of frequency of opiate use for nearly 300 British Columbia addicts [in the 1960s] ... occasional use (less than once weekly) patterns may be maintained for years ... and the urge to increase the dose is far from irresistible.[47]

Calls for publicly funded voluntary treatment outside of prison continued. In the late 1960s, drug use increased in and outside Canada. The increase was largely due to cannabis use associated with the 1960s counterculture.

THE 1960S COUNTERCULTURE, THE LE DAIN COMMISSION AND HEROIN

By the late 1960s, Canada was experiencing a youth-based counterculture movement that embraced the use of cannabis and other drugs, such as LSD. Cannabis offences rose swiftly in the late 1960s and early 1970s. Whereas previously law enforcement efforts centred almost solely on poor and working-class narcotic users, white, middle-class cannabis users were now targeted.[48] Counterculture youth were vocal about their cannabis use and university students across Canada called for the legalization of the drug.

United Empire Loyalists poster for a 1967 event at The Afterthought, a popular music venue on 4th Avenue, Vancouver, BC. Music posters in the 1960s often drew on psychedelic imagery. (Reprinted with permission from Bob Masse, www.bmasse.com.)

In the 1960s and early 1970s, Vancouver and Toronto's Yorkville neighbourhood were depicted by some media, politicians and law enforcement as "hippie" havens for youth and drug use. Music and films in the late 1960s and early 1970s normalized some illegal drug use, especially cannabis use. The 1969 US films *Easy Rider* and *Alice's Restaurant*, which were popular in Canada, normalized cannabis use and counterculture values. *Alice's Restaurant* also includes a narrative about heroin use, as a character, Shelly, dies from an overdose. Heroin is not demonized in the film, yet a distinction is made between cannabis use and heroin use. Unlike earlier films such as *Narcotic* or *Reefer Madness*, *Alice's Restaurant* and *Easy Rider* challenge conventional ideas about drugs and

Alice's Restaurant (1969) challenged conventional ideas about cannabis and heroin use. (Reprinted with permission from Photofest.)

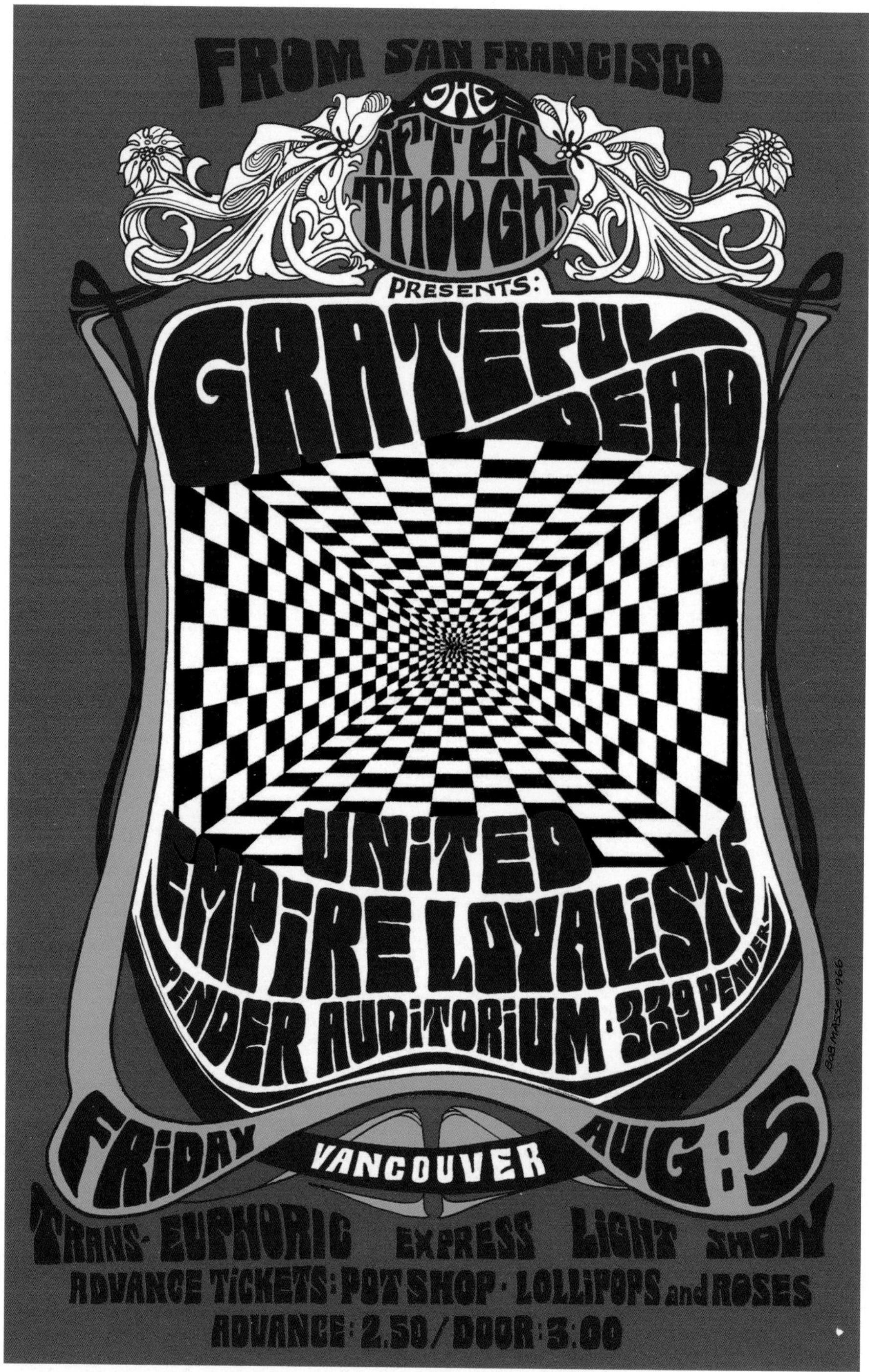

Grateful Dead poster for a 1968 event at The Afterthought, a popular music venue on 4th Avenue, Vancouver, BC. Psychedelic imagery on posters exemplified counterculture norms of experimental drug use and music. (Reprinted with permission from Bob Masse, www.bmasse.com.)

High (1967), directed by Larry Kent, links cannabis use to crime and murder, as depicted by the two lead actors, Astri Thorvik and Lanny Beckman. (Reprinted with permission from Photofest.)

the people who use them.

The media and politicians decried the counterculture as the downfall of youth, provoking a panic around cannabis and youth culture. Cannabis, or marijuana as it was officially referred to at the time, was depicted as a gateway drug to alleged harder substances such as heroin. Although this theory was discredited (and has been many times since), it continued to persist. Canadian filmmaker Larry Kent's 1967 film, *High*, depicts cannabis use leading to uninhibited sex, crime and murder.

On the music scene, many bands and songwriters espoused the benefits of cannabis and psychedelic drugs. The Velvet Undergound's 1967 song, "Heroin," was an exception, as its focus is on heroin use and disillusionment of conventional life — heroin use is not condemned. However, not all drugs were considered positive, nor were people who sold drugs. "The Pusher," a song written by Hoyt Axton and popularized by the band Steppenwolf in 1968, was featured on the soundtrack of *Easy Rider*. In it, drug dealers who sell "hard" drugs like heroin are depicted as "monsters" who should be shot. Although it may not be surprising that songwriter Hoyt Axton demonized "pushers," the popularity of Steppenwolf's cover of the song and the inclusion of it in *Easy Rider* suggests a line was drawn between recreational users of illegal drugs and "immoral drug dealers" who sold heroin and cocaine:

> Well, now if I were the president of this land
> You know, I'd declare total war on The Pusher man

In contrast, Curtis Mayfield's 1972 song, "Pusherman," featured on his album *Super Fly* and in the film of the same name, is more nuanced. In his song and film, the drug dealer is neither evil nor good. Rather, the dealer is depicted as a Black businessman with few legal options, a victim of the ghetto in racist America.

From 1967 to 2018, cannabis offences made up the majority of drug arrests in Canada. In 1970, total drug offences rose to 14,070, and cannabis charges in that year made up 93 percent of all drug offences. In

Super Fly (1972), directed by Gordon Parks, Jr., depicts a Black man with few legal options engaging in drug dealing. (Reprinted with permission from Photofest.)

Gerald Le Dain, third from left, sits as Chair of the Le Dain Commission along with fellow members Ian Campbell, Heinz Lehmann and Marie-Andrée Bertrand, circa 1970. (Reprinted with permission by the Le Dain family.)

In 1969, John Lennon and Yoko Ono met with members of the Le Dain Commission and with Prime Minister Pierre Elliott Trudeau in Ottawa. (Photo by Duncan Cameron, reprinted with permission from Library and Archives Canada.)

response to public pressure about increased illegal drug use and the arrest of white, middle-class youth for cannabis offences, the Commission of Inquiry into the Non-Medical Use of Drugs (the Le Dain Commission) was established in 1969 by Pierre Elliott Trudeau's Liberal-led federal government. The Commission released four reports between 1970 and 1973.

The Commission made many recommendations regarding drug policy in Canada, including heroin use and treatment. Amongst the reforms recommended, they included the expansion of publicly funded drug treatment and reduced criminal sanctions, and that heroin clinics be established for those who did not respond to conventional treatments such as MMT.[49] However, the federal Health Minister at the time, John Munro, rejected calls for heroin treatment. He claimed that the Le Dain Commission's recommendations were "so carefully hedged" that "he didn't think it should be tried in Canada." Instead, Munro suggested that methadone maintenance, rather than heroin maintenance, continue.[50]

On the international scene, in 1971, Canada signed the United Nations Convention on Psychotropic Substances, extending the Single Convention on Narcotic Drugs to include synthetic drugs, such as fentanyl, methadone, and amphetamines and Lysergic acid diethylamide (LSD). The list of criminalized drug continues to grow.

RESISTANCE TO CRIMINALIZATION PICKS UP

In 1971 the Division of Narcotic Control changed its name to the Bureau of Dangerous Drugs, clearly to better emphasize the conviction that certain drugs, the people who use these drugs and those who sell them are *dangerous*. As Canada entered the 1970s, cultural, political and economic shifts were also taking place that contributed to resistance to punitive drug policy. The Le Dain Commission findings and recommendations did however influence provincial policies. In BC, regional surveys showed that illegal drug use rates had increased and provincial prison admissions for drug offences rose from 1968 to 1971. In the same period, imprisonment for Government Liquor Act offences decreased substantially due to changes in the law.[51]

The BC Alcohol and Drug Commission was set up by the province in 1973, under the leadership of the New Democratic Party (NDP). The commissioners heard from people from across BC. Handwritten letters

Letter to Peter Stein, Chairman of the BC Alcohol and Drug Commission, from a man imprisoned at Matsqui wanting help for his "hard-core addiction":

October 9, 1974
My situation is very similar to the various aforementioned group [members of BC Drug Study Group at BC Penitentiary] as I too am a hard-core heroin addict. Presently I'm finishing a "10" year sentence at Matsqui (release date Oct. 26, 1974). I have 7 years solid time in, and I'm a little concerned about my future. The problem briefly is that, I know I will be using narcotics upon release, which if the drugs are illegal will eventually lead to another bust and back to prison.

What I want to know is can you recommend a Doctor who would be prepared to treat me for my addiction — "with narcotics" — ??

I know that you understand the problems facing addicts such as we are "hard-core" if you will and I don't use this term as a form of bragging but because it is an apt description of my condition.

If you could be of any help at all or can recommend an agency (other than the Narcotic foundation) or any individual who will treat me please answer at the above address. Time is of the essence!

Letter to Alex MacDonald, BC Attorney General, from a 42-year-old man requesting help to get a \ethadone carry so that he can work:

June 11, 1975
My job is on a fishing boat which will be out of Vancouver for 9 to 12 days this year ... I used to receive carries of 14 day supply of methadone every fishing season up to and including 1974. I never abused this privilege. However, this year I was turned down by my team [at the methadone clinic at 307 West Broadway, Vancouver] ... Is there any possible way that you can help me?

Letter to Peter Stein, Chair, BC Drug and Alcohol Commission, from a man concerned about no longer having access to legal methadone after his doctor moves away:

were sent to Peter Stein, Chair of the Commission, and Alex MacDonald, Attorney General, from people who used drugs (legal and illegal), and their parents and friends. One woman, following the death of her son from an overdose, urged the Commission to recognize and regulate the prescription of legal pharmaceutical drugs. Others asked for advice and the names of methadone providers in their area. Many of these people were telling officials that the criminalization of their addiction did not offer "help" to them.

Letter to Peter Stein, Chair, BC Drug and Alcohol Commission, from a man concerned about no longer having access to legal methadone after his doctor moves away:

June 26, 1975
I have overdosed twice after being cut off the [methadone] program and also lost my job … I feel more young people will become addicted to heroin because it is now readily available because of the methadone clinic's closure … I do not want massive amounts of methadone, only enough (40 –50mg a day) so my spirits are bright and I am a ready and willing worker with the energy to carry me through the day. Hopefully this will come to your attention because I am barely making it through the day on the 25mg a day I buy on the illicit market in Vancouver and it's costing me a fortune … Thank you for your time on reading this.[52]

Following their review of legislation, policies, and existing programs in BC, the commissioners argued that rather than looking for an "unobtainable 'cure,' … [such as] total abstinence," they should focus on the "whole person, and not on his drug use."[53] The forward-thinking commissioners recommended utilizing and providing voluntary recreation, social, education and health services to replace a singular focus on drug use and abstinence. The Commission approached drug use as a health and social issue, recommending that simple possession of illegal drugs and use of drugs no longer be criminalized.[54] The commissioners also recommended setting up a heroin clinic in Vancouver for a small number of heroin users.[55] In 1974, the Canadian Bar Association also passed a resolution calling for the establishment of heroin maintenance.

At the same time, the RCMP continued to view heroin as an evil to be eliminated and were opposed to setting up heroin clinics. In their 1975–76 annual report, they state: "Suppressing the illegal trafficking and use of heroin continues to be our top priority. Canada still supports a heroin addict population of approximately 16,000 to 20,000. The cost to Canadian society, in terms of lost productivity, welfare payments and other community losses, is staggering."[56] Rather than envisioning the enforcement of Canada's drug laws and policies as costly and harmful to society, the RCMP justified their profiling of people who used and sold illegal heroin by drawing on familiar tropes.

Unfortunately, the recommendations for heroin clinics by the federal Le Dain Commission and the BC Alcohol and Drugs Commission in the 1970s were not implemented. Instead, abstinence-based programs prevailed and limited MMT remained the only drug substitution therapy available in Canada. In the 1970s, MMT was controversial and rarely available outside of city centres. The rules and policies for MMT were also punitive; therefore, retention was low.[57]

Many of the recommendations put forth by the BC Alcohol and Drug Commission were disregarded due to the election of the (very) conservative Social Credit government in 1974. The Social Credit party pointedly rejected the Commission's recommendations to provide more than abstinence-based services, and instead enacted the Heroin Treatment Act in 1978. The Act allowed, without a criminal charge, the involuntary prison treatment of those labelled heroin "addicts" for up to three years.

Dr. Guy Richmond, former prison doctor at Oakalla Prison Farm, critical of the Heroin Treatment Act:

Abstention is unpredictable; it's a spontaneous and free act on the part of the user. It happens in spite of us. Enforced abstinence and forced withdrawals have done nothing to prevent the addict from racing to his first fix after [prison] release. To submit the narcotic user to compulsory treatment may require action which is unconstitutional or socially and professionally unethical. Section 16 of the bill stipulates so many offenses that most narcotic users would engage in that they would never be free under this act.[58]

The Heroin Treatment Act was a crushing blow to drug reform advocates and even more so to people who used heroin, disregarding their civil liberties and allowing for compulsory treatment.[59] It is important to note that in 1982 Brenda Ruth Schneider challenged the Heroin Treatment Act, however, in *Schneider v. the Queen*, the Supreme Court upheld the Act. By 1975, the medical officer of the federal BC Penitentiary noted that over 70 percent of all prisoners were there due to drug-related offences. In the same year, police reported drug offences reached 60,020. A far cry from 1960, there were a total of 467 drug convictions (88 percent were for possession) in that year. Of the total possession convictions in 1960, 91 percent were for heroin possession.[60] Even though their numbers were small, people who used illegal heroin continued to be subject to police violence, surveillance and arrest.

John Conroy, Member of the Canadian Bar Association, says the Heroin Treatment Act results in violent body searches:

Here is a case I was recently involved with. The police came into a room and saw a particular person throw heroin capsules into his mouth. Usually in such cases they apply a choke hole as a means of getting the substance out of the mouth. In this case, they took handcuffs, pried open the person's mouth, attached the handcuffs to the person's tongue, and then they ripped it for 13 stitches to get the capsules out.

This kind of brutality is a consequence of the kind of laws that we have had for the last 70 years pertaining to narcotics ... Prohibition not only doesn't work, it makes things worse. Regulation is the only sensible approach.[61]

A Vancouver man who used heroin explained that police violence was common in the 1960s and 70s, including the practice of choking and beating suspected heroin users: "Oh, they choke ya, jump up and down on your gut. Stick keys in your mouth. Or handcuffs, and turn 'em. Things like that. Anything to get the stuff outta ya, y'know. They've even killed people in the process."[62] Police violence and profiling, discrimination, stigma, limited services and long prison sentences were a central part of the lives of people who used illegal heroin.

The Main Block of Okalla Prison Farm, Lower Mainland Regional Correctional Centre, 1976. This was the destination for many heroin users in BC, and by the 1970s, cannabis users too. (Reprinted with permission from Heritage Burnaby.)

PRISON FOR ADDICTION CONTINUES

The countercultural era did not bring a relaxing of the criminalization of drug users, despite the seemingly loosened attitudes toward drug use expressed by a large segment of society at the time. Even the federal and provincial commissions, who based their deliberations on research evidence and consistently recommended a change in approach, did not affect the way people who used criminalized drugs were treated. Drug services for "addicts" in Canada remained abstinence-based outside of limited access to MMT. The lack of diverse services coupled with harsh drug laws resulted in criminal records and prison time for individuals who used heroin (and other criminalized drugs). As Canadians moved into the 1980s, they continued to consume legal and illegal drugs, and people who used illegal heroin continued to be vilified and denied access to legal heroin maintenance clinics.

END NOTES

1. Department of National Health and Welfare, 1955, p. 34
2. Carstairs, 2006; Government of Canada, 1950, 1962; Giffen, Endicott and Lambert, 1991; Stevenson et al., 1956
3. Government of Canada, 1962, p. 124
4. Department of National Health and Welfare, 1961, p. 105
5. Province of BC Attorney-General, 1963, p. EE 49
6. Province of BC Attorney-General, 1963, p. 24; see Anderson, 1993 and Schroeder, 1976
7. Province of BC Attorney-General, 1964, p. T60
8. Province of BC Attorney-General, 1964, p. 37
9. Province of BC Attorney-General, 1963
10. Province of BC Attorney-General, 1963
11. Province of BC Attorney-General, 1964, p. T40-41
12. Province of BC Attorney-General, 1965, p. AA25
13. Province of BC Attorney-General, 1965, p. AA18
14. Department of National Health and Welfare, 1966, p. 13
15. Department of National Health and Welfare, 1966, p. 14
16. Province of BC Attorney-General, 1968, p. FF61
17. RCMP, 1965
18. RCMP, 1969
19. RCMP, 1969, p. 18.
20. RCMP, 1969, p. 18
21. Health Canada, 2020
22. NAPRA, n.d.
23. Zacune, 1971; Spear and Glatt, 1971, p. 144
24. Zacune, 1971; Spear and Glatt, 1971
25. Ministry of Health, 1926
26. Krakowski and Smart, 1972
27. Zacune, 1971
28. Porter and Earl, 1963, p. 5
29. Strang and Gossop, 1994
30. Busby, 2019
31. Spear and Glatt, 1971, p. 146
32. For a more in-depth discussion of Lady Frankau, see Spear, 1994.
33. Frankau, 1964, p. 421
34. Frankau, 1964, p. 421
35. CBC Radio, 1960
36. Halliday, 1963
37. NAFBC, 1956–57b
38. Paulus and Halliday, 1967
39. NAFBC, 1956–57a
40. Murphy, 1972, p. 3
41. McDonald, 1971, p.1
42. McDonald, 1971, p. 9
43. Murphy, 1972, p. 7
44. McDonald, 1971, 15
45. Murphy, 1972
46. Murphy, 1972, p. 41
47. Murphy, 1972, pp. 31, 32
48. Martel, 2006
49. Canada, 1973
50. *Globe and Mail*, 1972
51. Province of BC Attorney-General, 1971, p. X49, 1976
52. BC Alcohol and Drug Commission, BC Archives
53. Stein et al., 1974b, p. 36
54. Stein et al., 1974b, p. 37
55. Stein et al., 1974b, p. 16, 37
56. RCMP, 1975–1976, p. 18
57. Stein et al., 1974a, 1974b
58. Richmond, 1978, p. 21
59. *Schneider* v. *Queen*, 1982
60. Government of Canada, 1962, p. 124
61. Conroy, 1978, pp. 24, 30
62. Stoddart, 1991, p. 91

8

Harm Reduction Comes to Canada

The 1980s and 1990s

The 1980s and 1990s are the decades that neoliberal economic, social and political policies took hold in Canada and other nations. Neoliberalism privileges the market above all else, alongside privatization and deregulation. Individual responsibility is the mantra of neoliberalism. For example, poverty is framed as stemming from laziness rather than economic and social policies. Drug use and its consequences are framed as one's personal responsibility rather than influenced by colonialism, racial profiling and punitive drug laws and policies. The love of the market led to severe cutbacks in health, education, housing and social supports, which had an impact, especially for poor and marginalized people. Yet, as several political analysts note, the idea of a smaller, less involved state did not mean a weak state, so drug law enforcement continued to be prioritized.

Although cannabis offences made up the largest category of total drug offences in the 1980s, the RCMP note in their annual 1985–86 report that heroin continued to be their top enforcement priority; however, cocaine was now identified as a growing problem. The justification of policing illegal drug use and trafficking continued to draw from long-held stereotypical tropes about the dangers of heroin. The fact that the overwhelming majority of drug offences in Canada at that time were cannabis-related rather than heroin-related is less visible and not as publicized. From its onset, one of the achievements of prohibition is to collapse different types of drugs into one all-encompassing category of illegal drugs. So, over time, the purported dangers of opium were extended to heroin, cocaine and even cannabis. In 1986, illegal drug use (rather than social and economic difficulties) was framed by Prime Minister Brian Mulroney as an epidemic. He had and gave no evidence to support the claim that drug use was destroying the social fabric of the nation. "A drug free world, we can do it!" — the slogan of the 1998 United Nations General Assembly Special Session on Drugs — exemplified the era and the enormous struggle that was to take place in Canada for alternative drug policies. Canada and other United Nations members signed the 1988 Convention against Illicit Traffic in Narcotic Drugs and Psychotropic Substances. This agreement expanded international efforts to suppress markets for illicit drugs and to criminalize a growing list of legal chemicals used to create illegal drugs.

Punitive drug laws and abstinence-based services continued in Canada. Given that access to safe legal heroin as a substitution drug in Canada was banned, overdose death from illegally obtained heroin continued to be a risk in the 1980s and 1990s. In 1980, there were 74,196 drug offences reported by the police across Canada. And, similar to the 1970s era, the majority were cannabis-related and for simple possession. In 1980, most heroin-related offences (342) were in BC, 63

The Doctor Game

Among other advocacy, Dr. Ken Walker wrote a weekly column, "The Doctor Game," for *The Globe and Mail* under his pen name, Dr. W. Gifford-Jones. In his column he advocated for legal heroin to be prescribed to terminal patients. In 1984, he was awarded the prestigious Michener Award for his journalism about prescribing heroin:

January 3, 1980: "A Renewed Resolve to Seek Heroin Relief for Dying Patients"
April 15, 1982: "Cancer Group Vetoes Heroin for Patients"
June 24, 1982: "Letters Support Heroin Treatment"
January 6, 1983: "British Sanity Needed in Debate over Heroin"
May 3, 1984: "Medial Use of Heroin Is Not Banned by Treaty"
February 14, 1986: "Many Hospitals Unconvinced of Need for Heroin Treatment"
March 10, 1987: "Heroin Critics Are Experts in Non-Scientific Method"

percent for simple possession.[1] The 1982 annual crime report showed a decrease in total drug offences from 1981 to 1982. However, it was explained that the decrease was due to a shift by police from cannabis enforcement toward heroin and cocaine enforcement. There were 583 heroin offences reported in 1981 compared to 734 offences in 1982 (up 25.9 percent).[2] Although cannabis offences continued to make up the majority of drug offences, law enforcement continued to crack down on the small population of people who used heroin.

In the late 1970s, Dr. Ken Walker (aka Dr. Gifford-Jones) began advocating for the availability of legal heroin to ease the pain experienced by his terminal patients. In April 1983, Dr. Walker also organized the W. Gifford-Jones Foundation to promote the therapeutic use of heroin for terminal patients.

Dr. Walker's efforts over many years led to the Government of Canada lifting the 1950s ban on licenses for heroin importation for medical use in 1984. However, prescribing heroin as a substitution drug for those labelled addicted remained illegal. Unfortunately, after the ban was lifted, it was almost impossible for doctors to prescribe the drug due to strict security criteria; therefore, suppliers eventually stopped providing heroin for therapeutic use.[3]

Dr. Ken Walker was awarded the 1984 Roland Michener Award for public service journalism for his articles in the *Globe and Mail* on the merits of prescribing heroin to terminal patients. Criticized by the RCMP and even the Canadian Cancer Society; Dr. Walker, undeterred, tirelessly championed for the therapeutic use of heroin in Canada. (Reprinted with permission from Ken Walker.)

Drugstore Cowboy (1989), directed by Gus Van Sant, highlights that the best source of drugs is pharmacies. (Reprinted with permission from Photofest.)

Abstinence-based drug services and limited access to MMT continued. And illegal drug overdoses began to rise; in 1988 there were 39 illegal drug overdoses in BC, rising to 331 by 1993.[4] As the 1990s advanced, Vancouver became world-renowned for its rising illegal heroin overdose deaths and high hepatitis C and HIV/AIDS rates. For decades, people who used drugs like heroin turned to the illegal market to purchase them. Yet, heroin was not always affordable or available. Nor was purity assured because drugs purchased on the illegal market are often adulterated with other unknown substances.

In Canada, people who used narcotics did seek out legal sources, as portrayed in films like the 1989 *Drugstore Cowboy*. In this movie, people who use heroin turn to the safest and purest source of some drugs — the legal drugstore with its vast array of pharmaceutical drugs, including opioids and stimulants. However, in the era, outside of limited access to MMT, diverse drug substitution (providing heroin, morphine or other narcotics) programs, which could stem the rising illegal heroin overdose deaths by providing safe drugs, were not set up.

HARM REDUCTION COMES TO CANADA

Harm reduction, an alternative approach to drug use, emerged in the UK and the Netherlands in the 1980s. As noted in Chapter 1, central to harm reduction practice is to save lives, to mitigate the harms associated with drug use and drug prohibition rather than perceived harms from drug addiction. Although harm reduction services do not reject abstinence or abstinence-based treatment programs, they are not the sole goal.

In defiance of federal law criminalizing drug paraphernalia, and to protect people who inject drugs from infectious diseases such as HIV, some early harm reduction needle programs were set up at CACTUS in Montreal, Alexander Park in Toronto, and the Downtown Eastside Youth Society in Vancouver between 1987 and 1989. These programs were non-judgmental and practical, providing education, support and equipment. In 1992, Canada's drug strategy included the reduction of harm, but most government funding went to abstinence-based programs and criminalization.

HARM REDUCTION AND WOMEN

Across Canada, at the grassroots level, ideas about people who use illegal drugs such as heroin started to shift slightly. However, rarely did the needs of women, especially pregnant women and mothers, influence conventional and emerging harm reduction services. In the 1990s, women living in BC and the rest of Canada continued to struggle against drug policies and other neoliberal policies. On the neoliberal front, for example, cuts to social services hit women and mothers, especially single mothers, very hard. Activists brought to our attention that drug policies and practices are gendered. This is due to the fact that the regulation of women, especially racialized and poor women, intersects with the regulation of sexuality, reproduction, mothering and drug consumption. Since the emergence of drug prohibition, women have been depicted as more deviant and immoral than men when they use illegal drugs. When they have children, women are constructed as bad mothers who place their children at risk. If they are pregnant and suspected of using drugs, they are seen as even more deviant and unfairly framed as damaging the developing fetus. However, prior to the 1990s, moral condemnation of pregnant women and mothers who used drugs did not lead to more supportive services in Canada. In fact, in some places the exact opposite occurred.

Indigenous, Black and poor women who were suspected of drug use while pregnant or parenting were profiled by some social workers and medical staff in and outside of Vancouver. It is assumed that using heroin is a risk. However, heroin is only one factor among many that shapes pregnancy and mothering. Worldwide, researchers acknowledge that poverty is the number one contributor to poor maternal outcomes and family instability. Marginalization and lack of access to publicly funded maternity, healthcare and social and economic supports negatively impact pregnancy and homelife. Yet these facts were ignored in Canada and child apprehension was routine for poor women suspected of illegal drug use, especially for Indigenous and Black mothers who faced systemic racism in child protection and health services.

Due to the systemic discrimination, racial profiling, child apprehensions and punitive "treatment" of their children, in April 1991 women in Vancouver came together to form the Drug and Alcohol Meeting Support for Women (DAMS). DAMS was the first women-centred harm reduction program for pregnant women, mothers and their children in Canada. It emerged on the cusp of a public health crisis in Vancouver's DTES, which was facing rising numbers of illegal drug overdose deaths and HIV/AIDS, as well as a hepatitis C outbreak. DAMS initially met in a number of places, including the basement of Christ Church Cathedral, and eventually settled into Blood Alley in the DTES.

This groundbreaking group emerged to address the unmet needs of women who used drugs and of their children.[5] To counter the harms stemming from drug prohibitionist policies, DAMS advocated for the adoption of harm reduction practices, especially in relation to pregnancy and mothering. Rather than focus on abstinence, the primary goals of DAMS were family stability and reunification as a response to child protection practices by the state, especially the apprehension of children, which had been a routine practice in Canada since the 1950s.[6] DAMS also worked with women where they were at. For example, if a woman wished to further her education, find safe stable housing or substitute illegal drug use with methadone maintenance, support and referrals were provided. DAMS also worked with like-minded doctors and social workers. DAMS looked to women-centred harm reduction programs outside of Canada that provided health and social and economic supports for pregnant women who used drugs and their children. DAMS, like most early harm reduction services, was grassroots and initially had no funding. Because abstinence was not its goal, it did not fit into the parameters of government funding criteria. As so often happens when innovative grassroots services are set up, people volunteered their time to keep the program going until some funding was eventually secured.

Inspired by Dr. Mary Hepburn's unique and pragmatic Women's Reproductive Health Services set up in the mid-1980s in Glasgow, Scotland, and in recognition of the needs of pregnant women and mothers, harm reduction services for women were established inside and outside the DTES. These programs demonstrated that our ideas about maternal drug use and parenting are terribly flawed. Poverty, racial profiling, colonialism, health and social inequality, violence and disparities in access to healthcare, economic and social supports shape maternal outcomes and parenting, not just drugs. DAMS was followed by Sheway, a pregnancy outreach program, in 1993, Fir Square Combined Maternity Care Unit, the first women-centred harm reduction maternity program, in BC Women's Hospital in 2003.

ILLEGAL DRUGS AND OVERDOSE DEATH

Even while some harm reduction services such as DAMS were set up, heroin overdoses continued to increase in the 1990s. In 1992, 162 people died from an illegal drug overdose in BC, and the largest percentage (65 percent) of people who died from an overdose death in BC lived in Vancouver. Heroin was associated with 90 percent of all overdose deaths in BC in 1993. Significantly, more than half of these deaths involved heroin and alcohol combined.[7]

TASK FORCE INTO ILLICIT NARCOTIC OVERDOSE DEATHS IN BRITISH COLUMBIA

Due to the rise in deaths, in 1993 the BC Minister of Health and Attorney General announced the appointment of Chief Coroner Vincent Cain to lead an eight-month task force of inquiry into the number of people dying from heroin overdose. The task force began their work in January 1994 and concluded with the release of the *Report of the Task Force into Illicit Narcotic Overdose Deaths in British Columbia*. Chief Coroner Cain argues in the report that criminalization, which he refers to as the "'War on Drugs,'… is an expensive failure."[8] The task force recommended, among other actions, the decriminalization of possession of all drugs and the legalization of "soft drugs" such as cannabis, expanded harm reduction services and a review of the possibility of providing a "heroin maintenance program."[9]

The task force also recommended that methadone services expand in BC alongside other harm reduction services. However, the response by all levels of government to Cain's report was inaction. This, not surprisingly, led to rising numbers of preventable illegal heroin overdose deaths. As well, a social justice movement for harm reduction services emerged, along with a critique of MMT, conventional abstinence-based programs and drug prohibition.

Decrimalization versus Legalization

Decriminalization refers to eliminating altogether or reducing to fines or warnings the criminal penalties for personal possession of criminalized drugs. Legalization refers to setting up a new regulatory system that eliminates criminal sanctions for possession, production, distribution and sale of currently criminalized drugs. Thus, the illegal drug market would decrease substantially as people would have legal access to safe, regulated drugs. Some sanctions could apply for producing or selling drugs outside the legal framework.

METHADONE MAINTENANCE THERAPY

As noted in earlier chapters, publicly funded drug treatment was not available until the late 1950s and 1960s. Treatment was abstinence-based and those people who did not respond well to this model, or would not comply with the rules, were kicked out with nowhere else to turn. There were no alternative models of treatment in Canada until MMT was introduced. Methadone is a synthetic opioid that can be consumed orally. In the late 1950s, for the first time in Canada, methadone was prescribed to help patients' withdrawal (or detox) from narcotics. This was done in a clinic or medical setting. However, prescribing methadone for maintenance purposes (also known as drug substitution) was not fully considered until the 1960s. Since then, MMT policy in Canada from the 1960s to the 1990s shifted constantly, from federal control (doctors had to receive approval from the federal government to prescribe methadone to a patient) to provincial control, from private clinics to public clinics, and then back to private physicians prescribing the drug, a reduction in doses and shifting requirements for daily pick-up and urine testing. These rollercoaster transitions negatively impacted individuals who were on MMT or hoped to access the drug. One patient noted that when she was first prescribed methadone through the BC

Narcotic Drug Foundation in the 1960s, she was told, "Look you've tried this [abstinence-based treatment] several times, you've tried withdrawal, this is methadone maintenance. In all probability, it's a lifetime program." Yet, instead of offering consistency, her dose and pick-up times were shifted dramatically as new rules were enforced.

Drug services in Canada, including MMT, were punitive. In many regions, they were unavailable. In order receive treatment, patients had to agree that they had a disease, even if they framed their own drug use differently. Instead of social supports, treatment was medicalized. In the early 1990s in Vancouver, to be eligible for MMT, a Physician-Patient Methadone Contract was typically signed by the patient which stated: "I state that I am addicted to narcotic drugs, and have made serious attempts through self-help groups, outpatient clinics, and/or residential treatment programs, to control my addictive condition (disease) and have been unsuccessful." Following the doctor's assessment, the individual had to agree to comply with a set of rules laid out in the contract, such as attending a counselling program, picking up methadone daily, not attempting to pick up methadone early and providing random and sometimes witnessed urine specimens. Failure to pick up methadone for two successive days would result in discontinuance in the program. Strict adherence to the rules was a condition of receiving MMT.

One woman who used heroin in the 1990s noted:

> The only alternative people are given is methadone and methadone is a really tough one because that is like the hardest habit to kick. God only knows what it does because it is not organic ... It was invented by the Nazis ... we owe it all to the Nazi scientists.[10]

The rigidity of the MMT program, and the stigma and discrimination people were subjected to by the program, made it near impossible for many heroin users to benefit from it. Daily pick-up and witnessed urine testing were difficult for people. Imagine trying to work or to socialize with family and others when you had to be at the clinic every day at a specific time. One Vancouver woman describes her MMT experience:

> When I was on the methadone program and having to go every day and have to go to the bathroom with the door open and drink my little methadone there and never be able to take a holiday and never be able to carry for two or three days to get away, like normal people … they encourage you to stay in the same rut that you are in.[11]

Failure to provide a urine sample when requested was considered the same as a positive test for drugs, resulting in further restrictions or being expelled from the program.

Women and Indigenous MMT patients were subjected to racist and gendered attitudes by physicians and staff. A woman describes her methadone clinic and how it drove her out of the MMT program:

> I was so sick, because usually when you decide to go on methadone, you are pretty desperate. This doctor, he keeps asking me how I made my money to buy drugs, during my [first] visit with him to see if I was eligible for the program. I told him I sold drugs. But he keeps insisting, "Well, how do you really make your money?" Finally, I realize he is implying that I am prostituting, and finally I realize if I don't just agree this is what I do, I'm probably not going to get on the program. Because you see he had a set idea of who I was, and by trying to state otherwise I appeared to be lying and not complying … So I just let him think what he wanted to because I needed to get on the program. But you know, I only lasted about four weeks because I couldn't follow all the rules.[12]

METHADONE PATIENTS ASSOCIATION

Although MMT had been available since the early 1960s in some regions of Canada, it was not seen as a harm reduction service. This is due not only to the fact that the term "harm reduction" was not employed then, but also rather than providing a non-judgmental service (an essential principle of harm reduction), MMT rules were rigid and punitive throughout the early years into the 1990s. So, in January 1995, the

Methadone Patients Association (MPA) in BC was formed. This group of methadone patients felt they needed to respond to changes to methadone treatment protocols, including the need for daily prescribing and pick-up. For MMT patients who responded well to the substitution drug, in the midst of an illegal drug overdose crisis, it was life-saving. The MPA advocated for the establishment of a harm reduction model of MMT and proposed the decriminalization of heroin use and the establishment of diverse and welcoming withdrawal and drug treatment services. The MPA also included representatives from the Ministry of Health's Pharmacare and Alcohol and Drug programs, the Colleges of Physicians and Surgeons and Pharmacists, academia and law enforcement. The group sought to make sure that the needs of people on methadone or those trying to access methadone were met.

Yet rather than less punitive drug policies, in 1997 the Canadian Drugs and Substances Act (CDSA) replaced the Narcotic Control Act.

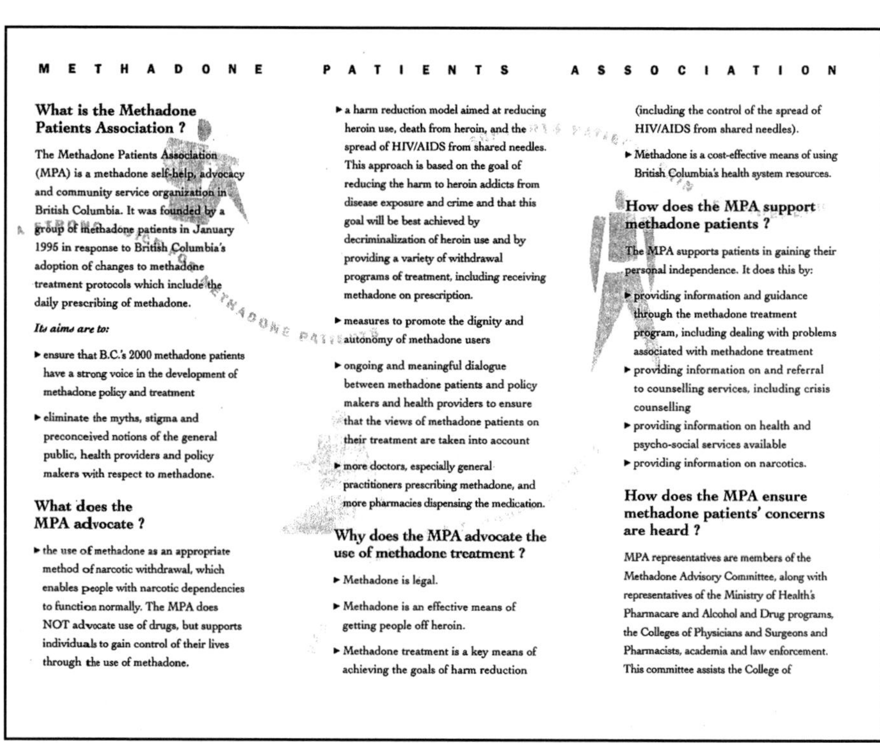

METHADONE PATIENTS ASSOCIATION

What is the Methadone Patients Association ?

The Methadone Patients Association (MPA) is a methadone self-help, advocacy and community service organization in British Columbia. It was founded by a group of methadone patients in January 1995 in response to British Columbia's adoption of changes to methadone treatment protocols which include the daily prescribing of methadone.

Its aims are to:

- ensure that B.C.'s 2000 methadone patients have a strong voice in the development of methadone policy and treatment
- eliminate the myths, stigma and preconceived notions of the general public, health providers and policy makers with respect to methadone.

What does the MPA advocate ?

- the use of methadone as an appropriate method of narcotic withdrawal, which enables people with narcotic dependencies to function normally. The MPA does NOT advocate use of drugs, but supports individuals to gain control of their lives through the use of methadone.
- a harm reduction model aimed at reducing heroin use, death from heroin, and the spread of HIV/AIDS from shared needles. This approach is based on the goal of reducing the harm to heroin addicts from disease exposure and crime and that this goal will be best achieved by decriminalization of heroin use and by providing a variety of withdrawal programs of treatment, including receiving methadone on prescription.
- measures to promote the dignity and autonomy of methadone users
- ongoing and meaningful dialogue between methadone patients and policy makers and health providers to ensure that the views of methadone patients on their treatment are taken into account
- more doctors, especially general practitioners prescribing methadone, and more pharmacies dispensing the medication.

Why does the MPA advocate the use of methadone treatment ?

- Methadone is legal.
- Methadone is an effective means of getting people off heroin.
- Methadone treatment is a key means of achieving the goals of harm reduction (including the control of the spread of HIV/AIDS from shared needles).
- Methadone is a cost-effective means of using British Columbia's health system resources.

How does the MPA support methadone patients ?

The MPA supports patients in gaining their personal independence. It does this by:

- providing information and guidance through the methadone treatment program, including dealing with problems associated with methadone treatment
- providing information on and referral to counselling services, including crisis counselling
- providing information on health and psycho-social services available
- providing information on narcotics.

How does the MPA ensure methadone patients' concerns are heard ?

MPA representatives are members of the Methadone Advisory Committee, along with representatives of the Ministry of Health's Pharmacare and Alcohol and Drug programs, the Colleges of Physicians and Surgeons and Pharmacists, academia and law enforcement. This committee assists the College of

A 1999 Vancouver MPA flyer advocating for methadone patients' rights and harm reduction models. (Reprinted with permission from the author).

The CDSA sets out penalties for drug offences that remained very punitive. Mandatory minimums, a maximum life sentence for trafficking heroin and seven years for personal possession of heroin are features of the CDSA.

VANDU AND THE PORTLAND HOTEL SOCIETY

As the 1990s progressed, illicit overdose deaths and HIV/AIDS and hepatitis C rates continued to rise in BC, and particularly in Vancouver's DTES. Activists appealed to the city of Vancouver and other levels of government, demanding recognition of the crisis and a change in health and drug policy to prevent deaths and infections. Linking these infection rates and deaths to prohibitionist policies, they called for harm reduction services including expanded needle distribution, the opening of an official safer injection site and heroin maintenance. In response to the crisis, and the inaction at all levels of government, people who used drugs and supporters set up their own unofficial safer injection sites in Vancouver, such as the Back Alley on Powell Street that ran from 1995 to 1996. Again, without official funding, it was grassroots activists and people who used the Back Alley who kept the temporary service going. After the police shut the Back Alley down, activists opened another unofficial safer injection site at 327 Carroll Street. Similar to the Back Alley, it provided a safe space for people who used illegal drugs, but it lasted for less than a year before it was forced to close. These sites assured that people who used drugs there would not die of an overdose death, and their shuttering by police led to meetings and new strategies by activists initiating change.

Meanwhile, cannabis activists continued to defy the law, advocating for cannabis legalization and legal access to medical cannabis. At the same time that a social justice for harm reduction emerged in Vancouver, so too did the social justice movement for cannabis legalization and medical cannabis.

In 1997, people who used drugs and various allies came together in Oppenheimer Park and the Foursquare Street Church to identify issues

VANDU logo. (Reprinted with permission from VANDU.)

in the DTES. These meetings culminated in the official establishment of the first drug user union in Canada in 1998 — the Vancouver Area Network of Drug Users (VANDU). VANDU, a pivotal organization in the social justice movement for drug reform, was co-founded by Bud Osborn, poet and social justice activist, and Ann Livingston, longtime activist for the rights of people who use criminalized drugs. Mellissa Eror was elected as the first president of VANDU. VANDU advocated for the human rights of its members and lobbied for safer injection sites, heroin-assisted treatment and an end to drug prohibition. They also began to provide weekly meetings, support, harm reduction supplies (needles, pipes and, today, naloxone) and education to people who use drugs. VANDU continues to act as a unique peer-led union that has gained international recognition for its activism and services. It remains a vital organization in the DTES and an inspirational model for other drug user groups outside of Vancouver.

Our Mission

The Vancouver Area Network of Drug Users is a group of users and former users who work to improve the lives of people who use illicit drugs through user-based peer support and education.

VANDU consists of a network of groups including:

-**MIND BODY LOVE** our youth outreach distributes drug information at raves. (phone: 604-215-4681)

-the **Downtown Eastside User Group** meets weekly providing peer support and a voice for people who use drugs.

-the **Methadone Committee** meets weekly to lobby for the humane and fair treatment of people on methadone.

VANDU's office is located at:
524 Powell St.
Vancouver, BC V6A 1G9
hours are 10 AM to 4 PM
Mondays to Thursdays
604-253-5485 (mes: 683-4797)

VANDU is a health initiative and is funded through Lookout Emergency Aid Society by the Vancouver / Richmond Health Board.

VANDU

The Vancouver Area Network of Drug Users

membership

An early VANDU flyer. (Reprinted with permission from the author.)

The Portland Hotel Society (PHS), a non-profit social, health and housing agency in the DTES (founded in 1991 by Liz Evans, with Mark Townsend, Kerstin Stuerzbecher, Dan Small and Tom Laviolette), helped to organize many pivotal harm reduction and drug policy events in the DTES, including "The Killing Fields" in the summer of 1997. The protest and memorial was held in the DTES to honour those who had died from overdoses and HIV/AIDS and to point to institutional and government inaction. The grounds of Oppenheimer Park were covered with wooden crosses bearing the name of each person who had lost their life. The

a thousand crosses in oppenheimer park

when eagles circle oppenheimer park we see them
feel awe feel joy feel hope soar in our hearts
the eagles are symbols for the courage in our spirits
for the fierce and piercing vision
for justice in our souls
the eagles bestow a blessing on our lives

but with these thousand crosses
planted in oppenheimer park today
who really see them feel sorrow feel loss feel rage
our hearts shed bitter tears these thousand crosses are symbols
of the social apartheid in our culture
the segregation of those who deserve to live
and those who are abandoned to die
these thousand crosses silently announce a social curse
on the lives of the poorest of the poor in the downtown eastside
they announce an assault on our community

these thousand crosses announce a deprivation of possibility
for those of us who mourn here
the mothers and fathers and sisters and brothers
the uncles, aunts, grandmothers and grandfathers
the sons and daughters the friends and acquaintances
of those members of our community
of a thousand dreams of a thousand hopes
of a thousand yearnings for real community
lost to us but memorialized today

(Excerpt of 1997 poem by Bud Osborn, reprinted with permission from Leslie Ottavi.)

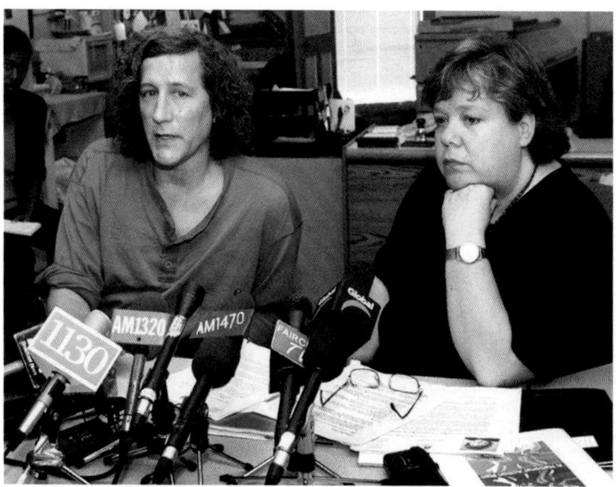

Bud Osborn and Libby Davies speak to the press about the overdose crisis and solutions to end it — safer injection sites and heroin-assisted treatment — on August 12, 1998. (Photo by Dick Clark, reprinted with permission from *The Province*.)

event was memorialized in a poem by Bud Osborn. This was one of many public events PHS and others helped organize in the DTES in the 1990s.

Through the efforts of Bud Osborn, PHS and other advocates, the Vancouver-Richmond Health Board finally declared a public health emergency in 1997. Speaking at a press conference in August 1998, Bud Osborn and then-NDP MP Libby Davies spoke again about the overdose crisis and offered concrete solutions: safer injection sites and heroin-assisted treatment so that people who used illegal opioids would no longer be vulnerable. As Libby Davies said: "These deaths are preventable. It's the responsibility of all levels of government to deal with the crisis. We ignore it at our peril."

OUT OF HARM'S WAY

Following up on the urgency to set up alternative drug policy, on November 20, 1998, the Portland Hotel Society, Carnegie Community Association and numerous volunteers hosted a free public international forum, Out of Harm's Way, on the overdose crisis, addiction, crime and solutions. The groundbreaking event took place under tents set up in Oppenheimer Park in the DTES of Vancouver.

Hundreds of people gathered in the morning for breakfast, live music and introductions. Poet and social justice activist Bud Osborn opened the forum with a poem that he wrote for the event, titled "A Song of Hope." Bud Osborn's poem voices the pain people experience from the war on drugs and concludes with these words:

SO WHETHER YOU DENY IT
OR WHETHER YOU EMBRACE IT
WE ARE EACH OTHERS' ONLY BROTHERS AND SISTERS
WE ARE EACH OTHERS' ONLY CHANCE
FOR A LIFE IN COMMON AND REAL BEAUTY
WE ARE ALL EACH OTHER HAS
WE ARE ALL
SOME-BODY
(Reprinted with permission from Leslie Ottavi.)

The Out of Harm's Way public tent event at Oppenheimer Park, November 20, 1998. (Reprinted with permission from Brian Murphy).

The international and Canadian panelists then gave accounts of pragmatic and successful heroin substitution programs, safer injection sites and harm reduction programs set up in Germany, Switzerland and the UK. Speaking about heroin, Warner Schneider, Drug Policy Co-ordinator for Frankfurt, Germany made clear that heroin substitution programs allow people "to lead an ordinary life." Canadian Dr. Bruce Alexander also spoke about the need for not only heroin substitution programs, but also cocaine and other stimulant substitution programs. The panelists made clear that any expansion of harm reduction services must be accompanied by a shift in perspective and delivery, advocating a social, health and human

Dear Friend,

Out Of Harm's Way - Friday November 20th . 1998

Please find enclosed information on the upcoming forum "Out of Harm's Way" which is being held in Oppenheimer Park, Vancouver, BC. The forum is a response to the fact that drugs, crime and addiction continue to present a major challenge to our community, the province of BC and the rest of Canada. As yet, there is no consensus on a comprehensive plan to tackle this situation.

The conference will be hosted by Daniel Richler, presenter of CBC TV's "Big Life" and Ian Mulgrew, columnist with the Vancouver Sun.

The day will feature presentations from:

Out of Harm's Way invitation. (Reprinted with permission from Portland Hotel Society.)

The June 1999 VANDU rally at the BC legislature in Victoria. (Photo by Elaine Brier, reprinted with permission.)

rights approach. The panel discussion was followed by an open mic "town hall" forum where attendees asked questions, but also voiced their own concerns.

Tragically, the speakers' and community recommendations were not fully taken up in Canada at that time.

PUBLIC HEALTH EMERGENCY DECLARED

Thanks to the efforts of activists, the Vancouver/Richmond Health Board finally declared a public health emergency in 1997. The declaration of a public health emergency was a direct result of extensive activism by harm reduction advocates, including Bud Osborn, the co-founder of VANDU. This time was different, though. Demands for drug policy reform came from those most affected, as people with lived experience of illegal drug use and their allies led the work for change. The founding of VANDU epitomized the advocacy efforts of drug users focused on the human rights and needs of their members. VANDU members also disrupted conventional myths about people who used heroin and other illegal drugs. For the first time, rather than a fixed stereotype of the heroin user, VANDU's members were organized and politicized and they demonstrated publicly. VANDU members were also diverse, with a wide range of experiences with heroin and other illegal drugs. Rather than be discounted, VANDU members asserted that their lived experience of drug use, solutions to save lives and to end drug prohibition are valid.

On June 15, 1999, VANDU, with the BC Anti-Prohibition League,

Young New Democrats and From Greif to Action, demonstrated for drug reform and harm reduction services at the BC Legislature in Victoria, BC. They collectively made clear that Canada's war on drugs was actively killing people.

HARM REDUCTION IS PART OF SOCIAL JUSTICE

The social justice movement for harm reduction (including heroin-assisted treatment and safer injection sites) and an end to drug prohibition that emerged in Vancouver in the 1990s[13] continues today throughout Canada. To be clear, harm reduction is not a panacea, and harm reduction services are not necessarily liberatory. However, for grassroots groups such as drug user unions, harm reduction services are "on the ground responses" to the changing needs of their members, who experience ongoing structural violence stemming from drug prohibition, colonialism and economic and social policies that negatively impact their everyday lives. Continued activism and harm reduction work is necessary because although harm reduction services have expanded (despite a lack of diverse services), so too has the criminalization of drugs and the people who use them.

VANDU demonstrates at the BC legislature in Victoria, BC, demanding action to save lives. (Photo by Elaine Brier, reprinted with permission.)

There is a direct relationship between discriminatory policies and stigmatization for both women and men who use illicit drugs. Discriminatory drug laws and policies "activate stigma" against people who use criminalized drugs and produce social inequality. The failure to provide services and implement alternative drug policies (diverse harm reduction, safe supply, family supports) assures that state violence and discrimination and stigma will be ongoing. The experiences and outcomes of drug use are shaped by one's social status and environment. Consequently, Indigenous peoples, poor people and people of colour bear the brunt of drug prohibitionist policies in Canada.

The 1990s social justice movement also communicated loudly and clearly that drug prohibitionist policies create a lethal environment. Without access to safe legal drugs, people who use criminalized drugs buy on the illegal market. In the illegal market, drug prices are high and drug quality and quantity are always in question. Illegal drug overdose death is preventable, yet our policies sustain them.

END NOTES

1. Statistics Canada, 1982
2. Statistics Canada, 1984
3. Gifford-Jones, 2000
4. Cain, 1994, p. 5
5. Facilitated early on by Margaret Michaud, Olive Phillips and Susan Boyd
6. Stevenson et al., 1956
7. Cain, 1994, p. 11
8. Cain, 1994, p. vi
9. Cain, 1994, pp. xi, 91
10. Boyd, 1999, p. 144
11. Boyd, 1999, p. 149
12. Boyd, 1999, p. 146
13. Boyd, MacPherson and Osborn, 2009; Campbell, Boyd, N. and Culbert, 2009

9

Struggling for Heroin-assisted Treatment

The 2000s

Responding to rising illegal drug overdose deaths, and the rates of hepatitis C and HIV/AIDs, a social justice movement for harm reduction and drug reform emerged in the DTES of Vancouver in the 1990s. However, even though awareness of the issues increased, Vancouver's promised safer injection site did not immediately open, heroin-assisted treatment was not set up, and harm reduction services remained underfunded. Illegal drug overdose deaths continued. So, on July 11,

Longtime activist Dean Wilson at the July 2000 "Two Thousand Crosses" event at Oppenheimer Park to mourn and honour lives lost due to punitive drug policies. (Photo by Elaine Brier, reprinted with permission.)

Insite, Canada's first safer injection site in Vancouver. (Photo by Steve Rolles, Transform, reprinted with permission)

2000, family members and concerned citizens gathered once again in Oppenheimer Park.

These events and others set the stage for city-wide consultation in 2001 about drug issues. Drawing from these Vancouver consultations and services outside of Canada that had already developed alternative drug policies and harm reduction programs, Vancouver's first Drug Policy Coordinator, Donald MacPherson, authored his report, *A Framework for Action: A Four-Pillar Approach to Drug Problems in Vancouver*. With support from Mayor Philip Owen and later Mayor Larry Campbell in 2002, MacPherson's report was adopted as official policy. MacPherson recommended changes in drug policy, including the opening of safer injection sites and HAT. However, the long-anticipated safer injection site was delayed.

Without official approval, Dr. Peter's Center, an HIV/AIDS health care facility in Vancouver's west end, integrated a nurse-supervised injection site into its health program and care residence in 2002. Repeated calls for a federally sanctioned supervised injection site finally resulted in Portland Hotel Society opening Insite in the DTES in 2003, Canada's first sanctioned safer injection site. Activists in other regions of Canada planned to open federally approved sites, too.

Activists also hoped to establish smoking rooms in safer injection sites. Crack cocaine, a form of cocaine that is smoked and sold cheaply, became available in some cities across Canada from the late 1980s on. However, it was not until the early 2000s that some formal initiatives in Toronto, Ottawa, Winnipeg and Vancouver were set up to provide education and safe equipment (such as Pyrex stems and mouthpieces). These harm reduction initiatives reflected changing drug use across Canada; in fact, at that time, women were more likely than men to smoke crack than to inject.

Inside the safer injection site Insite. (Reprinted with permission from Vancouver Coastal Health.)

However, the political environment in Ottawa changed. In 2007, the Liberal-led federal government lost to the Conservatives under Stephen Harper. The Conservatives introduced their new National Anti-Drug Strategy in the same year. It supported harsher law enforcement and rejected harm reduction services. Abstinence-based services were prioritized by the Harper Government, and they set about overturning existing policies and pushed forward law-and-order crime bills.

They also fought to close Insite. Rejecting research findings on the effectiveness of Insite and the fact that not one overdose death had occurred at the site, the government spent millions of taxpayer dollars to discredit and close Insite. Originally, Insite was set up as a three-year pilot project. By the end of that three-year period, the Harper-led Conservative party was in power and adamantly opposed Insite. In August 2007, a constitutional challenge to the federal government's proposal to shut Insite was launched by the Portland Hotel Society and two Insite users, longtime activist Dean Wilson and Shelly Tomic. In September 2011, the Supreme Court of Canada ruled that the closing of Insite would be a violation of the *Canadian Charter of Rights and Freedoms*. Thus, Insite remained open; however, in direct response to the

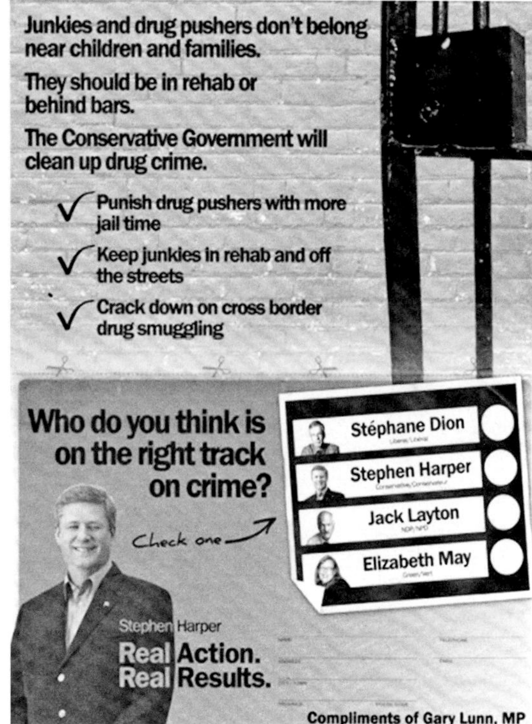

Prior to the 2011 federal election, Saanich-Gulf Island Conservative MP Gary Lunn sent out this flyer to his constituents outlining the party's mandate. (Reprinted with permission from the author).

ruling, the Conservatives set about changing the requirements for opening more safer injection sites, making it impossible for other cities to open them.

The Conservatives also set about reintroducing discriminatory language to describe people who used heroin. Prior to the May 2011 federal election, members of the Conservative party sent out flyers to their constituents that emphasized their stigmatizing and discriminatory law-and-order stance toward people who used or sold heroin, and their opposition to any drug service that was not abstinence-based. Abstinence or prison was the Conservative party mantra. The term "junkie" was employed in the flyer, a shorthand label for people who use heroin and one that is easily recognizable now (after decades of myth making). To be clear, supervised injection sites are not only confined to people who use heroin, but the term "junkie" resonates as synonymous with degradation, deviance and crime.

In 2012, the Conservative federal government finally passed their long sought-after legislation, the Safe Streets and Communities Act. The Act introduced a number of changes to the Controlled Drugs and Substances Act, including an escalating system of punitive mandatory minimum sentences. People who used illegal heroin and other drugs were further criminalized by the Act.

At the BC provincial level, there were contradictory policies. While the province and Vancouver City supported Insite and were undertaking HAT studies, the police were moving in opposite directions. Even though most people who use drugs do not suffer from mental illness, since the early 2000s the Vancouver Police Department (VPD) has positioned itself as being at the forefront of managing mental health and addiction regulation. In reports spanning from 2003 to 2013, the VPD set themselves up as reluctant experts linking dangerousness, mental illness and addiction. Researchers conclude that this "is partially achieved by emphasizing the twinning of mental health with addiction (dual diagnoses) and a focus on illegal drug consumption … Mental illness is thus framed as encompassing addiction." In the VPD reports, the DTES of Vancouver is depicted "as a deviant space predominantly populated by people with mental health and addiction problems."[1]

Using a case study approach and before-and-after photographs (a common technique used by media, governments and prohibitionist organizations to visually depict the supposed ravishes of drug use), the VPD report describes the life of a young white man, identified as having a dual diagnosis. In the first few photos, he is depicted at as a bright, happy boy and young adult. In sharp contrast, the later photos depict him as an adult in physical disarray, and it is made clear in the text that his physical disintegration is due to drug use and mental illness, ultimately leading to his death. While the VPD report assumes that most people who use illegal drugs have mental health problems, this is not the case.[2] It is worth noting here that a few years later, in 2017, the province of BC cemented the twinning of mental health and addiction. The Ministry of Mental Health and Addiction was created, purporting to coordinate service networks and to "lead the response to the overdose crisis." And in October 2021, Prime Minister Trudeau announced a new ministerial post, appointing Dr. Carolyn Bennett as the first Minister of Mental Health and Addictions.

HEROIN-ASSISTED TREATMENT

Other nations responded to illegal heroin use differently than in Canada. In the early 1990s, HAT trials were set up in Switzerland as a harm reduction measure to counter increasing heroin injecting, an open drug scene and rising HIV infection rates. Clinics were set up for medically supervised heroin injections on site for the small percentage of people that conventional substitution programs fail. Unlike safer injection sites where people bring illegal drugs to consume in a medical setting, HAT consists of people receiving prescribed heroin in a medical setting.

Other European nations (Netherlands, Spain, Germany) followed suit, setting up further clinical trials and then permanent programs. The European programs were built on growing evidence of the feasibility and efficacy of HAT as a model of treatment.[3] Rather than being constituted as an "evil" drug, heroin is conceptualized as a medical treatment in this setting. Rather than forcing abstinence on this population, safe daily doses of heroin are seen as contributing to health and wellbeing. Since the 1950s, numerous Canadian reports and studies, a Royal Commission of Inquiry, a BC Commission and a BC task force recommended the setting up HAT.

The site of NAOMI, the first pilot HAT program in Canada, at the Crosstown Clinic in Vancouver. (Reprinted with permission from Providence Health Care.)

In 2005, Canada established the first HAT clinical trial outside of Europe — the North American Opiate Initiative (NAOMI). Participants were recruited in Montreal and Vancouver. The Vancouver site, Crosstown Clinic, is on the western border of the DTES.

Even though the NAOMI results were positive, a permanent HAT program was not established at the end of the study in Montreal or Vancouver.[4] The follow-up to the NAOMI study turned out to be unlike that of every other nation that has conducted a HAT trial. The Declaration of Helsinki guidelines developed by the World Medical Association to guide ethical medical research state:

> [the] well-being of the individual research subject must take precedence over all other interests.... At the conclusion of the study, patients entered into the study are entitled to be informed about the outcome of the study and to share any benefits that result from it, for example, access to interventions identified as beneficial in the study or to other appropriate care or benefits.... Some research populations are particularly vulnerable and need special protection. These include those who cannot give or refuse consent for themselves and those who may be vulnerable to coercion or undue influence.[5]

Nevertheless, despite these guidelines and the recommendations of the WHO and the 2011 UNAIDS report, *Ethical Engagement of People Who Inject Drugs in HIV Prevention Trials*,[6] that clinical-trial participants be offered continued treatment at the end of a trial if the treatment is found to be effective, a permanent HAT program was not set up in Canada at that time.

Excerpt of a poem entitled CAUTION, by a SNAP member who received HAT during the first clinical trial:

NAOMI, she was a gift of freedom, a taste,
but she didn't give me her number!!![7]

Leaving aside the ethics of failing to establish a permanent HAT program,[8] in 2011, another HAT clinical trial was set up in Vancouver: the Study to Assess Longer-term Opioid Medication Effectiveness (SALOME). This study aimed to compare the effectiveness of hydromorphone and diacetylmorphine as a drug substitution treatment. Hydromorphone is an opioid that is commonly prescribed for pain management, and it is also sold on the illegal market as dilaudid. Prior to the SALOME trail, hydromorphone was not approved by Health Canada as a substitution drug for the treatment of heroin or opioid dependence. Nor was hydromorphone used as a drug substitution in other nations. Rather than challenge negative stereotypes about heroin, the SALOME researchers argued that since hydromorphone was already prescribed for pain relief and held few negative associations, it would be more acceptable as a substitution. Once again, the establishment of a permanent drug substitution program was not a component of the SALOME trial.[9]

SNAP

Responding to the political changes in Ottawa and the failure to establish a permanent HAT program following the end of the first Canadian HAT trial (NAOMI), in January 2011, Dave Murray, who had been a research participant in the NAOMI trial, organized an independent, peer-run mutual support group to meet weekly at the VANDU site in the DTES. As noted earlier, VANDU is Canada's oldest drug user union with a long history of activism. The peer-run group organized by Dave Murray was supported by VANDU. Initially named the NAOMI Patients Association (NPA) and later named SALOME/NAOMI Association of Patients (SNAP), the group understood their unique status: at that time, they were the only Canadians — or North Americans for that matter — to be recipients of HAT. All the members of NPA had been research subjects in the NAOMI trial at the Crosstown Clinic.

SNAP Flyer (2012)

SNAP is a unique group of people who were participants in the NAOMI and/or SALOME heroin-assisted therapy (HAT) clinical trials in Vancouver, BC. We are an independent group dedicated to supporting each other and educating peers, researchers, government, and the public. We advocate for the human rights of people who use opiates, the establishment of permanent and less medicalized HAT programs in Canada, and an end to drug prohibition.

We are also dedicated to:

- Influencing decisions about our health care and drug control.
- Advising future studies on HAT and drug substitution trials and programs.
- The right to a stable life and improvement in quality of life.
- Having the continuous choice of diverse routes of administration — injection, oral and smoking.
- Having access to safe affordable housing, social, legal and medical support, and nutritious food for self and family.
- Support to move life forward (school, trade, family reunification).

The SNAP logo, a 2013 painting by Vancouver artist Mark Scofield. (Reprinted with permission from SNAP.)

The change in name from NPA to SNAP reflected members, old and new, who also became research subjects in the second HAT trial, SALOME, launched in December 2011. Similar to NAOMI, SALOME had no exit strategy or plans for establishing a permanent HAT program if the study found HAT to be effective.

Led by extensive advocacy efforts on the part of SNAP, Pivot Legal Society and others since late 2012, Providence Health

An NPA event at Simon Fraser University's Woodward's site in Vancouver, with members Dave Murray, Dianne Tobin, Jewel Chapman and researcher/collaborator Susan Boyd, in November 2011. (Reprinted with permission from Canadian Drug Policy Coalition.)

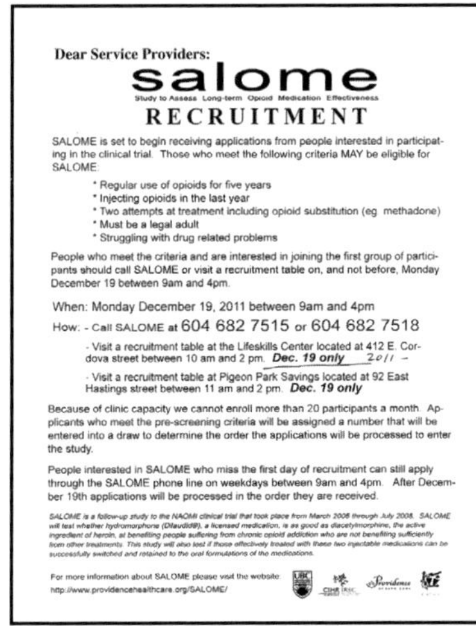

Dear Service Providers:

salome

Study to Assess Long-term Opioid Medication Effectiveness

RECRUITMENT

SALOME is set to begin receiving applications from people interested in participating in the clinical trial. Those who meet the following criteria MAY be eligible for SALOME:

* Regular use of opioids for five years
* Injecting opioids in the last year
* Two attempts at treatment including opioid substitution (eg. methadone)
* Must be a legal adult
* Struggling with drug related problems

People who meet the criteria and are interested in joining the first group of participants should call SALOME or visit a recruitment table on, and not before, Monday December 19 between 9am and 4pm.

When: Monday December 19, 2011 between 9am and 4pm

How: - Call SALOME at 604 682 7515 or 604 682 7518

- Visit a recruitment table at the Lifeskills Center located at 412 E. Cordova street between 10 am and 2 pm. ***Dec. 19 only*** 2011 –

- Visit a recruitment table at Pigeon Park Savings located at 92 East Hastings street between 11 am and 2 pm. ***Dec. 19 only***

Because of clinic capacity we cannot enroll more than 20 participants a month. Applicants who meet the pre-screening criteria will be assigned a number that will be entered into a draw to determine the order the applications will be processed to enter the study.

People interested in SALOME who miss the first day of recruitment can still apply through the SALOME phone line on weekdays between 9am and 4pm. After December 19th applications will be processed in the order they are received.

SALOME is a follow-up study to the NAOMI clinical trial that took place from March 2005 through July 2008. SALOME will test whether hydromorphone (Dilaudid®), a licensed medication, is as good as diacetylmorphine, the active ingredient of heroin, at benefiting people suffering from chronic opioid addiction who are not benefiting sufficiently from other treatments. This study will also test if those effectively treated with these two injectable medications can be successfully switched and retained to the oral formulations of the medications.

For more information about SALOME please visit the website: http://www.providencehealthcare.org/SALOME/

A SALOME recruitment poster posted at VANDU in 2011. (Reprinted with permission from the author.)

Dr. Scott MacDonald, a leading Canadian expert on diacetylmorphine and injectable opioid agonist therapy, at Crosstown Clinic. (Reprinted with permission from Scott MacDonald and Providence Health Care.)

Two SNAP members reflect on the group's activism

P1: These [SNAP] groups, it's the first time in my life I've ever witnessed people, you know, working towards, you know …

P2: A bunch of fucking junkies got something done.

P1: Yeah, I mean, it's not the drug that fucks us up, it's the fucking lifestyle that we wind up living to, you know? I mean, you know, it's so simple. It's a no-brainer, but … for me to go and tell one person that and hope they listen … [it] is not going to change anything. The only way anything is going to change is by doing what we're doing.[10]

Care Society (PHCS) and some of the SALOME team strove for a feasible exit strategy for research participants. PHCS physicians, including Dr. Scott MacDonald and those at Crosstown Clinic, successfully submitted Special Access Program requests to Health Canada to continue prescribing heroin to eligible patients exiting the SALOME trial.

In Canada, all drugs included in Schedule I of the Controlled Drugs and Substances Act, including heroin, are deemed the most dangerous of all controlled substances and given the most punitive of penalties. Until NAOMI, physicians in Canada could not legally prescribe heroin to patients for addiction treatment. In addition, Health Canada's permission was limited to this one specific clinical trial, and a special section 56 exemption to Canada's CDSA was necessary to allow NAOMI researchers and staff to receive and administer heroin to research participants without being arrested. Onsite, research participants inject themselves with prepared doses of heroin, prescribed by a doctor, with supervision from nurses and other staff if needed. Similar approvals made the later SALOME clinical trial possible. At this time, outside of a clinical trial, heroin had not been approved as a drug substitution treatment option. On September 20, 2013, for the first time since heroin was criminalized, Health Canada approved twenty-one SAP requests for research participants exiting SALOME to receive legally prescribed heroin as a substitution drug.

HEALTH CANADA'S SPECIAL ACCESS TO DRUGS

The Special Access Program (SAP) provides access to non-marketed drugs for practitioners treating patients with serious or life-threatening conditions when conventional therapies have failed, are unsuitable or are unavailable. The SAP authorizes a manufacturer to sell a drug that cannot otherwise be sold or distributed in Canada. Drugs considered for release by the SAP include pharmaceutical, biologic and radio-pharmaceutical products not approved for sale in Canada.

SAP allows for physicians to submit a request on behalf of a patient for a drug not yet approved in Canada. However, before the research participants could celebrate their victory, then Conservative federal Minister of Health Rona Ambrose sent out a press release and announced that her government would stop SAP requests for heroin. The press release below was released on September 21, 2013:

> Our Government takes seriously the harm caused by dangerous and addictive drugs. These drugs tear families apart, promote criminal behaviour, and destroy lives. That is why our Government is focused on preventing children and youth from using drugs in the first place and strongly deterring existing use of harmful and addictive drugs. Health Canada has a "Special Access Program," which is designed to give Canadians with rare diseases or terminal illnesses access to medications that are not otherwise approved for use in Canada. For example, a doctor who is treating a child with a rare form of cancer can apply to Health Canada for access to potentially life-saving medicines, which otherwise would not have been approved for medical treatment. This is what the Special Access Program is designed to do. Earlier today, officials at Health Canada made the decision to approve an application under the Special Access Program's current regulations to give heroin to heroin users — not to treat an underlying medical condition, but simply to allow them to continue to have access to heroin for their addiction even though other safe treatments for heroin addiction, such as methadone, are available. This decision is in direct opposition to the government's anti-drug policy and violates the spirit and intent of the Special Access Program. I am taking immediate action to protect the integrity of the Special Access Program and ensure this does not happen again. The Special Access Program was designed to treat unusual cases and medical emergencies; it was not intended as a way to give illicit drugs to drug addicts. Our policy is to take heroin out of the hands of addicts, not to put it into their arms. Our Government will continue to invest in drug treatment and prevention programs that work to keep our children and youth off drugs, and will continue to protect Canadian families and communities.

Minister of Health Ambrose quickly announced new regulations for Health Canada's SAP, eliminating prescription heroin for the treatment of addiction.

In response to these new regulations, five plaintiffs — Larry Love, Deborah Bartosch, Charles English, Douglas Lidstrom and Dave Murray, all former SALOME participants — along with co-plaintiff PHCS, filed a constitutional challenge in the Supreme Court of British Columbia to overturn the federal government's decision to prevent further SAP requests for HAT (*Providence Health Care Society v. Canada*).[11]

The notice of civil claim was submitted on behalf of the plaintiffs and "on behalf of all persons with severe opioid addiction who have previously not responded to other available treatment."[12] Pivot Legal Society initiated the constitutional challenge on behalf of the individual plaintiffs and others and PHCS retained Joseph Arvay as legal counsel. Since its inception in 2001, Pivot Legal Society in Vancouver has collaborated with grassroots organizations and marginalized people to challenge legislation, policies and practices that "undermine human rights, intensify poverty, and perpetuate stigma." [13] Challenging punitive drug policies are an integral component of their ongoing work.

SNAP members argued that in the midst of a preventable public health crisis — illegal opioid overdose deaths — having access to HAT saved their lives.[14] The plaintiffs stated in their individual affidavits that denying their SAP applications following the new regulations forced them to use illegal heroin and made them vulnerable to all of the associated risks, including infection, overdose death and arrest. One SNAP member who had long advocated for HAT argued, "I'd say the doctor should have everything in his tool bag and recognize the fact that everyone's different ... what will work for me might not work for you."[15]

Because HAT was an effective treatment for SALOME participants, the new federal regulations were unconstitutional and infringed on their rights as set out in the *Canadian Charter of Rights and Freedoms*. Because the Charter case would not be heard for at least another year, in May 2014, BC Supreme Court Chief Justice Hinkson granted an injunction, in effect approving an exemption from the new federal regulations for the participants in SALOME.[16] Former SALOME research participants could receive HAT if their physicians deemed it the best treatment option, and SAP concurred. Hinkson's judgment was a victory for patients exiting the SALOME trial. Unfortunately, the decision only applied to former SALOME participants and not to other people labelled with severe opioid addiction who had previously not responded to other available treatment. Since November 2014, about one hundred people receive HAT through the injectable opioid agonist treatment (iOAT) program at Crosstown Clinic. The Charter case was never heard because, following a federal election in October 2015, the newly elected Liberal-led government reinstated the former SAP policy for diacetylmorphine only.

This time, due to extensive activism by SNAP, Pivot and others, including the Charter challenge for HAT, a permanent program was established at Crosstown Clinic in Vancouver.[17] However, unlike Switzerland's twenty-three HAT clinics and the Netherlands' eleven HAT clinics,[18] outside of Crosstown Clinic, two other smaller HAT programs have been established in Vancouver and another in Surrey, BC. No other province in Canada provides HAT. Instead, low-barrier hydromorphone programs have been set up in BC and some other provinces. Health Canada now allows for prescribing injectable hydromorphone for those diagnosed with severe opioid use disorder.[19] The increase in hydromorphone programs is curious, given the limited evidence of hydromorphone effectiveness in the treatment of addiction in contrast to the substantial body of international and Canadian research results demonstrating the efficacy of HAT.[20]

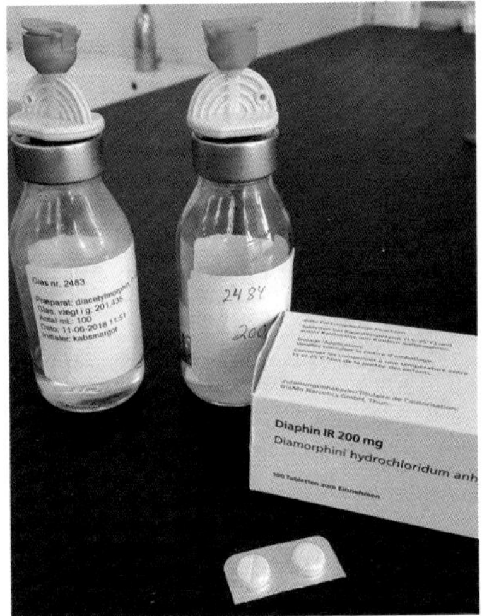

Diamorphine (legal heroin). (Photo by Steve Rolles, Transform, reprinted with permission.)

This is not to suggest rejecting hydromorphone programs. Rather, I am questioning the rejection of further HAT programs (and other flexible drug substitution programs). Not all opi-

Poppy batik by artist Elaine Alfoldy. (Reprinted with permission.)

oid users respond positively to hydromorphone programs. The failure to include and expand access to legal heroin (whether iOAT, oral or other modes of ingestion) for those who would benefit will have a negative impact, including overdose death. Activists and their allies have also questioned why diverse forms of heroin are not available, such as smokeable heroin, liquid heroin and heroin in pill form, especially for those people who do not want to inject. These advocates look to poppy tea, liquid forms of opium and pills as potential sources.[21] Activists and allies also look to other HAT programs and drug user union activism in and outside of Canada for inspiration. They also note that legal heroin continues to be prescribed to some patients in the UK, including young children, for acute pain and hospice care. As well, for a century legal, safe, heroin has been prescribed in the UK to some people dependent on the drug. And since the 1990s, heroin-assisted programs have been set up in a number of other nations.

A Danish HAT Model

Anyone for Coffee and Heroin? Inside a Danish Narcotics Dispensary is a 2011 documentary that examines the first year of a heroin-assisted treatment program (not a trial) called "Poppy" in Copenhagen, Denmark. The film follows the lives of both staff and patients at Poppy. The out-patient Poppy clinic is informal and welcoming, bright and airy, with sun streaming in from large windows. At the Poppy clinic, the walls are painted white and covered in large colorful abstract paintings. Patients at the Poppy clinic received legally prescribed heroin and had all-day access to a kitchen, meals, a living room area, a gym and a sun deck on the roof. The patients at Poppy also had access to social and legal support, housing and therapy. In the documentary, housing in Denmark is depicted as consisting of one-bedroom apartments rather than single-room occupancies or small studio apartments so favored for the poor by all levels of government in Canada.

A DOUBLE STANDARD: WOMEN SUSPECTED OF DRUG USE

There are few harm-reduction programs specifically for women (in all their diversity) and their children in Canada. As well, mothers suspected of using drugs are vulnerable to child protection services investigations and apprehension of their children. In 2014, this fact was once again made public in Canada when the Ontario government established an independent review of drug hair testing practices conducted by Motherisk Drug Testing Laboratory (MDTL) at Toronto's Hospital for Sick Kids. Between 2005 and 2015, MDTL tested more than 24,00 hair samples from 16,000 people for drug consumption, mostly from poor

Kent Monkman, *The Scream*, 2017. Acrylic on canvas, 84" x 126". (Reprinted with permission from the artist, Collection of the Denver Art Museum.)

pregnant women and mothers living in Ontario. However, about 8,000 BC, 1,400 New Brunswick and 900 Nova Scotia hair samples were also tested. The testing results were introduced as evidence in court and resulted in both temporary and permanent loss of custody of children. Tragically, it was later discovered that the hair testing results were unreliable, giving false positive results for drug consumption when in fact the result was negative. Relying on the evidence of false positive tests, many of these stolen children never came home, and other children suffered harm in foster care. Poor and Indigenous women were overrepresented, and although not evident in the review sample of cases chosen, Black women and their children were also thought to be negatively impacted. The Motherisk tragedy is not an isolated event, rather it is part of a continuum of state and gendered violence against poor, Indigenous and Black women and their families in Canada. These women have been legally denied the right to be with and care for their own children.[22] The lifelong suffering and harms experienced by mothers and their children, families and communities due to child protection policies are horrific.

Women, especially Indigenous women, have been vocal about the violence of child apprehension in Canada and government discrimination and underfunding of Indigenous child welfare systems in comparison to non-Indigenous services. However, it is difficult for individual mothers who are suspected of drug use to speak publicly about their experiences, to access services or to rally for change. This is because any admission of past or current drug use to healthcare providers, housing authorities, social workers, schools or partners can be used as evidence to deny them custody of their children. For example, if a woman who is raising children asks her doctor to consider prescribing her a safe supply of hydromorphone so that the risk of overdose death from a poisoned drug supply is lessened for her, the doctor may contact child protection services due to their flawed assumptions about drugs, risk and parenting.

In all of this, individual mothers and drugs are blamed for destroying family life and putting children at risk. The stereotypes and policies that equate drug use with poor parenting are never held up to scrutiny. Nor are the more systemic sources of family disruption and risk for children considered, such as colonialism and systemic racism, neoliberal social service cuts, economic policies that drive up unemployment and poverty and gendered violence that destroys family life. Across Canada, marginalized mothers, especially Indigenous mothers, whose children have been taken from their care are at much greater risk of accidental non-fatal drug overdose[23] and other health risks.[24] And although not all child apprehensions stem from allegations of drug use, they are significant.

THE STRUGGLE CONTINUES

Throughout Canada, end-prohibition groups and harm reduction advocates called on governments at every level to take further actions to stem the harms of drug prohibition. Due to the governments' failure to do so, activists set about providing those services, often risking arrest. Advocates and their allies also launched Charter challenges to secure safer injection sites and HAT. However, the struggle continued, and the next decade brought with it new challenges for people who use drugs.

END NOTES

1. Boyd, Boyd and Kerr, 2015, p. 636
2. Fraser, 2017; Fraser, Moore and Keane, 2014; Reinarman and Granfield, 2015
3. Strang, Groshkova and Metrebian, 2012; Strang et al., 2015
4. Oviedo-Joekes et al., 2008; Strang et al., 2015
5. World Medical Association, 2004
6. Arosteguy, 2011
7. From a writing workshop conducted by SNAP (formally NPA) members and the author in the fall of 2011. See Boyd, Murray and NAOMI Patients Association, 2017, p. 365
8. see Boyd, Murray, SNAP and MacPherson, 2017; Boyd and NPA, 2013; Small and Drucker, 2006
9. Oviedo-Joekes et al., 2016
10. Boyd, Murray, SNAP and MacPherson, 2017
11. Providence Health Care Society v. Canada (Attorney General), Notice of Civil Claim, BCSC S138411 (November 13, 2013)
12. Providence Health Care Society v. Canada (Attorney General), Notice of Civil Claim, BCSC S138411 (November 13, 2013), p. 1
13. See https://www.pivotlegal.org/our_story
14. Boyd et al., 2017
15. Boyd et al., 2017
16. Providence Health Care Society v. Canada (Attorney General), BCSC 936 (May 29, 2014)
17. Boyd and Norton, 2019
18. Strang et al., 2015, p. 149
19. Health Canada, 2019
20. See Fairbairn et al., 2019; Oviedo-Joekes et al., 2016; Strang et al., 2012, Strang et al., 2015
21. In fact, in the fall of 2021, longtime cannabis activist Dana Larsen opened The Coca Leaf Cafe in Vancouver. The menu includes coca leaf tea.
22. Boyd, 2018
23. Thumath et al., 2021
24. Kenny et al., 2021

10

A Poisoned Heroin Supply

The 2010s and 2020s

The struggle for harm reduction drug policies continued through the 2010s and into 2020s. Although progress was made in relation to setting up more harm reduction services, Canada's drug control regime and the United Nations Office on Drugs and Crime continued to negatively impact individuals and their families. The ongoing criminalization of people who use heroin and/or other illegal drugs contravenes the United Nations Universal Declaration of Human rights, UN Convention of the Rights of the Child, UN Convention on the Elimination of all Forms of Discrimination Against Women, UN Commission on the Status of Women, UN Declaration on the Rights of Indigenous Peoples and the goals of the Joint UN Programme on HIV and AIDS. Yet, drug prohibition continues, as does the illegal drug overdose crisis and a lack of a safe supply, including heroin substitution programs in Canada. By 2010 it was widely acknowledged by people who use drugs that illegal drug overdose deaths were rising. So, drug user unions and allies once again stepped in to fill in the gap produced by government inaction.

In 2012, VANDU responded to the overdose crisis by opening an unsanctioned overdose prevention site (OPS) in-house. An OPS usually refers to smaller safer injection sites, often a one-room set-up in an existing service, such as VANDU's. Outside of BC, other regions called on the government to take action to save lives.

In Toronto, to remember and honour the lives of people who have

Raffi Balian, longtime harm reduction and drug reform activist and coordinator of COUNTERfit Harm Reduction at South Riverdale Community Health Service, stands next to the Drug User Memorial in January 2017. Raffi, internationally and nationally recognized for his work and activism, passed away on February 16, 2017. (Photo by Carlos Osorio, reprinted with permission from Getty Images.)

died from a preventable overdose, on August 20, 2013, a day before International Drug User Memorial Day, a beautiful and harrowing public sculpture was unveiled, created by local artist Rocky Dobey in collaboration with COUNTERfit Harm Reduction, community harm reduction allies and South Riverdale Community Health Centre. The Drug User Memorial includes the names of people who have died from a preventable overdose. The memorial is also a permanent protest, a reminder that these deaths are the result of government inaction and failed drug policy.

Activists in Ottawa and Toronto had long called for more funding to set up life-saving harm reduction services, including supervised consumption sites, and an evaluation report in 2012 supported the opening of three sites in Toronto and one in Ottawa. However, they were not set up at that time. Illegal drug overdose deaths continued in these two cities.

A PUBLIC HEALTH EMERGENCY DECLARED IN BC

Meanwhile, in BC, illegal drug overdoses continued to rise. After years of inaction, on April 14, 2016, Dr. Perry Kendall, the provincial health officer of BC, declared a public health emergency due to the illegal overdose death crisis in the province. However, on the ground, people who used drugs continued to die. Therefore, in September 2016, in violation of the law, activists Ann Livingston, Chris Ewart and Sarah Blythe set up an unsanctioned OPS in a tent in the DTES. As mentioned above, OPS usually refers to more informal supervised injection and/or smoking sites set up in tents, trailers or in a room of an existing service. Inside the tent set up in the DTES, harm reduction supplies were available along with tables and chairs. Risking arrest, activists volunteered to provide live-saving services to people who use drugs.[1]

In September 2016, activists Chris Ewart, Sarah Blythe and Ann Livingston set up an unsanctioned OPS in a tent in the DTES. (Reprinted with permission from journalist Christopher Cheung.)

In December 2016, on the advice of Dr. Perry Kendall, BC Health Minister Terry Lake enacted a ministerial order to fund and set up OPSS across the province (without federal approval) as one strategy to curb overdose deaths. However, not all sanctioned OPSS are equal in BC and many municipalities do not even have one. In the face of the growing illegal drug overdose death crisis, activists called for innovative drug substitution programs to be set up, especially HAT programs. Public forums were initiated by advocates to educate the public about HAT.

A 2017 public forum on HAT, one of many held in Vancouver over the years around the illegal drug overdose crisis. (Reprinted with permission from poster designer Iva Cheung and Pivot Legal Society.)

Across Canada, activists also organized to bring attention to the overdose crisis. In 2017, with the Canadian Association

Outside Queen's Park in Toronto, on the first National Day of Action on the overdose crisis in February 2017, harm reduction activist Zoë Dodd speaks, with Marjie Francis on the left and Matt Johnson on the right. (Photo from Zoë Dodd, reprinted with permission.)

of People who Use Drugs (CAPUD), activists in Toronto, Ottawa, Montreal, Edmonton, Calgary, Vancouver, Victoria and Nanaimo gathered in each city to demand action from governments to prevent overdose deaths and to end the war on drugs — a war on people. Many banners read: "They talk we die."

As well, responding to inaction by governments, the Toronto Harm Reduction alliance and allies came together to form the Toronto Overdose Prevention Society (TOPS). They opened an unsanctioned OPS injection tent in August 2017 in Moss Park, located on the east side of Toronto. TOPS volunteers managed the OPS tent site and later a trailer.

The Moss Park OPS was officially sanctioned and relocated to South Riverdale Community Health Service in July 2018, where other harm reduction services and supplies are provided as well, including drug checking and a Safer Opioid Supply Program, which was made more possible to implement when new regulations to address the overdose death crisis were introduced in 2017 and 2019 by the federal government.

The unsanctioned OPS tent in Moss Park on August 13, 2017, with harm reduction advocates Matt Johnson, Zoë Dodd and Nick Boyce. (Photo by Joanna Lavoie, reprinted with permission from Joanna Lavoie and Metroland.)

The new federal regulations made it easier to provide methadone, injectable hydromorphone and diacetylmorphine, also referred to as heroin-assisted therapy (HAT) and diacetylmorphine-assisted therapy (DAM).[2] A new "List of Drugs for an Urgent Public Health Need" was developed by Health Canada in 2017. The list includes drugs (and prescribing) that are not yet authorized by Health Canada. In order to obtain access to the drugs on the list (for one year, although it can be renewed), a territory or provincial public health authority must notify Health Canada of their particular public health need. In 2017, injectable and tablet-form Diaphin (a brand name for heroin) was added to the list for use in BC only as a substitution therapy for the treatment of "severe heroin dependence." In 2019, injectable heroin was approved for all of Canada as an opioid crisis substitution therapy for severe heroin dependence. However, rather than scale up HAT programs across Canada, more hydromorphone programs have been established. In Vancouver, Crosstown Clinic, and more recently two other clinics, plus another clinic in Surrey, BC are the only sites that provide HAT in Canada. Even though it saves lives, and in the face of a poisoned illegal drug supply that is killing people, provincial and municipal governments' resistance to HAT in Canada continues. [3] In BC, drug checking and Bad Dope Alerts were posted to stem preventable deaths. Because people still do not have access to a safe legal drug supply, these efforts are crucial.

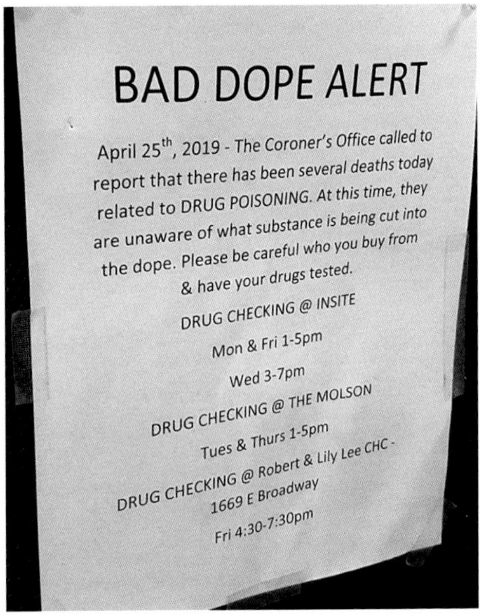

Bad Dope Alert flyer in Vancouver's DTES, 2019. (Photo by Steve Rolles, Transform, reprinted with permission.)

Across Canada, people with diverse social status have died from illegal overdose death, largely due to fentanyl poisoning of the illegal drug supply. However, in Canada, as with drug offences and prison statistics, poor, marginalized and racialized people are most vulnerable. For example, women made up about 24 percent of all BC illegal overdose deaths in 2019.[4] However, Indigenous women in BC are five times more likely to die from an illegal overdose than non-Indigenous women.[5] Preliminary findings suggest that Indigenous peoples in BC are three times more likely to die from an illegal overdose than non-Indigenous people.[6] Later research conducted during the COVID-19 pandemic

Filmmaker Elle-Máijá Tailfeathers' 2021 documentary, Kímmapiiyipitssini: The Meaning of Empathy, is an intimate story about community, substance use, overdose, resistance and harm reduction in Kainai First Nation. (Reprinted with permission from National Film Board)

concluded that even though Indigenous peoples make up a little over 3 percent of the population in BC, 16 percent of all overdose deaths in BC from January to May 2020 were Indigenous men and women, which is up from 9.9 percent in 2019. In fact, Indigenous women's rate of death from an overdose was 8.7 higher than the rate of non-Indigenous women in the province.[7] Culturally diverse and gender-appropriate overdose prevention sites are still lacking in BC and other provinces.[8]

SISTERSPACE, CANNABIS SUBSTITUTION AND DRUG TESTING

In response to the lack of services specifically for women (cis women, trans women, genderqueer women and non-binary people who are significantly femme-identified) who use drugs, in May 2017, SisterSpace opened in the Vancouver's DTES. It is the first women-only overdose prevention site in Canada. At the site women are provided a safe, comfortable (non-clinical) setting to use their drugs, talk amongst themselves and share information. SisterSpace provides harm reduction equipment, referrals and food, and their staff includes women with lived experience. In this, they offer a temporary reprieve from criminalization and gendered violence.[9]

SisterSpace, the first women-only OPS in North America, opened in May 2017. (Photo by SisterSpace, Atira Women's Resource Society, reprinted with permission.)

Meeting room of Sisterspace interior. (Photo by SisterSpace, Atira Women's Resource Society, reprinted with permission.)

Activists like Neil Magnuson, a longtime cannabis activist, also stepped in when the government did not. In April 2017, Magnuson set up the Cannabis Substitution Project at VANDU. Vancouver City Council did not reply to his earlier request for funding and permission, so he set up without their support. Keeping in mind that cannabis for recreational use was not legalized until October 2018, and medically approved cannabis could only be accessed online, Magnuson offered a range of cannabis products at a table set up inside the doorway of VANDU, including joints, edibles and seeds. As might be expected, the response was positive. Magnuson was quick to point out that many people told him they consumed cannabis to help them sleep, to address pain, to feel better and to "offset" street drug use. In fact, scientific studies support what he heard from people at VANDU every weekend.[10]

Cannabis Substitution Project poster in VANDU, 2017. (Photo by the author.)

Drug user unions also set up drug testing services so that people would know if the drugs they bought on the illegal market were adulterated. On April 14, 2019, groups across Canada protested on the National Day of Action on the Overdose Crisis, appealing to governments at all levels to take action to save lives. In BC, activists made clear that it was three years since the public emergency was declared in 2016, yet people were still dying every day — these deaths are preventable.

Neil Magnuson and Ann Genovy at the Cannabis Substitution Program hosted by VANDU in June 2017. (Photo by the author, reprinted with permission from Neil Magnuson and Ann Genovy.)

Drug testing signage in the window of VANDU, 2020. (Photo by the author.)

Donald MacPherson, Executive Director of the Canadian Drug Policy Coalition spoke at the National Day of Action on the Overdose Crisis on the steps of Vancouver Art Gallery on April 18, 2019. (Photo by Peter Kim, reprinted with permission from him and Canada Drug Policy Coalition.)

OUTSIDE OF BC THE STRUGGLE CONTINUES

Since the onset of the COVID-19 pandemic in March 2020, regions across Canada have experienced steep increases in overdose deaths. These deaths are linked to a poisoned illegal drug supply, drug prohibitionist policies, lack of a safe supply and COVID-19-related restrictions, such as limiting onsite access to harm reduction services and other social supports. Overdose deaths have been reported in every province and the Yukon and Northwest Territories.

Harm reduction services, including HAT, OPSS and iOAT, are not available in all regions across Canada. And funding and support for services can disappear depending on the results of federal, provincial and municipal election results. For example, since winning the provincial election in 2019 in Alberta, the United Conservate-led government has been busy slashing funding and cutting back social programs and supports for vulnerable people, including harm reduction services. Harm reduction allies have publicly contested provincial and municipal drug policies. After years of setting up some effective, hard-won harm reduction services in the province, the newly elected United Conservative party led by Jason Kenny, who oppose harm reduction in favour of abstinence-based services, announced that it would freeze all funding to supervised consumption sites until a review took place.

Contesting Alberta's flawed drug policy outside the McCauley Center, a provincial government building in Calgary, in March 2020. (Photo by Rebecca Haines-Saah, reprinted with permission.)

Following the review, the Alberta government released a controversial propogandist, and later discredited, report on March 5, 2020, recommending supervised consumption sites be shut down. A small group of harm reduction advocates responded right away, organizing a news conference disputing the findings and claims publicized in the report and publicly protesting outside of a government building

In protest of the sham report by the Alberta government on supervised consumption sites outside a provincial government building in Calgary, in March 2020. (Photo by Rebecca Haines-Saah, reprinted with permission.)

in Calgary. Other actions took place as well. Activists in Alberta point to the fact that in the first six months of 2020, 449 people died from a preventable illegal overdose death. They argue that OPSS and other harm reduction services are essential. It is estimated that in 2021, about 2.5 people per day in Alberta died from a preventable illegal overdose death.[11] The Alberta provincial government also moved to shut down iOAT sites in Calgary and Edmonton by cutting off their funding in March 2021. Due to condemnation from advocates and researchers, as well as a Charter challenge, the Alberta government back-peddled and announced that iOAT would continue to be funded, but only for those people already enrolled in the two existing programs. No new clients would be allowed to receive iOAT, leaving them vulnerable to arrest and death.

A DEATH EPIDEMIC

The fight for HAT in Canada is urgent because a poisoned illegal drug supply (due to fentanyl and its analogues) has led to overdoses of illegal opioids increasing in Canada since 2010. It is estimated that over 24,626 people have died across Canada from a preventable overdose between January 2016 and March 2021.[12] BC has been hit hard, with Ontario and Alberta right behind.[13] To be clear, because they have a much larger population, Ontario has recorded more deaths than BC. Yet, BC has the highest illegal overdose *rate* in Canada (deaths per 100,000 people). Drug user unions, harm reduction services and allies at the provincial and national level have strongly condemned all levels of government for failing to act quickly to provide a legal supply of drugs and have called for an end to criminalization.[14]

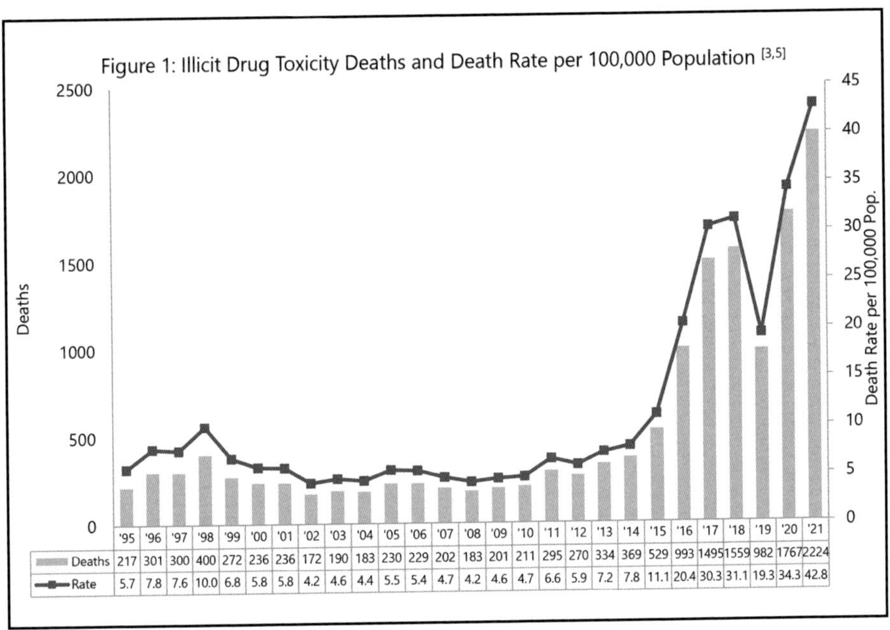

	'95	'96	'97	'98	'99	'00	'01	'02	'03	'04	'05	'06	'07	'08	'09	'10	'11	'12	'13	'14	'15	'16	'17	'18	'19	'20	'21
Deaths	217	301	300	400	272	236	236	172	190	183	230	229	202	183	201	211	295	270	334	369	529	993	1495	1559	982	1767	2224
Rate	5.7	7.8	7.6	10.0	6.8	5.8	5.8	4.2	4.6	4.4	5.5	5.4	4.7	4.2	4.6	4.7	6.6	5.9	7.2	7.8	11.1	20.4	30.3	31.1	19.3	34.3	42.8

BC Coroner's Office, February 2022[15]

In BC alone, there were an estimated 11,028 preventable illegal drug overdose deaths from January 1, 2010 to December 31, 2021.[16] Illegal overdose deaths in BC are higher than those of people dying from car accidents, homicides and suicides combined.[17] In BC, the city of Vancouver has been hit the hardest, followed by Surrey, Victoria and Abbotsford.[18] However, for the first time since the number of illegal overdose deaths began to rise, the BC Coroners Service announced that the number of deaths in the first half of 2019 decreased.[19] The expansion of harm reduction services was making a difference. Yet, this hopeful trend was about to change dramatically in and outside of BC. On March 17, 2020, BC declared another public health emergency due to the COVID-19 pandemic. Other provinces followed suit. As the two public health emergencies coalesced, a steep increase in illegal drug overdose deaths in BC was reported in the first half of 2020 and they continued to rise in 2021.[20] Other provinces reported sharp increases, too.

From March 2020 on, all levels of government acted swiftly setting up COVID-19 safety measures (from economic support to social distancing, online schooling, travel restrictions and testing). This response was in stark contrast to the measures taken by the federal and provincial governments following the illegal overdose death public health emergency declared in BC in August 2016. Governments had ignored for years the call for access to a safer supply of legal drugs to counter overdose deaths. In 2020, however, in order to stem the spread of COVID-19 infection (with drug users constructed as vectors of disease), to ensure physical distancing and self-isolation and to reduce the risk of drug withdrawal and overdose deaths, temporary changes in federal and BC prescribing policies for controlled drugs were enacted. The new policies allowed for a safer supply of legal substitution drugs (hydromorphone, Dexedrine) and home delivery of prescriptions to people using illegal drugs during the pandemic.[21] Unconscionably, heroin was not included in the list of drugs that doctors in BC can prescribe more easily during the pandemic. Compared to COVID-19 deaths, illegal drug overdose deaths are overlooked — many would even say it is an unacknowledged genocide. Drug user unions and their allies question why the lives of people who use criminalized drugs are seen as less worthy than those of others.

BC/Yukon Association of Drug War Survivors. (Reprinted with permission from BCYADWS.)

In order to stem rising preventable drug overdose deaths during the COVID-19 pandemic, drug user unions and allies called again for an immediate expansion of harm reduction services and access to safe, legal, unadulterated drugs, an end to drug prohibition and the decriminalization/legalization of possession for personal use of all illegal drugs. As early as 2019, people in BC with lived expertise of drug use[22] and their allies called for the establishment of a "heroin compassion club" — a cooperative model where people who use opioids (including fentanyl) could access unadulterated heroin.[23] In the same year, the BC/Yukon Association of Drug War Survivors (BCYADWS) demanded that the BC government immediately set up heroin buyer clubs.[24]

ACTIVISM DURING COVID-19

Activists and allies have fought on many fronts to save lives and to change drug policy in Canada. Their combined efforts have made some difference, but until city, provincial and federal officials take further action, people will continue to die. Due to COVID-19 restrictions, social distancing and isolation often prevent people from accessing important services. Many services have had to shut down their "onsite" programs. COVID-19 also disrupted the illegal drug market, leading to an even more toxic drug supply. Doctors in BC were reluctant to take up the new prescribing guidelines, especially for patients who identified as mothers.[25] In September 2020, Dr. Bonnie Henry, BC's provincial health officer, issued a new public health order to stem the tide of rising illegal drug overdose deaths. The new order allows registered nurses and psychiatric nurses to prescribe legal pharmaceuticals to people using illegal drugs. But heroin is not on the list of drugs that can be prescribed.

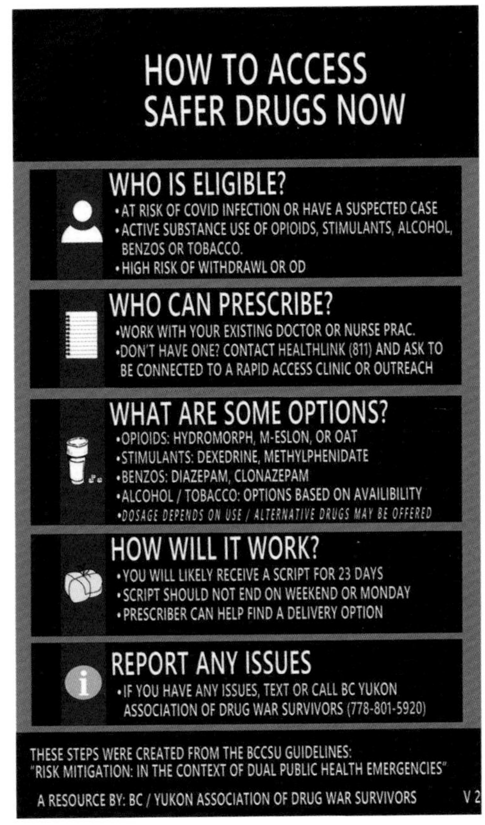

A 2020 BC/Yukon Association of Drug War Survivors flyer. (Reprinted with permission from BCYADWS.)

Crackdown, a monthly podcast, began airing in January 2019. The unique Vancouver-based program investigates pressing local, national and international issues, such as COVID-19, policing, illegal overdose deaths and solutions. *Crackdown*'s focus is: "The drug war, covered by drug users as war correspondents. A monthly podcast about drugs, drug policy and the drug war led by drug user activists and supported by research." (Reprinted with permission from *Crackdown*.)

There have been numerous marches demanding action during the COVID-19 pandemic across Canada. Following more than four months of steadily rising overdose deaths in Vancouver, activists, friends and family, under the leadership of VANDU, gathered on August 15, 2020, in memory of those who recently died.

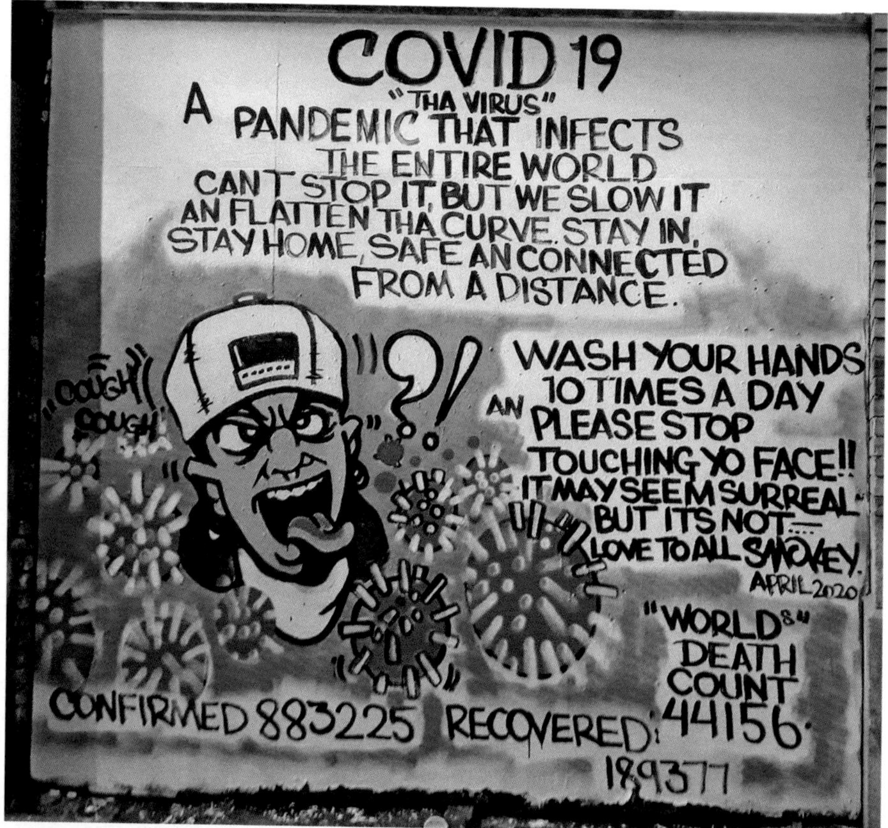

Graffiti artist Smokey D (a.k.a. Jamie Hardy) collaborated with activist Karen Ward on this COVID-19 mural in the DTES in April 2020. (Reprinted with permission from Jamie Hardy and Karen Ward.)

Kat Wahamaa and Tracy Scott, members of Moms Stop the Harm and Maple Ridge Street Outreach Society at "We speak their names, We march with rage" on August 20, 2020. (Photo by the author. Reprinted with permission from Kat Wahamaa and Tracy Scott.)

"We speak their names, We march with rage": the August 2020 VANDU march. (Reprinted with permission from VANDU.)

Responding to COVID-19 regulations, SisterSquare, the first women-only outdoor tent OPS in North America, was set up in May 2020 by Atira Women's Resource Society in a parking lot in the DTES. (Photo by Joshua Berson, reprinted with permission from Atira Women's Resource Society.)

WOMEN AND THE OVERDOSE CRISIS

Responding to government inaction early in the pandemic, and social distancing and COVID-19 restrictions in BC, activists in Vancouver set up outdoor pop-up OPS tents so that people could safely use their drugs and receive other services. For example, in May 2020, SisterSquare was set up on the corner of Jackson and Powell in a parking lot in the DTES.

SisterSpace and SisterSquare were set up to address the needs of women (in all their diversity). Women who use or used drugs are especially vulnerable to gender-specific institutional and state interventions and are underserved due to a lack of gender and culturally appropriate drug services. Women users continue to experience systemic discrimination, especially in relation to child protection practices and family court decisions that result in the apprehension of their children by the state and the loss of their children in custody disputes. For Indigenous, Black and poor women who use drugs, the threat of child apprehension and loss of custody is lifelong.

The entrance to SisterSquare in a parking lot in the DTES. (Photo by SisterSpace, reprinted with permission from Atira Women's Resource Society.)

ACROSS CANADA

In Manitoba, it is estimated that in 2020 that 372 people died of a preventable illegal drug overdose, a huge increase from the year before. Similar to other regions, COVID-19 restrictions have created barriers to harm reduction services, leaving them more vulnerable. Activists continue to respond to increases in illegal overdose deaths by setting up unsanctioned overdose prevention sites. In Winnipeg, the Manitoba Harm Reduction Network set up an unsanctioned OPS in a park in September 2021. Not only are these advocates risking arrest, but they are also doing the hard work of providing essential services and saving lives, while all levels of government fail to adequately do so. The government of Manitoba has not set up official OPSS, nor has it provided hydromorphone drug substitution or HAT services.

In September 2021, an unsanctioned OPS tent was set up in Winnipeg by Manitoba Harm Reduction Network, providing safe supplies and consumption space. (Photo by Jonny Mexico, reprinted with permission from him and Manitoba Harm Reduction Network.)

Ontario and Alberta have been hit hard, too. Other regions, such as Saskatchewan and Manitoba, are also experiencing increases in overdose deaths. For example, between January and March 2021, the illegal overdose rate in BC was 40 deaths per 100,000 people. Alberta's rate was 32, Ontario's rate was 19 and Quebec's rate was 4.6.[26] In the same three-month period, 517 people in BC, 722 people in Ontario, 353 people in Alberta and 99 people in Quebec died from a preventable illegal overdose. Keep in mind that these rates and numbers are only for a three-month period.

HARM REDUCTION'S LIMITS

Harm reduction and drug user unions have made clear that there is a limit to what harm reduction services can provide unless a safe supply of drugs become more available and drug prohibitionist policies end. With little support, drug user unions, people with experiential knowledge and harm reduction services are the frontline workers striving to reduce the harms caused by prohibition. On April 14, 2021, five years after the BC government announced a public health emergency stemming from rising illegal overdose deaths, the Drug User Liberation Front (DULF) organized a rally in Vancouver. Other organizations such as Moms Stop the Harm, VANDU and Canadian Drug Policy Coalition joined in. Cities outside of Vancouver also participated.

At the rally, DULF provided safe supplies as well as one individual dose of heroin, cocaine or methamphetamine in small, labelled cardboard boxes. The box labels included not only the type of drug but the percentage of each drug — the boxes with heroin contained 40 percent heroin and 60 percent caffeine.

BC Moms Stop the Harm, Day of Action, April 14, 2021. MSTH members gathered in Uplands Park in Victoria, BC, in remembrance of loved ones who died. (Photo by MSTH, reprinted with permission.)

Drug User Liberation Front logo. (Reprinted with permission from DULF.)

"No Compromise for Safe Supply" Vancouver rally organized by DULF on April 14, 2021. (Photo by Nathaniel Canuel and Canadian Drug Policy Coalition, reprinted with permission.)

Western Aboriginal Harm Reduction Society in Vancouver joins "No Compromise for Safe Supply," April 14, 2021. WAHRS members Brendin Edwards and Wally Merasty holding the banner. (Photo by Nathaniel Canuel and Canadian Drug Policy Coalition, reprinted with permission.)

Calls for an end to drug prohibition, access to safe legal drugs and decriminalization now are still a primary focus of heroin activism, but it is clear that people who used cocaine and methamphetamine are gravely impacted by the illegal overdose death crisis. In fact, at the end of 2021, the BC Coroners Service noted that in an illegal overdose death sub-sample of toxicology tests in the province, fentanyl or its analogues were detected in 90 percent of the samples, 74 percent of the samples also included a stimulant, 20 percent included one other opioid and 44 percent included at least one benzodiazepine — a poisoned illegal drug supply.[27] The consumption of alcohol in combination with illegal drugs also increases the risk of overdose. The BC Coroners Service also makes clear that prescribed safe supply (i.e., diacetylmorphine, hydromorphone) is not contributing to illegal drug overdose deaths in the province.[28]

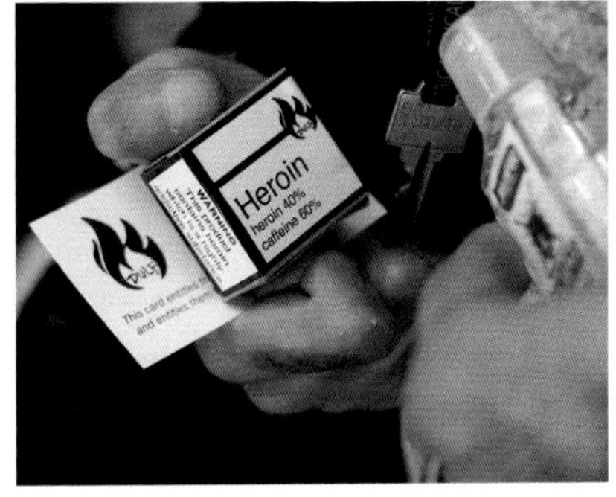

At the rally on April 14, 2021, DULF provided safe supplies, including individual doses of heroin packaged in small, labelled cardboard boxes. (Reprinted with permission from photographer Maggie MacPherson, www.maggiemacpherson.ca/.)

Some activists were also pointing to other issues that connected to drug prohibition. Police brutality and violence against women are part of the consequences of drug prohibition, including the missing and murdered women in Canada, who are largely Indigenous. Recent movements, such as Black Lives Matter and Idle No More, also bring attention to ongoing state violence and centuries of resistance. These movements intersect with the concerns of other groups, such as prison abolition and drug reform movements in and outside of Canada.

HARM REDUCTION SAVES LIVES

Consumption sites, overdose prevention sites, compassion clubs, drug user union services and other harm reduction initiatives save lives. The BC Coroners Service, for example, states that no deaths have been reported at any supervised consumption or OPS in BC.[29] The same goes for supervised consumption sites across Canada. As this book goes to press, there are thirty-eight federally approved supervised consumption sites (as they are called now) across Canada, and many more unsanctioned OPSs have been set up by activists. In BC, there are also many more provincially approved OPS. However, a further shift in drug policy to more flexible and diverse services are still needed to end the illegal overdose death epidemic. The BC government and its health authorities have not established more HAT programs throughout the province, nor have they supported recent calls for heroin buyer clubs or compassion clubs. Instead, law enforcement has accelerated their response and heroin possession offences have been rising in BC and the rest of Canada.

Given the illegal overdose death epidemic in Canada, it might be assumed that illegal opioid consumption is high. This is not the case. The 2017 *Canadian Tobacco, Alcohol, and Drugs Survey* revealed that heroin use rates in the previous year were too variable to validate (similar to the 2015 survey results) and of those surveyed, 0.7 percent are lifetime heroin users.[30] Amongst those who used a prescribed pain reliever, 2.9 percent noted "problematic use," including "to get high."[31] Yet, it is still the small, visible and poor population of illegal opioid users in Canada who are heavily policed.

CONTEMPORARY DRUG OFFENCES AND USE

In 2020, there were 66,827 drug offences across Canada, compared to 70,140 in 2019. Until 2019, the overwhelming majority of all drug offences in Canada were for drug possession. However, in 2020, 48 percent of all drug offences were for drug possession, up from 46 percent in 2019 and down from 72 percent in 2017.[32] The decrease in total drug offences and possession offences across Canada is due to fewer cannabis possession offences stemming from shifting police practices leading up to and following the enactment of the Cannabis Act (legalizing cannabis) in October 2018. Whereas cannabis possession offences decreased, in 2020 there were 2,755 heroin offences, 72 percent of which were for possession. In 2020, there were also an additional 5,142 opioid-related offences (other than heroin, but including fentanyl) in Canada, and 66 percent of these offences were for personal possession. Opioid-related offences increased sharply in 2020.[33] To be clear, in 2020 there were a total of 7,897 heroin and opioid-related offences across Canada. Since 2017, heroin and opioid-related offences are listed separately in police-reported crime statistics. Among the provinces, the highest rates of opioid-related offences and heroin offences were reported in BC.[34]

BC accounted for 45 percent of all heroin-related offences (85 percent of which were for possession) and 54 percent of opioid-related offences (69 percent of which were for possession) across Canada in 2020.[35] In Vancouver, there were 1,604 drug offences in 2020 (compared to 1,552 in 2019), 45 percent which were for possession.[36] As well, in 2020, 74 percent of heroin-related offences in Vancouver were for possession.[37] Given the extent of the illegal overdose death epidemic, it begs the question why our drug laws continue to criminalize personal possession in Canada and why enforcement continues to focus on possession of illegal drugs during an illegal drug overdose death crisis.[38]

CRIMINALIZING WOMEN AND INDIGENOUS AND BLACK PEOPLE

Given that criminalization is still the key response to drug use and the illegal overdose death epidemic, it is important to couple that with colonialism, white supremacy and racial injustice that have and still shape the criminal justice system. Reports from Indian Affairs (even in its early years), the North West Mounted Police and the RCMP show that Indigenous peoples have long been the subject of racialized police profiling and overrepresentation in arrests and prison time. An early 1922 RCMP report weighs in on Indian Act infractions, stating "The enforcement of the Indian Act imposed duties on our men in all the divisions. Convictions were numerous."[39] Intoxication offences were plentiful. Over-policing of Indigenous peoples in Canada persists to this day. In 1996, the *Royal Commission on Aboriginal Peoples* concluded that, for Indigenous peoples in Canada, criminalization is one of the key forms of colonial state violence.

A Statistics Canada report examining police-reported crime in mostly Indigenous rural communities (the majority of which are policed by the RCMP) found that, in 2018, the police reported rates for drug offences for Indigenous peoples was more than three times higher than non-Indigenous people (735 compared to 219). Tellingly, drug use rates are similar for Indigenous and non-Indigenous people.[40] Canadian scholars Akwasi Owusu-Bempah and Alex Luscombe note that there is "little information on racial disparities in drug arrests" in a Canadian context.[41] This is due to the fact that Statistics Canada did not request information on race from police services. Recently, in order to fill this gap, researchers and news reporters have submitted freedom of information requests to specific police services across Canada for data on rates of arrests by race for drug and other offences.

Reports pointing to the over-policing of Indigenous and Black people in Canada also note that racial injustice is systemic. Like Indigenous peoples, drug-use surveys demonstrate that Black people use criminalized drugs at the same rate as white people. Yet, arrest data from five major cities (Vancouver, Calgary, Regina, Ottawa and Halifax) in Canada in 2015 also found that Black and Indigenous peoples were racially profiled by law enforcement and grossly overrepresented in cannabis possession arrests.[42] In Vancouver, the arrest rate for cannabis possession was 21.5 per 100,000 people for Indigenous men, 23.3. for Black men and 5.5 for white men. Calgary, Halifax, Ottawa and Regina also showed similar racial differences for cannabis possession arrests.[43] In Toronto, Black people make up about 8 percent of the population. Yet, Black people made up 28 percent of Toronto's non-cannabis drug possession offences, even though their drug use rates were actually lower than other racial groups. Black people are also more vulnerable to police violence in Toronto.[44] Many drug arrests lead to prison time.

In BC, a ten-year study on arrest data in the cities of Duncan, Nelson, Prince George, Surrey and Vancouver from 2011 to 2020 also found that Indigenous men and women and Black men were overrepresented in arrest data. In the city of Vancouver, the Indigenous arrest rate is ten times higher than the white arrest rate. The Black arrest rate is 4.7 times higher than the white rate. The study also found that Hispanic and Arab/West Asian people are over-represented in Vancouver's arrest data. As well, over 41 percent of the arrests occurred in District Two, an area that includes the DTES. The study analyzed only incidents that involved single-charge arrests (61 percent of the arrests were for one crime only) rather than multiple charges. Unfortunately, the Vancouver police data did not include incidents where people were released on the street, and only those people brought into the station are included. Because drug possession and administration of justice arrests often occur on the street, they are under-represented in the data. Even so, the study found that Indigenous and Black people are over-represented for these crimes. In Vancouver, Prince George and Surrey, Indigenous women are "grossly" over-represented in arrests. As well, in contrast to negative stereotypes, Indigenous and Black people were "under-represented" in serious violent crime arrests.[45]

Low-level offences, such as drug possession and administration of justice offences, can lead to prison time. Although Indigenous peoples make up about 5 percent of the Canadian population, in 2020, Indigenous adults accounted for 30 percent of people incarcerated in federal prisons.[46] For Indigenous women, prison time is even more likely: they make up about 41 percent of all federally incarcerated women.[47] In BC in 2020–2021, 46.5 percent of all women in provincial prisons in BC were Indigenous (compared to 34.5 percent of men).[48] In Manitoba and Saskatchewan, the percentage of Indigenous peoples in provincial jails are the highest in the country.

We must recognize that the prison statistics, especially provincially, don't tell the whole story. Many people in provincial prisons have not been convicted of a crime. For example, roughly 65 percent of people in BC provincial jails in 2020 were awaiting trial — they had not been charged (that is, they were on "remand").[49] In addition, only the "most serious offence designation" is included in prison statistics. This statistical practice renders lesser offences invisible. Administration of justice offences account for about 10 percent of all offences in Canada, although, BC, Saskatchewan and Prince Edward Island report higher percentages. These offences include failure to appear, breach of a probation order and failure to comply with a probation order. These breaches may stem from, for example, a failure to attend a court date or a court-mandated addiction counselling session, being in a "red zone" (a street or area of town a person is ordered to stay out of) or consuming illegal drugs or alcohol. For some people who use criminalized drugs, administration of justice offences snowball into prison time and are referred to as the "revolving door" of the criminal justice system. Women and poor and marginalized people who use illegal drugs are especially vulnerable to administration of justice arrests.[50]

Federally, in 2017–2018, "18 percent of all prisoners were serving sentences for drug-related offences."[51] Of those admissions to federal prisons in 2017–2018, women make up about 6 percent of the total population.[52] However, a higher percentage of women in prison is serving sentences for drug-related crimes than men. Women federal prisoners in Canada were almost twice as likely as their male counterparts to be serving time for drug-related offences. In 2015, almost 27 percent of female prisoners were serving time for drug-related offences (compared to 16.7 percent of men), even though they consume less drugs than men and are less likely to be engaged in high-level drug selling.[53] In 2019–2020, 11.6 percent of all women and 7.5 percent of all men in provincial prisons in BC were in prison due to a drug charge. This is especially the case for Indigenous and Black women. The "stigmatization of women who use drugs is highly racialized,"[54] as are most criminal justice encounters. It isn't that Indigenous and Black women and men in Canada are more "criminal" than their white counterparts, but rather, as noted above, they are certainly more likely to be criminalized than their white counterparts.

The criminalization of heroin (and other drugs) and resulting encounters with law enforcement (and other institutions) have an effect. Although not all encounters with law enforcement result in arrest, due to systemic discrimination and colonial violence, conflict with the law, arrests and the trauma of street checks and drug confiscation by police are higher for poor and racialized people in Canada.[55] And these encounters can result in prison time.

END NOTES

1. Boyd, MacPherson and VANDU, 2019, p. 95
2. Government of Canada, 2017
3. Boyd et al., 2017; Boyd and NPA, 2013
4. BC Coroners Service, 2021a
5. First Nations Health Authority, 2017
6. First Nations Health Authority, 2017

7. First Nations Health Authority, 2020
8. Boyd, Collins et al., 2018
9. Boyd, Lavalley et al., 2020
10. See Lucas, Boyd, Milloy and Walsh, 2021
11. Health, Government of Alberta, 2020
12. Government of Canada, 2021a
13. Government of Canada, 2021a; BC Coroners Service, 2021a
14. BCYADWS, 2019; Boyd, Murray, SNAP and MacPherson, 2017; CAPUD, 2019
15. BC Coroners Service, 2022, p. 3
16. BC Coroners Service, 2022
17. BC Coroners Service, 2021a
18. BC Coroners Service, 2021a
19. BC Coroners Service, 2021a
20. BC Coroners Service, 2021a
21. BC Centre on Substance Use, 2020
22. See CRISM PWLE, 2019
23. Thomson et al., 2019
24. BCYADWS, 2019
25. BCYADWS, Personal communication, June 13, 2020; Winter, 2020
26. Numbers rounded off, see Government of Canada, 2021a
27. BC Coroners Service, 2021b
28. BC Coroners Service, 2021a, p. 4
29. BC Coroners Service, 2021a
30. Statistics Canada, 2017
31. Statistics Canada, 2017
32. Moreau, 2019; Moreau, 2021; Moreau, Jaffray and Armstrong, 2020
33. Moreau, 2021
34. Moreau, 2021
35. Moreau, 2021
36. Statistics Canada, 2021
37. Statistics Canada, 2021
38. Moreau, 2021; Statistics Canada 2021
39. RCMP, 1922, p. 18
40. Allen, 2020
41. Owusu-Bempah and Luscombe, 2021
42. Owusu-Bempah and Luscombe, 2021
43. Owusu-Bempah and Luscombe, 2021
44. Ontario Human Rights Commission, 2020; see also Commission on Systemic Racism in the Ontario Criminal Justice System, 1995
45. Wortley, 2021
46. Malakieh, 2019, Table 4, p. 20; Department of Justice Canada, 2021
47. Correctional Service Canada, 2019b
48. Greiner, 2021
49. Greiner, 2021
50. Bennett and Larkin, 2018; Burczycka and Munch, 2015; Public Safety Canada, 2016
51. Correctional Service Canada, 2019a
52. Correctional Service Canada, 2019b
53. Corrections and Conditional Release Statistical Overview, 2015
54. Boyd, 2015; Dell and Kilty, 2012; Maynard, 2017
55. Bennett and Larkin, 2018; Crompton, 2019; Owusu-Bempah, 2017; Owusu-Bempah and Luscombe, 2021; Wortley, 2021

A 2018 Poster for an ADDICQ Montreal's "Support. Don't Punish" campaign, delivered to Prime Minister Trudeau's county office in Montreal. There are three ADDICQ [Quebec Association for the Defense of Rights and Inclusion of People Who Consume Drugs] chapters federated within the AQPSUD [Quebec Association for Drug User Health Promotion]. (Reprinted with permission from artist JF Mary.)

11

Our Drug Policy Is Killing People

Decriminalizing and Legalizing Heroin Use

Examining Canada's history of heroin criminalization is a way to understand the systemic discrimination against people who use illegal heroin and other opioids. Rooted in racial colonialism, white supremacy and Christian perspectives, ideas about intoxication, sobriety, morality, punishment and citizenship have shaped drug policy in Canada. Our longstanding ideas about heroin, addiction and the people who use heroin are deeply flawed. Across Canada, drug user unions, family members, harm reduction advocates and practitioners, human rights and justice organizations and other allies continue to make clear that lives are at stake. As this book goes to press, it is estimated that over 24,626 people across Canada have died from a preventable illegal drug overdose since 2016. And the number of deaths is rising. Each day in Canada, roughly nineteen people die from a preventable illegal drug overdose.[1] Our drug policy is killing people every day — our beloved children, sisters, brothers, partners and friends. The struggle continues to change drug laws and policies.

A critical and historical approach helps to understand the roots of heroin prohibition and the current preventable illegal drug overdose epidemic. Drug prohibition has a serious impact on people — denying access to legal and safe sources of heroin and other drugs produces harm, especially overdose death. Illegal fentanyl on its own, or mixed into heroin, cocaine and methamphetamine, is implicated in the majority of overdose deaths in Canada.[2] People who occasionally use heroin or other illegal drugs also need access to a safe supply. For those who use drugs regularly, understanding drug use as a "habit" rather than a disorder brings to the forefront the social, political and cultural factors that shape drug use. Our historical and ongoing failure to understand this binary framing of heroin as good or bad closes off diverse alternative perspectives.

The history of heroin prohibition intersects with the regulation of other criminalized drugs, colonialism, white supremacy and systemic racism. It is important to be specific when investigating the history of regulation and resistance to regulation of illegal drugs. For example, the history of cannabis regulation differs from heroin regulation, as do resistance strategies and the call for legalization. Yet, key injustices are the same: no access to a legal supply. The unequal enforcement of drug laws in Canada has led to the overrepresentation of poor and racialized people for stop and search, arrests and imprisonment.[3]

Drug policies are not fixed, as evidenced by rapid federal and BC provincial prescribing policy changes temporarily set in place in 2020 to provide a safer supply of some legal substitution drugs during the COVID-19 pandemic. Canada's laws, policies and social, economic and political systems are produced by people with specific political intentions. They are not "natural" or inherent. Change is always possible.

From its inception, heroin prohibition has worked to brutally punish a small segment of the population, especially those who are racialized and poor. Negative heroin discourse and stereotyping of people who use heroin has shaped drug law, policing, prisons, policy and treatment options — and for mothers, child apprehension. Over the decades, fears about opium dens, cocaine, heroin, cannabis, crack cocaine, methamphetamine, grow ops and so on have circulated, informing policies. At the same time, vocal law and order pundits and moral reformers clamored for harsh drug policies. Yet, a singular focus on the purported "evils" of specific drugs like heroin renders invisible the structural violence of drug prohibition that negatively impacts the lives of people. Our flawed ideas about specific drugs and the people who use them have worked to criminalize and pathologize individuals.

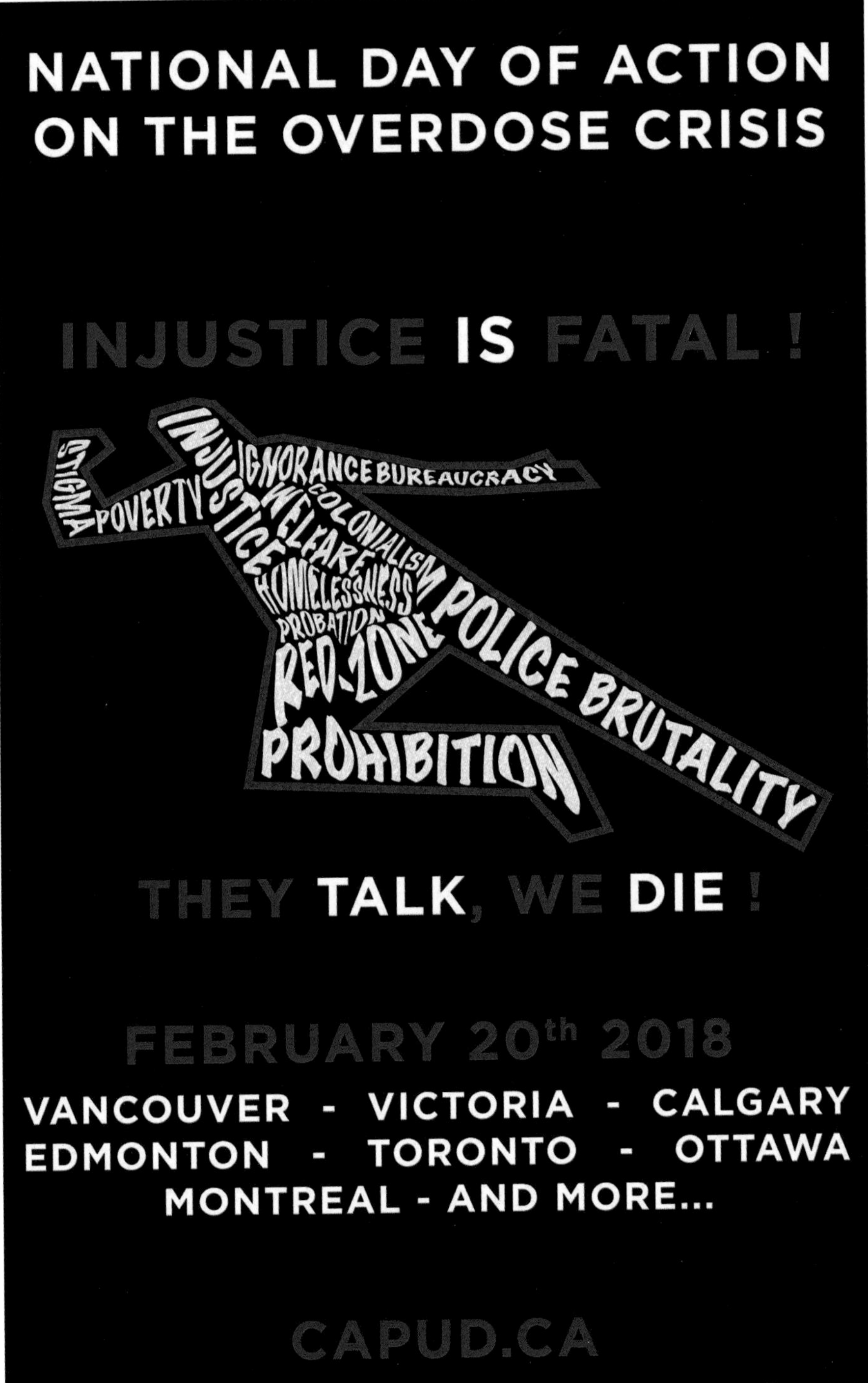

"They Talk We Die!" a National Day of Action organized by the Canadian Association of People Who Use Drugs. (Poster art by JF Mary, reprinted with permission.)

Although the term "criminal addict" is no longer used in Canada to characterize people who use heroin and/or other criminalized drugs, drug policy remains racialized and gendered, and poor heroin users continue to be seen as other. People who use heroin and other illegal drugs have been made to be the problem, so we lose sight of the violence of prohibition.

DECRIMINALIZING DRUG USE IS STILL A STRUGGLE

In Canada, calls for drug law/policy reform are not new. To be clear, there is an incredible imbalance of power between people who use criminalized drugs and the Canadian state. Yet, activism for drug law reform has had successes. To stem the harms of drug prohibition, in August 2020, the Public Prosecution Service of Canada advised prosecutors to cease prosecuting simple drug possession cases unless there were other safety concerns. In February 2021, in recognition of systemic criminalization of marginalized people, especially Black and Indige-

March during a National Day of Action to end prohibition, not just reform drug laws, in Vancouver on February 21, 2017. (Photo by the Canadian Drug Policy Coalition, reprinted with permission.)

nous people in Canada, Bill C-22, an Act to amend the Criminal Code and the Controlled Drugs and Substance Act was submitted to Parliament (and resubmitted in December 2021). The Act seeks to repeal all mandatory minimum penalties for drug offences and to allow greater use of conditional sentences and diversion measures for simple drug possession offences.

Most drug war resistors argue that the Act is a half measure. For long-time activists — drug user unions, harm reduction advocates and national non-profits such as Canadian Drug Policy Coalition, Canadian HIV Legal Network, Canadian Students for Sensible Drug Policy and Pivot Legal Society — drug prohibition and punitive laws, particularly for personal use, must stop.

CALLS FOR DECRIMINALIZATION STEP UP

In 2020, the city council in Vancouver, the Health Minister of BC and the Police Chiefs of Canada called for the decriminalization of simple possession of all illegal drugs in order to stem illegal overdose deaths. Further, the City of Vancouver approached Health Canada to request a federal exemption from the Controlled Drugs and Substances Act (CDSA) to allow for the decriminalization of simple possession of drugs for personal use. In April 2021, the City presented a submission to decriminalize personal possession.[4] A few months earlier, in February 2021, BC's Minister of Mental Health and Addictions requested that the federal Health Minister provide a province-wide exemption to the CDSA for simple drug possession. On June 11, 2021, Health Canada's own Expert Task Force on Substance Use strongly recommended that "bold" actions are needed, including decriminalization and a central public health framework to regulate all drugs and safer supply.[5]

However, as this book goes to print, the federal government continues to reject the decriminalization of simple drug possession and many other measures that have been recommended over many decades. Canada is out of step with other nations and jurisdictions who have adopted decriminalization for personal possession of small amounts

Mural by Bob High (Robert Nightingale) in the DTES, 2019. (Reprinted with permission from Robert Nightingale and photographer Steve Rolles, Transform.)

of drugs and who have set up more drug substitution programs that include safe, legal heroin.

Across Canada, people who use drugs and allies have led the way, demanding an end to drug prohibition. They have ruptured our ideas about who the heroin or illegal drug user is. They are also demanding less medicalization of people who use drugs — for example, establishing compassion clubs in existing drug user unions rather than conventional drug substitution programs whose criteria include being diagnosed with opioid substance disorder.

In response to inadequate action on safe supply by all governments, on July 14, 2021, the Drug User Liberation Front (DULF), VANDU and allies hosted D-Day, a rally held outside of the Vancouver Police Department where organizers provided a tested supply of heroin, cocaine and methamphetamine to drug user organizations to distribute to their members "in an ethical way." The rally was followed by a march and street party with an information booth, free food, music, overdose prevention services and drug checking (they also provided free masks and hand sanitizer). The event highlighted the rising overdose deaths in BC and across Canada, offered viable solutions and recognized the many lives stolen due to unjust Canadian drug policies and systemic violence.

DULF's co-founders, Eris Nyx and Jeremy Kalicum, and VANDU's Executive Director, Brittany Graham, stepped up their advocacy by submitting a formal request to the federal government on August 31, 2021, requesting a 56(1) exemption to the CDSA to ensure the "equitable application of public health protections to vulnerable Canadians" and allow DULF through VANDU to operate a Safe Supply Fulfillment Centre and Cocaine, Heroin and Methamphetamine Compassion Clubs in Vancouver. A 56(1) exemption from the CDSA can be granted by the Minister of Health to exempt a person or controlled drugs from the application of the Act (therefore a person cannot be arrested for a drug crime), if deemed necessary for a medical or scientific purpose or if it is in the public's interest. For example, federally approved supervised injection sites in Canada have a 56(1) exemption. In order to save lives, the 56(1) exemption allows people to bring, and use, an illegal drug inside the site without fear of arrest.

DULF poster for the D-Day rally in July 2021. (Reprinted with permission from DULF.)

Introduced as a motion by Councillor Jean Swanson to support DULF and VANDU's application, Vancouver city councillors voted on October 7, 2021, to support the request as long as an amendment was added ensuring that the drugs would be purchased through legal sources. Fair Price Pharma, a new Canadian non-profit pharmaceutical company, offered to supply DULF with injectable pharmaceutical heroin.[6] Legal sources for cocaine and methamphetamine would also be attained by DULF. In order to reduce illegal overdose deaths, and if the compassion club is successful in finding legal sources for other drugs, adult members of the compassion club would be able to buy legal, safe doses of cocaine, heroin or methamphetamine. And if the province of BC fully funds the compassion club, the cost of these legal drugs would not fall on members, DULF or VANDU. New policy changes by Health Canada in early 2022, will make the prescribing of heroin for injection use in a clinical setting simpler; however, it is restricted to people diagnosed with severe opioid use disorder.

On the same day that DULF and VANDU submitted their request to the federal government for compassion clubs, on August 31, 2021, the Canadian Association of People Who Use Drugs (CAPUD) and four plaintiffs submitted a constitutional challenge in the Supreme Court of BC. They assert that the criminalized regime under the CDSA violates their human rights protected under the *Canadian Charter of Rights and Freedoms*. To address this violation, the challenge proposes decriminalization in relation to all drug possession and drug trafficking offences related to people who sell drugs out of necessity.

As this book goes to press, in response to the preventable illegal drug overdose crisis, over forty-three cities across Canada (including Montreal, Toronto and Vancouver) have already indorsed decriminalization.[7] On December 9, 2021, after months of collaboration between more than twenty human rights and social justice organizations (such as CAPUD, Canadian Drug Policy Coalition and the HIV Legal Net-

Dustin Klaudt, the laywer for CAPUD and plaintiffs, Natasha Touesnard, Executive Director of CAPUD, and Matthew Bonn, CAPUD Program Coordinator, outside the Supreme Court of BC after filling their constitutional challenge to the CDSA on August 31, 2021. (Reprinted with permission from Natasha Touesnard, Matthew Bonn and Dustin Klaudt.)

work) released their policy platform: "Decriminalization Done Right: A Rights-based Path for Drug Policy." The platform was endorsed by more than one hundred other organizations across Canada. It calls for several actions, including: "*Full decriminalization of all drug possession for personal use – as well as sharing or selling of drugs for subsistence, to support personal drug use costs, or to provide a safe supply.*"[8] The report also calls for a redistribution of funds from policing and law enforcement to alternative voluntary services and health, education, housing and social services.[9]

In December 2021, New Democratic Party MP, Gord Johns introduced Bill-216, a private member's bill: Health-based Approach to Substance Use Act, to the House of Commons. The Act seeks to repeal personal possession offences, expunge certain drug-related convictions, expand safer supplies and to develop a national strategy to address harms.

Urgent requests for decriminalization and a compassion club model are responses to Canada's failed drug policy. Outside of establishing more life-saving programs, demands for decriminalization have stepped up in Canada. "Decriminalization Done Right" is a comprehensive policy framework and provides a vital first step. It recognizes that decriminalization alone, without expanding legal sources of drugs (as a VANDU and DULF compassion club model would do), will not curtail illegal drug overdoses. That is because people will still need to buy their drugs from the illegal market, a poisoned drug supply. The adoption of a comprehensive decriminalization framework is a necessary step as Canadians move toward a fundamental shift in policy – legal regulation that eliminates punishment and prohibition in its entirety and the systemic social and political violence that fuels it. Laws and policies can support, rather than destroy lives. Local, provincial and national drug user unions, people who use(d) drugs and their allies have shown us what we need to do to save lives and to have a more just future. Our failure to prioritize people's lives must end.

END NOTES

1. Government of Canada, 2021a
2. BC Coroner Service, 2021b
3. Boyd, 2017; Owusu-Bempah and Luscombe, 2021
4. Without consultation with those most impacted by drug policy (such as VANDU), the City presented an unnecessarily complicated submission. Their proposal included highly unrealistic limits (daily amounts of a drug a person can have in their possession) for personal possession and increased police involvement.
5. Health Canada Expert Task Force on Substance Use, 2021
6. The non-profit company (incorporated in November 2020) was formed by Dr. Perry Kendall, BC's former provincial health officer, and Dr. Martin Schechter, lead investigator of both NAOMI and SALOME trials in Canada.
7. Moms stop the harms, 2021
8. CAPUD, CDPC, HIV Legal Network, et al., 2021, p.3
9. CAPUD, CDPC, HIV Legal Network, et al., 2021, p.3

APPENDIX
Methodology and Theory

Heroin: An Illustrated History is a history of the regulation of heroin in Canada. This book is informed by critical feminist, sociological and historical scholarship on drug control in Canada,[1] international research[2] and critical race theory.[3] These works and others highlight international and domestic drug control, fueled by structural violence, white supremacy, colonialism and the intersection of race, class, gender and sexuality oppression in the production of drug policy and law. A critical perspective on heroin (opioid) regulation, with a focus on international, federal and provincial policies in BC and across Canada draws our attention to the drivers of the contemporary illegal drug overdose death epidemic in Canada.

In this book, I draw from primary and secondary sources. Primary sources include archival material:

- House of Commons debates;
- RCMP Annual Reports (1922–2019);
  annual reports of criminal statistics (1923–2020, the titles of which vary over the years);
- BC Corrections data on drug offence and prison populations;
- BC annual reports of the Inspector of Gaols;
- Annual reports from the BC Director of Corrections;
- reports by the Department of Pensions and National Health (1936, 1941, 1945);
- Department of National Health and Welfare Annual Reports (1949–1950, 1951, 1954, 1955, 1956, 1960, 1965, 1966, 1970, 1975–1976, 1980–1981, 1989–1990, 1990–1991);

- the Board of Pension Commissioners for Canada and the Federal Appeal Board; and
- Royal BC Museum Archives, including the BC Alcohol and Drug Commission, the Narcotic Addiction Foundation of British Columbia annual reports and City of Vancouver Archives.

Primary source material is also drawn from:

- Legal material from BC Supreme Court 2014 constitutional challenge, *Providence Health Care Society et al.* v. *Canada* and the decision by the Honourable Chief Justice Hinkson; and
- news media, especially *The Globe and Mail*, *The Province* and *The Sun* (1890–2019).

I also draw on primary source research used in my earlier studies:

- fictional drug films (1912–2019);
- National Film Board drug documentaries; and
- CBC radio documentaries about illegal drugs (1957–1969).

At the onset of this project, I created a history timeline on the regulation of heroin, adding to the timeline as the project unfolded. The timeline has been long in the making; it was initially informed by a general history of Canadian drug prohibition that I wrote in 2017.[4] Research evidence for this book also draws from a nine-year research collaboration with SNAP, the drug user, peer-led and heroin-assisted treatment activist group, including interviews with their members.

The heroin project was supported by a four-year Social Science and Humanities Research Council grant that I received to study the specific history of heroin regulation in Canada that included, along with the primary sources, an analysis of media representations of heroin users and transcripts from a 2014 Charter challenge, *Providence Health Care Society et al.* v. *Canada.*

With the timeline of important events, people, legislation, policies and resistance in relation to heroin regulation compiled, I began archival searches for images to illustrate the history of heroin prohibition and harm reduction activism. At city, provincial and federal libraries, the United Nations Archives and Vancouver Police Museum and Archives, among others, I searched for visual material for historical events, persons and terms (such as heroin, diacetylmorphine, drug, drug advertisement, opium, opioids, prohibition, police and corrections). I strove to include the most representative images, and where more than one image was available, the clearest image (because some old images are of poor quality). I contacted other people in Canada's drug reform movement and non-profits associated with the events in the book asking if they could/would share posters, photos and other images of their involvement in drug reform. I also included photos taken from news media sources. Finally, many artists generously gave me permission to include their work in this book.

END NOTES

1. Boyd, N., 1984; Boyd, 2017; Carstairs, 2006; Comack, 1986; Giffen, Endicott and Lambert, 1991; Maynard, 2017; Owusu-Bempah and Luscombe, 2021; Solomon and Green, 1988
2. Acker, 2002; Berridge and Edwards, 1981; Musto, 1987; Reinarman and Levine, 1997; Warner, 2003
3. Hall, 1997; Million, 2013; Said, 2001; Thobani, 2007, 2021
4. Boyd, 2017

REFERENCES

Acker, C. 2002. *Creating the American Junkie: Addiction Research in the Classic Era of Narcotic Control.* Baltimore, MI: Johns Hopkins University Press.

Alexander, B. 2008. *The Globalization of Addiction: A Study in Poverty of the Spirit.* New York: Oxford Press.

Algren, N. 1949. *The Man With the Golden Arm.* New York: Doubleday

Allen, M. 2020. "Crime Reported by Police Serving Areas Where the Majority of the Population Is Indigenous, 2018." *Juristat,* Nov. 18. Ottawa, ON: Statistics Canada.

American Psychiatric Association. 2013. *Diagnostic and Statistical Manual of Mental Disorders,* fifth ed. Washington, DC.

Anderson, E. 1993. *Hard Place to Do Time: The Story of Oakalla Prison Farm 1912–1991.* New Westminster, BC: Hillpointe Publishing.

Anyone for Coffee and Heroin? Inside a Danish Narcotics Dispensary. 2011. Dir. by Ulrik Holmstrup. Denmark.

Arosteguy, J. 2011. "Ethical Engagement of People Who Inject Drugs in HIV Prevention Trials." *WHO/UNAIDS,* 1–29. https://www.unaids.org/en/resources/documents/2011/20110429-Ethical-engagement-people-inject-drugs-HIV-prevention-trials_en.

Bayer. 1899. Bayer's Pharmaceutical Specialties (advertisement). *The British Medical Journal,* April 8. London, UK: Wellcome Library.

BC Centre for Disease Control. 2021. "BC COVID-19 Dashboard." April 12. https://experience.arcgis.com/experience/a6f23959a8b14bfa989e3cda29297ded.

BC Centre on Substance Use 2020. "Risk Mitigation in the Context of Dual Public Health Emergencies." March. https://www.bccsu.ca/wp-content/uploads/2020/04/Risk-Mitigation-in-the-Context-of-Dual-Public-Health-Emergencies-v1.5.pdf.

BC Coroners Service. 2022. "Illicit Drug Toxicity Deaths in BC January 1, 2011 – December 31, 2021." February 9. https://www2.gov.bc.ca/assets/gov/birth-adoption-death-marriage-and-divorce/deaths/coroners-service/statistical/illicit-drug.pdf

___. 2021a. "Illicit Drug Toxicity Deaths in BC January 1, 2011–October 31, 2021." December 9. https://www2.gov.bc.ca/assets/gov/birthadoption-death-marriage-and-divorce/deaths/coroners-service/statistical/illicit-drug.pdf.

___. 2021b. "Illicit Drug Toxicity Type of Drug Data to October 31, 2021." December 9. https://www2.gov.bc.ca/assets/gov/birth-adoption-death-marriage-and-divorce/deaths/coroners-service/statistical/illicit-drug-type.pdf.

BCYADWS (BC-Yukon Association of Drug War Survivors). 2019. "Ministerial Order for Heroin Buyer Clubs Needed Immediately." News release, August 29.

Beech, C., and A. Gregersen. 1964. Three Year Follow-Up Study – Drug Addiction Clinic, Mimico. *Canadian Journal of Corrections* 6.

Bennett, D., and D. Larkin. 2018. *Project Inclusion: Confronting Anti-Homeless & Anti-Substance User Stigma in British Columbia*. Vancouver, BC: Pivot Legal Society.

Berridge, V., and G. Edwards. 1981. *Opium and the People: Opiate Use in Nineteenth Century England*. London, UK: Allan Lane.

Bewley-Taylor, D., and M. Jelsma. 2012. "Regime Change: Re-Visiting the 1961 Single Convention on Narcotic Drugs." *International Journal of Drug Policy* 23.

Blashfield, R., J. Keeley, E. Flnagan, and S. Miles. 2014. "The Cycle of Classification: DSM-I through DSM-5." *Annual Review Clinical Psychology* 10.

Boyd, J., S. Boyd, and T. Kerr. 2015. "Visual and Narrative Representations of Mental Health and Addiction by Law Enforcement." *International Journal of Drug Policy* 26, 7.

Boyd, J., A. Collins, S. Mayer, et al. 2018. "Gendered Violence and Overdose Prevention Sites: A Rapid Ethnographic Study During an Overdose Epidemic in Vancouver, Canada." *Addiction* 113, 12.

Boyd, J., J. Lavalley, S. Czechaczek, et al. 2020. "'Bed Bugs and Beyond': An Ethnographic Analysis of North America's First Women-Only Supervised Drug Consumption Site." *International Journal of Drug Policy* 78.

Boyd, N. 1984. "The Origins of Canadian Narcotics Legislation: The Process of Criminalization in Historical Context." *Dalhousie Law Journal* 8, 1.

Boyd, S. 1999. *Mothers and Illicit Drugs: Transcending the Myths*. Toronto, ON: University of Toronto Press.

___. 2008. *Hooked: Drug War Films in Britain, Canada, and the U.S.* New York: Routledge.

___. 2013. "A Canadian Perspective on Documentary Film: Drug Addict." *International Journal of Drug Policy* 24, 6.

___. 2015. *From Witches to Crack Moms: Women, Drug Policy, and Law*, 2nd edition. Durham, NC: Carolina Academic Press.

___. 2017. *Busted: An Illustrated History of Drug Prohibition in Canada*. Winnipeg, MB: Fernwood Publishing.

___. 2018. "Gendered Drug Policy: Motherisk and the Regulation of Mothering in Canada." *International Journal of Drug Policy* 68.

Boyd, S., A. Ivsins, and D. Murray. 2020. "Problematizing the DSM-5 Criteria for Opioid Use Disorder: A Qualitative Analysis." *International Journal of Drug Policy* 78.

Boyd, S., D. MacPherson, and B. Osborn. 2009. *Raise Shit! Social Action Saving Lives*. Halifax, NS: Fernwood Publishing.

Boyd, S., D. MacPherson, and VANDU. 2019. "The Harms of Drug Prohibition: Ongoing Resistance in Vancouver's Downtown Eastside." *BC Studies* 200.

Boyd, S., D. Murray and NAOMI Patients Association. 2017. "Ethics, Research and Advocacy: The Experiences of the NAOMI Patients Association in the Downtown Eastside of Vancouver." In *Critical Inquiries for Social Justice in Mental Health*, edited by M. Marrow and L. Halinka Malcoe (365–385). Toronto, ON: University of Toronto Press.

Boyd, S., D. Murray, SNAP, and D. MacPherson. 2017. "Telling Our Stories: Heroin-Assisted Treatment and SNAP Activism in the Downtown Eastside of

Vancouver." *Harm Reduction Journal* 14, 27.
Boyd, S., and A. Norton. 2019. "Addiction and Heroin-Assisted Treatment: Legal Discourse and Drug Reform." *Contemporary Drug Problems* 46, 3.
Boyd, S., and NPA. 2013. "Yet They Failed to Do so: Recommendations Based on the Experiences of NAOMI Research Survivors and a Call for Action." *Harm Reduction Journal,* 10, 6. http://www.harmreductionjournal.com/content/10/1/6.
Burczycka, M., and D. Munch. 2015. "Trends in Offences Against the Administration of Justice." *Jurista,* Oct. 15. Ottawa, ON: Statistics Canada.
Busby, M. 2019. "Drug Addicts to Receive Diamorphine Twice a Day in UK-First Scheme." *The Guardian,* Oct. 9. https://www.theguardian.com/society/2019/oct/09/drug-addicts-to-receive-diamorphine-twice-a-day-in-uk-first-scheme.
Cain, V. 1994. *Report of the Task Force into Illicit Narcotic Overdose Deaths in British Columbia.* Burnaby, BC: Office of the Chief Coroner.
Campbell, L., N. Boyd, and L. Culbert. 2009. *A Thousand Dreams: Vancouver's Downtown Eastside and the Fight for Its Future.* Vancouver, BC: Greystone Books.
Campbell, N. 2007. *Discovering Addiction: The Science and Politics of Substance Abuse Research.* Ann Arbor, MI: University of Michigan Press.
Canada. 1931. *Annual Report of the Department of Pensions and National Health for the Year ending March 31, 1930* (69–83). Ottawa, ON: Department of Pensions and National Health Ottawa.
___. 1955. *Proceedings.* Parliament. Senate. Special Committee on the Traffic in Narcotic Drugs in Canada. Ottawa, ON: Queen's Printer.
___. 1973. *Final Report of the Canadian Commission of Inquiry into the Non-Medical Use of Drugs.* Ottawa, ON: Information Canada. http://publications.gc.ca/site/eng/9.699765/publication. html.
___. 2021. "Opioid- and Stimulant-Related Harms in Canada." December. https://health-infobase.canada.ca/substance-related-harms/opioids-stimulants/.
CAPUD (Canadian Association of People Who Use Drugs). 2019. *Safe Supply Concept Document.* Feb. Vancouver, BC. https://vancouver.ca/files/cov/capud-safe-supply-concept-document.pdf.
CAPUD, Canadian Drug Policy Coalition, HIV Legal Network, et al. 2020. *Decriminalization Done Right: A Rights-Based Path for Drug Policy.* December 9. https://www.hivlegalnetwork.ca/site/decriminalization-done-right-a-rights-based-path-for-drug-policy/?lang=en.
Carstairs, C. 2006. *Jailed for Possession: Illegal Drug Use, Regulation, and Power in Canada, 1920–1961.* Toronto, ON: University of Toronto Press.
CBC (Canadian Broadcasting Corporation) Radio. 1957. "Assignment, Jack Webster." April 15.
___. 1959. "Assignment, Drug Addiction." November 21.
___. 1960. "God's Own Medicine" [Radio interview with Dr. George Stevenson]. May 29.
___. 1965. "Christian Frontiers." Street Haven, August 24.
City of Vancouver Archives. 1937. "Record of Narcotic Prescriptions and Purchases, 1937." Narcotics Register, Bertram Emery fonds, AM303-S2. Vancouver, BC:

City of Vancouver Archives.

Comack, E. 1986. "We Will Get Some Good Out of This Riot Yet: The Canadian State, Drug Legislation and Class Conflict." In *The Social Basis of Law: Critical Readings in the Sociology of Law*, edited by S. Brickey and E. Comack. Toronto, ON: Garamond.

Commission on Systemic Racism in the Ontario Criminal Justice System. 1995. *Report of the Commission on Systemic Racism in the Ontario Criminal Justice System*. Ottawa, ON.

Conroy, J. 1978. "The History of Opiates in BC and the Legal Ramifications of Bill 18." In *Some Implications of the* Heroin Treatment Act *(Bill 18)*, edited by M. Brunke. A series of speeches given at the "Public's Public Inquiry" of the *Heroin Treatment Act* on June 24, 1978. BC: Funded by the Non-Medical Use of Drugs Directorate Summer Programme #1216-9-99.

Correctional Service Canada. 2019a. "CSC Statistics – Quick Facts and Figures." Ottawa, ON: Correctional Service Canada. https://www.csc-scc.gc.ca/publications/092/005007-3024-eng.pdf.

___. 2019b. "The Federal Offender Population Profile 2018." Ottawa, ON: Corrections Service Canada. https://www.csc-scc.gc.ca/publications/005007-3033-en.shtml.

Corrections and Conditional Release Statistical Overview. 2015. Ottawa, ON. https://www.publicsafety.gc.ca/cnt/rsrcs/pblctns/ccrso-2015/index-en.aspx.

Courtright, D. 2001. *Dark Paradise: A History of Opiate Addiction in America*. Cambridge, MA: Harvard University Press.

Coutts, D. 1963. "The Oakalla Prison Farm Program for Treatment of Narcotic Addicts." *Canadian Journal of Corrections* 6.

CRISM PWLE National Working Group. 2019. "'Having a Voice and Saving Lives': A Survey by and for People Who Use Drugs and Work in Harm Reduction." Vancouver, BC: Centre on Substance Use.

Crompton, N. 2019. "VANDU: As VPD Budget Spirals Out of Control, Defunding Police in Our Community Alternative to Drug War." *Georgia Straight*, Dec. 2. https://www.straight.com/news/1332066/nathan-crompton-vpd-budget-spirals-out-control-defunding-police-our-community.

Culpeper, N. 1824. *The English Physician*, revised, corrected, and enlarged by James Scammon. Exeter, UK: James Scammon.

Dalrymple, W. 2019. *The Anarchy: The Relentless rise of the East India Company*. New York: Bloomsbury.

Delgamuukw v. BC, [1991] 3 W.W.R. 97 (BCS.C.).

Dell, C., and J. Kilty. 2012. "The Creation of the Expected Aboriginal Women Drug Offender in Canada: Exploring Relations Between Victimization, Punishment, and Cultural Identity." *International Review of Victimology* 19, 1.

Department of Justice Canada. 2021. Bill-C-22: Mandatory Minimum Penalties to Be Repealed. February 18. https://www.canada.ca/en/department-justice/news/2021/02/bill-c-22-mandatory-minimum-penalties-to-be-repealed.html.

Department of National Health and Welfare. 1945. *First Annual Report of the Department of National Health and Welfare for the Fiscal Year Ended March 31, 1945*. Ottawa, ON: Queen's Printer.

___. 1950. *First Annual Report of the Department of National Health and Welfare for the*

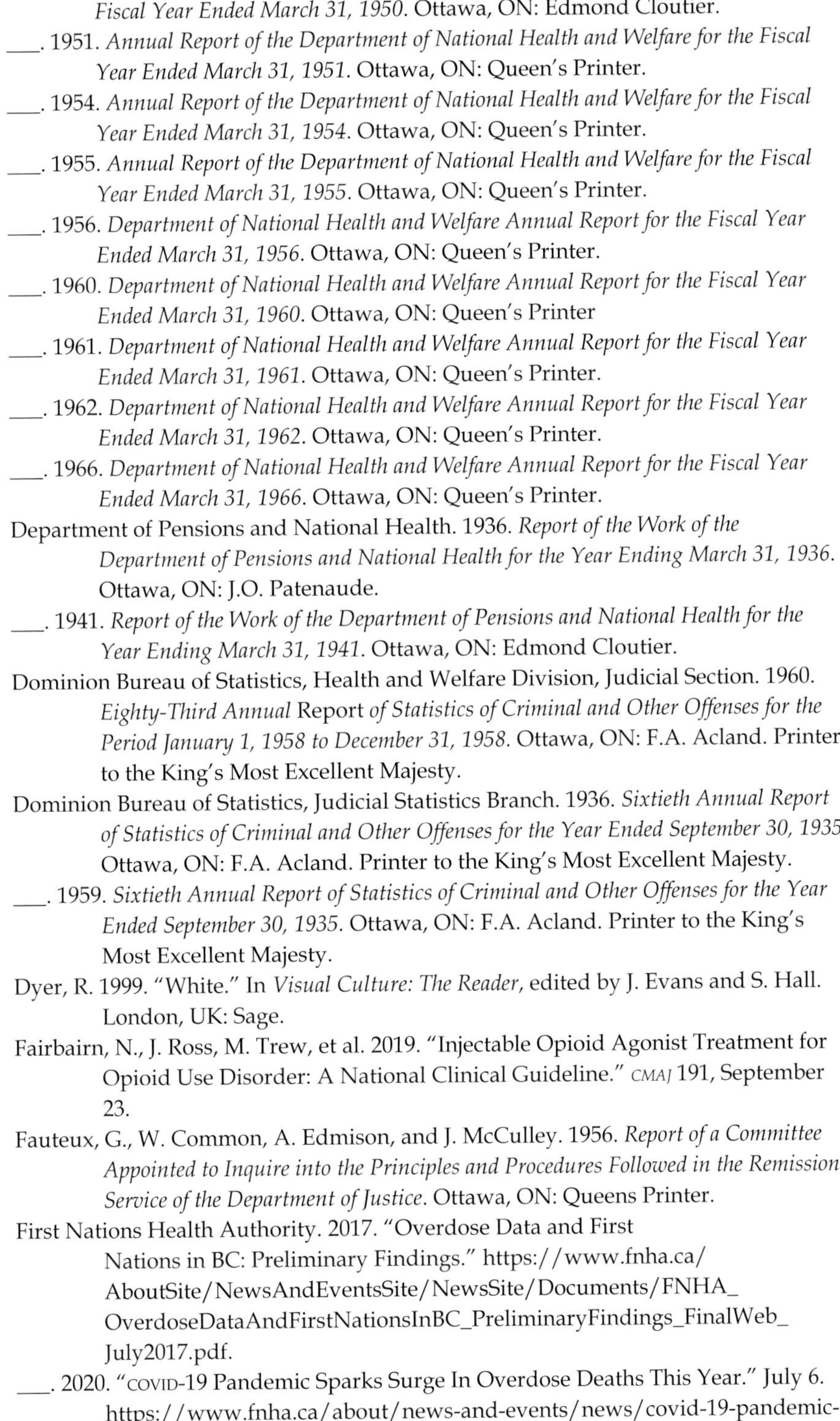

Fiscal Year Ended March 31, 1950. Ottawa, ON: Edmond Cloutier.

___. 1951. *Annual Report of the Department of National Health and Welfare for the Fiscal Year Ended March 31, 1951*. Ottawa, ON: Queen's Printer.

___. 1954. *Annual Report of the Department of National Health and Welfare for the Fiscal Year Ended March 31, 1954*. Ottawa, ON: Queen's Printer.

___. 1955. *Annual Report of the Department of National Health and Welfare for the Fiscal Year Ended March 31, 1955*. Ottawa, ON: Queen's Printer.

___. 1956. *Department of National Health and Welfare Annual Report for the Fiscal Year Ended March 31, 1956*. Ottawa, ON: Queen's Printer.

___. 1960. *Department of National Health and Welfare Annual Report for the Fiscal Year Ended March 31, 1960*. Ottawa, ON: Queen's Printer

___. 1961. *Department of National Health and Welfare Annual Report for the Fiscal Year Ended March 31, 1961*. Ottawa, ON: Queen's Printer.

___. 1962. *Department of National Health and Welfare Annual Report for the Fiscal Year Ended March 31, 1962*. Ottawa, ON: Queen's Printer.

___. 1966. *Department of National Health and Welfare Annual Report for the Fiscal Year Ended March 31, 1966*. Ottawa, ON: Queen's Printer.

Department of Pensions and National Health. 1936. *Report of the Work of the Department of Pensions and National Health for the Year Ending March 31, 1936*. Ottawa, ON: J.O. Patenaude.

___. 1941. *Report of the Work of the Department of Pensions and National Health for the Year Ending March 31, 1941*. Ottawa, ON: Edmond Cloutier.

Dominion Bureau of Statistics, Health and Welfare Division, Judicial Section. 1960. *Eighty-Third Annual* Report *of Statistics of Criminal and Other Offenses for the Period January 1, 1958 to December 31, 1958*. Ottawa, ON: F.A. Acland. Printer to the King's Most Excellent Majesty.

Dominion Bureau of Statistics, Judicial Statistics Branch. 1936. *Sixtieth Annual Report of Statistics of Criminal and Other Offenses for the Year Ended September 30, 1935*. Ottawa, ON: F.A. Acland. Printer to the King's Most Excellent Majesty.

___. 1959. *Sixtieth Annual Report of Statistics of Criminal and Other Offenses for the Year Ended September 30, 1935*. Ottawa, ON: F.A. Acland. Printer to the King's Most Excellent Majesty.

Dyer, R. 1999. "White." In *Visual Culture: The Reader*, edited by J. Evans and S. Hall. London, UK: Sage.

Fairbairn, N., J. Ross, M. Trew, et al. 2019. "Injectable Opioid Agonist Treatment for Opioid Use Disorder: A National Clinical Guideline." CMAJ 191, September 23.

Fauteux, G., W. Common, A. Edmison, and J. McCulley. 1956. *Report of a Committee Appointed to Inquire into the Principles and Procedures Followed in the Remission Service of the Department of Justice*. Ottawa, ON: Queens Printer.

First Nations Health Authority. 2017. "Overdose Data and First Nations in BC: Preliminary Findings." https://www.fnha.ca/AboutSite/NewsAndEventsSite/NewsSite/Documents/FNHA_OverdoseDataAndFirstNationsInBC_PreliminaryFindings_FinalWeb_July2017.pdf.

___. 2020. "COVID-19 Pandemic Sparks Surge In Overdose Deaths This Year." July 6. https://www.fnha.ca/about/news-and-events/news/covid-19-pandemic-sparks-surge-in-overdose-deaths-this-year.

Flint, M. 1964. "Narcotic Addiction in Women Offenders." *Canadian Journal of Corrections* 6.

Frankau, L. 1964. Treatment in England of Canadian Patients Addicted to Narcotic Drugs. *Canadian Medical Association Journal* 90, 6.

Fraser, S. 2017. "The Future of 'Addiction': Critique and Composition." *International Journal of Drug Policy* 44.

Fraser, S., D. Moore, and H. Keane. 2014. *Habits: Remaking Addiction.* Basingstoke, UK: Palgrave Macmillan.

Fraser, S., and K. Valentine. 2008. *Substance and Substitution: Methadone Subjects in Liberal Societies.* NewYork: Palgrave Macmillan.

Gardner, Ray. 1958. "The Streets of Canada: Hastings." *Maclean's Magazine,* Mar. 1. https://archive.macleans.ca/article/1958/3/1/the-streets-of-canada-hastings.

Giffen, P., S. Endicott, and S. Lambert. 1991. *Panic and Indifference: The Politics of Canada's Drug Laws.* Ottawa, ON: Canadian Centre on Substance Abuse.

Gifford-Jones, W. 2000. *You're Going to Do What?: The Memoir of Dr. W. Gifford-Jones.* Toronto, ON: ECW Press.

Globe and Mail. 1909. "Nations United in Good Cause." May 8.

___. 1972. "Munro Won't Let Heroin Be Used as Treatment." March 23.

Gomes, T., R. Murray, G. Kolla, et al. 2021. *Changing Circumstances Surrounding Opioid-Related Deaths in Ontario During the COVID-19 Pandemic.* On behalf of the Ontario Drug Policy Research Network, Office of the Chief Coroner for Ontario and Ontario Agency for Health Protection and Promotion. Toronto, ON: Ontario Drug Policy Research Network.

Government of Canada. 1949. *Seventy-Fourth Annual Report of Statistics of Criminal and Other Offences for the Year Ended September 30, 1949.* Ottawa, ON: Dominion Bureau of Statistics.

___. 1950. *Seventy-Fifth Annual Report of Statistics of Criminal and Other Offences for the Period October 1, 1949 to December 31, 1950.* Ottawa, ON: Health and Welfare Division, Dominion Bureau of Statistics.

___. 1952. *Seventy-Fifth Annual Report of Statistics of Criminal and Other Offenses for the Year Ended September 30, 1950.* Ottawa, ON: Health and Welfare Division, Dominion Bureau of Statistics.

___. 1962. *Eighty-Fifth Annual Report of Statistics of Criminal and Other Offences for the Period January 1, 1960 to December 31, 1960.* Ottawa, ON: Health and Welfare Division, Dominion Bureau of Statistics.

___. 1969. *Ninety-Second Annual Report of Statistics of Criminal and Other Offenses for the Period January 1, 1967 to December 31, 1967.* Ottawa, ON: Health and Welfare Division, Dominion Bureau of Statistics.

___. 2017. "Regulations Amending the Food and Drug Regulations (Importation of Drugs for an Urgent Public Health Need)." *Canada Gazette,* 151, 14, July 12. http://www.gazette.gc.ca/rp-pr/p2/2017/2017-07-12/html/sor-dors133-eng.html.

___. 2019. "Government of Canada Approves New Treatment Options for Opioid Use Disorder and Supports Research, Treatment and Harm Reduction Projects in Ontario." https://www.canada.ca/en/health-canada/news/2019/05/government-of-canada-approves-new-treatment-options-for-opioid-use-disorder-and-supports-research-treatment-and-harm-reduction-projects-in-ontario.html.

___. 2021a. "Opioid- and Stimulant-Related Harms in Canada." December. https://health-infobase.canada.ca/datalab/national-surveillance-opioid-mortality.html

___. 2021b. "Treaty Texts: Treaty No. 6." https://www.rcaanc-cirnac.gc.ca/eng/1100100028710/1581292569426.

Green, M. 1986. "A History of Canadian Narcotics Control: The Formative Years." In *The Social Dimensions of Law,* edited by N. Boyd. Scarborough, ON: Prentice-Hall.

___. 2013. "Nonmedical Drug Use." *The Canadian Encyclopedia.* https://www.thecanadianencyclopedia.ca/en/article/nonmedical-drug-use.

Greenfield, T., and F. Hamilton. 1948. "The Hopheads Are Ahead." *Maclean's Magazine*, 29, 62, Nov. 15.

Greiner, L. 2021. BC prison statistics requested from BC Corrections and Ministry of Public Safety and Solicitor General.

Hall, S. 1997. *Representations: Cultural Representations and Signifying Practices.* London, UK: Sage.

Halliday, R. 1963. "Management of the Narcotic Addict." *British Columbia Medical Journal*, 5, 10.

Hansard. 1920. House of Commons Debates, 13th Parliament, 4th Session, 1. Ottawa, ON.

___. 1954. House of Commons Debates, 22nd Parliament, 1st Session, 5. Ottawa, ON.

Hart, C. 2017. "Viewing Addiction as a Brain Disease Promotes Social Injustice." *Nature Human Behaviour* 1, 0055.

Health Canada. 2019. "Notice of Compliance Information." Health Canada, May. https://health-products.canada.ca/noc-ac/info.do?lang=en&no=22105.

___. 2020. *Statistics on the Marketed Drugs in Canada.* Report prepared on November 2, 2020 by Information Dissemination Unit, Health Products and Food Branch, Therapeutic Product Directorate. Ottawa, ON: Health Canada.

___. 2021. *Recommendations on the Federal Government's Drug Policy as Articulated in a Draft Canadian Drug and Substances Strategy*, Report 2, June. Ottawa, ON: Health Canada Expert Task Force on Substance Use.

Health Canada Expert Task Force on Substance Use. 2021. "Recommendations on the Federal Government's Drug Policy as Articulated in a Draft Canadian Drugs and Substances Strategy." Health Canada, June 11. https://www.canada.ca/content/dam/hc-sc/documents/corporate/about-health-canada/public-engagement/external-advisory-bodies/reports/report-2-2021/report-2-HC-expert-task-force-on-substance-use-final-en.pdf.

Health, Government of Alberta. 2020. *Alberta COVID-19 Opioid Response Surveillance Report.* Edmonton, AB.

Heritage Burnaby. 2022. "Oakalla Prison Collection." https://search.heritageburnaby.ca/list?q=%22Oakalla+Prison%22&p=1&ps=.

Hewitt, S. 2006. *Riding to the Rescue: The Transformation of the RCMP in Alberta and Saskatchewan, 1914–1939.* Toronto, ON: University of Toronto Press.

Hodgson, B. 1999. *Opium: A Portrait of the Heavenly Demon.* Vancouver, BC: Greystone Books.

International Narcotics Control Board. 2020. *Narcotic Drugs Estimated World Requirements for 2020.* Vienna, Austria: United Nations.

Jackel, S. 2008. "Emily Murphy." *The Canadian Encyclopedia.* https://www.thecanadianencyclopedia.ca/en/article/emily-murphy.

Jellinek, E.M. 1960. *The Disease Concept of Alcoholism.* New Haven. CT: Hillhouse.

Josie, G. 1947. *A Report on Drug Addiction in Canada.* Ottawa, ON: Department of National Health and Welfare.

Keane, H. 2002. *What's Wrong with Addiction?* New York: New York University.

Kenny, K., C. Barrington, and S. Green. 2015. "'I Felt for a Long Time Like Everything Beautiful in Me Had Been Taken Out': Women's Suffering, Remembering, and Survival Following the Loss of Child Custody." *The International Journal of Drug Policy* 26.

Kenny, K., A. Krusi, C. Barrington, et al. 2021. "Health Consequences of Child Removal Among Indigenous and Non-Indigenous Sex Workers: Examining Trajectories, Mechansisms and Resiliencies." *Sociology of Health & Illness.* https://doi.org/10.1111/1467-9566.13364.

King, M. 1908. *The Need for the Suppression of the Opium Traffic in Canada.* Ottawa, ON: S.E. Dawson.

Krakowski, M., and R. Smart. 1972. *Report on the Evaluation of the Narcotic Addiction Unit's Methadone Maintenance Treatment Program.* Toronto, ON: Centre for Addiction and Mental Health.

Levine, H. 2015. "Discovering Addiction: Enduring Conceptions of Habitual Drunkenness in America." In *Expanding Addiction: Critical Essays,* edited by R. Granfield and C. Reinarman. New York: Routledge.

Lucas, P., S. Boyd, M.J. Milloy, and Z. Walsh. 2021. "Cannabis Significantly Reduces the Use of Prescription Opioids & Improves Quality of Life in Authorized Patients; Results of a Large Prospective Study." *Pain Medicine* 22, 3.

MacLeod, A. 1963. "Custody for Treatment under the Narcotic Control Act." *Canadian Journal of Corrections* 3.

MacPherson, D. 2001. "A Framework for Action: A Four-Pillar Approach to Drug Problems in Vancouver." Vancouver, BC: City of Vancouver.

Malakieh, J. 2019. "Adult and Youth Correctional Statistics in Canada, 2017/2018." *Juristat,* Canadian Centre for Justice Statistics, Ottawa, ON: Statistics Canada.

Martel, M. 2006. *Not This Time: Canadians, Public Policy, and the Marijuana Question 1961–1975.* Toronto, ON: University of Toronto Press.

Maynard, R. 2017. *Policing Black Lives: State Violence in Canada from Slavery to the Present.* Winnipeg, MB: Fernwood Publishing.

McDonald, L. 1971. "The Matsqui Institution (Matsqui Prison Story)." For the Commission of Inquiry into the Non-Medical Use of Drugs. March 15. Commission Project NO.: 80. RG 33, Series 101, VOL 158, Reel M-4223. Library and Archives Canada.

Million, D. 2013. *Therapeutic Nations: Healing in an Age of Indigenous Human Rights.* Tucson, AZ: University of Arizona Press.

Ministry of Health. 1926. *Report of the Departmental Committee on Morphine and Heroin Addiction (Rolleston).* London, UK: HMSO.

Moms stop the harms. 2021. "Moms Stop the Harms Takes Their Message to Municipalities." https://www.momsstoptheharm.com/

actions/2020/11/24/moms-stop-the-harm-takes-its-message-to-municipalities.
Moreau, G. 2019. "Police-Reported Crime Statistics in Canada, 2018." *Juristat*, July 22. Ottawa, ON: Statistics Canada.
___. 2021. "Police-Reported Crime Statistics in Canada, 2020." *Juristat*, July27. Ottawa, ON: Statistics Canada.
Moreau, G., B. Jaffray and A. Armstrong. 2020. "Police-Reported Crime Statistics in Canada, 2019." *Juristat*, Oct. 29. Ottawa, ON: Statistics Canada. https://www150.statcan.gc.ca/n1/pub/85-002-x/2020001/article/00010-eng.htm.
Murphy, B. 1972. *A Quantitative Test of the Effectiveness of an Experimental Treatment Programme for Delinquent Opiate Addicts*. Ottawa, ON: Information Canada.
Murphy, E. 1920. "The Grave Drug Menace." *Maclean's Magazine, XXXIII*, 3, Feb. 15. https://archive.macleans.ca/article/1920/2/15/the-grave-drug-menace.
___. 1922a. "'Joy Shots That Lead to Hell'." *Maclean's Magazine*, June 15. https://archive.macleans.ca/article/1922/6/15/joy-shots-that-lead-to-hell.
___. 1922b. "Curbing Illicit Vendors of Drugs." *Maclean's Magazine*, July 1922. https://archive.macleans.ca/article/1922/07/15/curbing-illicit-vendors-of-drugs.
___. 1922c. *The Black Candle*. Toronto, ON: Thomas Allen.
Musto, D. 1987. *The American Disease: Origins of Narcotic Control*, expanded ed. New York: Oxford University Press.
___ (ed.). 2002. *Drugs in America: A Documentary History*. New York: New York University Press.
NAFBC (Narcotic Addiction Foundation of British Columbia). 1956–57a. *Narcotic Addiction Foundation of British Columbia Annual Report, 1956–1957*. Vancouver, BC.
___. 1956–57b. *Narcotic Addiction Foundation of British Columbia Annual Report, 1956–1957*. Memo. Vancouver, BC.
NAPRA (National Association of Pharmacy Regulatory Authorities). n.d. "Drug Scheduling in Canada - General Overview. https://napra.ca/drug-scheduling-canada-general-overview.
Narcotic Control Act (NCA), S.C. 1961, c.35.
National Film Board. 1948. *Drug Addict* [Motion picture]. Royal Canadian Mounted Police (Producers), and R. Anderson (Director). Canada.
Ontario Human Rights Commission. 2020. *A Disparate Impact: Second Interim Report on the Inquiry into Racial Profiling and Racial Discrimination of Black Persons by the Toronto Police Service*. Government of Canada.
Oviedo-Joekes, E., D. Guh, S. Brissette, et al. 2016. "Hydromorphone Compared with Diacetylmorphine for Long-Term Opioid Dependence: A Randomized Clinical Trial." *JAMA Psychiatry* 73, 5, May. doi: 10.1001/jamapsychiatry.2016.0109.
Oviedo-Joikes, E., B. Nosyk, S. Brissette, et al. 2008. "The North American Opiate Medication Initiative (NAOMI): Profile of Participants in North America's First Trial of Heroin-Assisted Treatment." *Journal of Urban Health* 85, 6.
Owusu-Bempah, A. 2017. "Race and Policing in Historical Context: Dehumanization and the Policing of Black People in the 21st Century." *Theoretical Criminology* 21, 1.

Owusu-Bempah, A., and A. Luscombe. 2021. "Race, Cannabis and the Canadian War on Drugs: An Examination of Cannabis Arrest Data by Race in Five Cities." *International Journal of Drug Policy* 91.

Paulus, I., and R. Halliday. 1967. "Rehabilitation and the Narcotic Addict: Results of a Comparative Methadone Withdrawal Program." *Canadian Medical Association Journal* 96.

Pienaar, K., and E. Dilkes-Frayne. 2017. "Telling Different Stories, Making New Realities: The Ontological Politics of 'Addiction' Biographies." *International Journal of Drug Policy* 44.

Porter, M. 1955. "The Dope Craze That's Terrorizing Vancouver." *Maclean's Magazine*, 68. Feb. 1.

Porter, M., and L. Earl. 1963. "In Canada: Terror In Britain: Help. "*Star Weekly Magazine*, April 27.

Price, H. 1946. "The Criminal Addict." *Annual Report of the RCMP for the Year Ended March 31, 1946*, Appendix A-2, 73–82. Ottawa, ON: Edmond Cloutier.

Province of BC, Attorney-General. 1953. *Annual Report of the Inspector of Gaols for the Year Ended March 31st, 1952*. Victoria, BC: Don McDiarmid.

___. 1954a. *Annual Report of the Inspector of Gaols for the Year Ended March 31st, 1953*. Victoria, BC: Don McDiarmid.

___. 1954b. *Annual Report of the Inspector of Gaols for the Year Ended March 31st, 1954*. Victoria, BC: Don McDiarmid.

___. 1955. *Annual Report of the Inspector of Gaols for the Year Ended March 31st, 1955*. Victoria, BC: Don McDiarmid.

___. 1956. *Annual Report of the Inspector of Gaols for the Year Ended March 31st, 1956*. Victoria, BC: Don McDiarmid.

___. 1957. *Annual Report of the Inspector of Gaols for the Year Ended March 31st, 1957*. Victoria, BC: Don McDiarmid.

___. 1959. *Annual Report of the Director of Correction for the Year Ended March 31, 1958*. Victoria, BC: Don McDiarmid.

___. 1963. *Annual Report of the Director of Correction for the Year Ended March 31, 1962*. Victoria, BC: A. Sutton.

___. 1964. *Annual Report of the Director of Correction for the Year Ended March 31, 1963*. Victoria, BC: A. Sutton.

___. 1965. *Annual Report of the Director of Correction for the Year Ended March 31, 1964*. Victoria, BC: A. Sutton.

___. 1968. *Annual Report of the Director of Correction for the Year Ended March 31, 1967*. Victoria, BC: A. Sutton.

___. 1971. *Annual Report of the Director of Correction for the Year Ended March 31, 1970*. Victoria, BC: A. Sutton.

___. 1980. *Corrections Branch Annual Report for the Period January 1, 1979 to March 31, 1980*. Victoria, BC: Office of Attorney General.

Public Safety Canada. 2016. *Corrections and Conditional Release Statistical Overview 2015*. February. Ottawa, ON: Public Safety Canada.

___. 2019. *2018 Annual Report: Corrections and Conditional Release Statistical Overview*. Ottawa: Public Works and Government Services Canada. https://www.publicsafety.gc.ca/cnt/rsrcs/pblctns/ccrso-2018/ccrso-2018-en.pdf.

Ranta, L. 1952. *Drug Addiction in Canada: The Problem and its Solution*. Vancouver,

BC: Health and Auxiliary Division's Special Committee on Narcotics Community Chest and Council of Greater Vancouver. In G. Stevenson, L. Lingley, G. Trasov, and H. Stansfield, 1956, *Drug Addiction in British Columbia: A Research Survey,* unpublished manuscript. Vancouver, BC: University of British Columbia.

RCMP (Royal Canadian Mounted Police). 1922. *Report of the Royal Canadian Mounted Police for the Year Ended September 30, 1921*. Ottawa, ON: F.A. Acland Printer.

___. 1925. *Report of the Royal Canadian Police for the Year Ended September 30, 1924.* Ottawa, ON: F.A. Acland Printer.

___. 1960. *Report of the Royal Canadian Police for the Year Ended March 31, 1959*. Ottawa, ON: The Queen's Printer.

___. 1961. *Report of the Royal Canadian Police for the Year Ended March 31, 1960*. Ottawa, ON: Roger Duhamel Printer.

___. 1965. *Report of the Royal Canadian Police for the Year Ended March 31, 1965*. Ottawa, ON: Roger Duhamel Printer.

___. 1966. *Report of the Royal Canadian Police for the Year Ended March 31, 1966*. Ottawa, ON: Roger Duhamel Printer.

___. 1967. *Report of the Royal Canadian Police for the Year Ended March 31, 1965*. Ottawa, ON: Roger Duhamel Printer.

___. 1969. *Report of the Royal Canadian Police for the Year Ended March 31, 1968*. Ottawa, ON: Queen's Printer.

___. 1975–76. *Annual Report 1975–1976*. Ottawa, ON: Solicitor General Canada.

Reinarman, C. 2005. "Addiction as Accomplishment: The Discursive Construction of Disease." *Addiction Research & Theory* 13.

Reinarman, C., and R. Granfield. 2015. "Addiction Is Not Just a Brain Disease: Critical Studies of Addiction." In *Expanding Addiction: Critical Essays,* edited by R. Granfield and C. Reinarman. New York: Routledge.

Reinarman, C., and H. Levine. 1997. *Crack in America: Demon Drugs and Social Justice.* Berkely, CA: University of California Press.

Richmond, G. 1975. *Prison Doctor*. New Westminster, BC: Antonson Publishing.

___. 1978. "My Experience with the Addict-Prisoner." In *Some Implications of the Heroin Treatment Act (Bill 18)*, edited by M. Brunke. A series of speeches given at the "Public's Public Inquiry" of the *Heroin Treatment Act* on June 24, 1978. BC: Funded by the Non-Medical Use of Drugs Directorate Summer Programme #1216-9-99.

Robins, L., D. Davis, and D. Goodwin. 1974. "Drug Use in the U.S. Army Enlisted Men in Vietnam: A Follow-up on Their Return Home." *American Journal of Epidemiology* 99.

Robins, L., J. Helzer, M. Hesselbrock, and E. Wish. 2010. "Vietnam Veterans Three Years after Vietnam: How Our Study Changed Our View on Heroin." *American Journal on Addictions* 19.

Robinson, S., and B. Adinoff. 2016. "The Classification of Substance Use Disorders: Historical, Contextual, and Conceptual Considerations." *Behavioral Sciences* 16, 1. https://doi.org/10.3390/bs6030018.

Rolles, S., A. Schlag, F. Measham, et al. 2021. "A Multi Criteria Decision Analysis (MCDA) for Evaluating and Appraising Government Policy Responses to Non-Medical Heroin Use." *International Journal of Drug Policy* 91.

Said, E. 2001. *Orientalism* (25th anniversary ed.). New York: Vintage Books.
Schneider v. Queen 1982. 2 SCR. 112, Supreme Court of Canada. Case Number, 16255.
Schroeder, A. 1976. *Shaking It Rough: A Prison Memoir*. Halifax, NS: Goodread.
Simons, N. 1986. "Liquor Control and the Native Peoples of Western Canada." Unpublished MA thesis, School of Criminology, University of Ottawa.
Small, D., and E. Drucker. 2006. "Policy Makers Ignoring Science and Scientists Ignoring Policy: The Medical Ethical Challenges of Heroin Treatment." *Harm Reduction Journal* 3, 16.
Sneader, W. 1998. "The Discovery of Heroin." *Lancet*, 352.
Solomon, R., and M. Green. 1988. "The First Century: The History of Nonmedical Opiate Use and Control Policies in Canada, 1870–1970." In *Illicit Drugs in Canada,* edited by J. Blackwell and P. Erickson (pre-publication ed.). Toronto, ON: Methuen Publications.
Spear, B. 1994. "The Early Years of the 'British System' in Practice." In *Heroin Addiction and Drug Policy: The British System*, edited by J. Strang and M. Gossop. New York: Oxford Press.
Spear, H., and M. Glatt. 1971. "The Influence of Canadian Addicts on Heroin Addiction in the United Kingdom." *British Journal of Addiction, Alcohol Other Drugs* 66, 2.
Statistics Canada. 1977. *Crime and Traffic Enforcement Statistics 1975*. Ottawa, ON.
___. 1982. *Crime and Traffic Enforcement Statistics 1980*. Ottawa, ON.
___. 1984. *Crime and Traffic Enforcement Statistics 1982*. Ottawa, ON.
___. 2017. "Canadian Tobacco, Alcohol and Drugs Survey: 2017 Detailed Tables." https://www.canada.ca/en/health-canada/services/canadian-tobacco-alcohol-drugs-survey/2017-summary/2017-detailed-tables.html.
___. 2019a. "Incident-Based Crime Statistics, by Detailed Violations, Police Services in British Columbia." Table-35-10-0184-01. Ottawa, ON.
___. 2019b. "Incident-Based Crime Statistics, by Detailed Violations, Police Services in Canada." Table-35-10-0177-01. Ottawa, ON.
___. 2021. "Incident-Based Crime Statistics, by Detailed Violations, Police Services in British Columbia." Table-35-10-0184-01. Ottawa, ON.
Stein, P., I. Peters, G. Creech, et al. 1974a. *Annual Report to the Legislature of the Alcohol and Drug Commission, January 1 to December 31, 1974*. Victoria, BC: K.M. MacDonald, printer to the Queen.
___. 1974b. *Special Report to the Legislature of the Alcohol and Drug Commission*. March 15. Victoria, BC: K.M. MacDonald, printer to the Queen.
Stepler, J. 1949. "Killer of Men and Morals." *The Province Magazine*, Feb. 26.
Stevenson, G., L. Lingley, G. Trasov, and H. Stansfield. 1956. *Drug Addiction in British Columbia: A Research Survey*. Unpublished manuscript. Vancouver, BC: University of British Columbia.
Stoddart, K. 1991. "It's Easier for the Bulls Now: Official Statistics and Social Change in a Canadian Heroin-Using Community." *Journal of Drug Issues* 21, 1.
Strang, J., and M. Gossop (eds.). 1994. *Heroin Addiction and Drug Policy: The British System*. Oxford, UK: Oxford University Press.
Strang J., T. Groshkova, and N. Metrebian. 2012. *New Heroin-Assisted Treatment: Recent Evidence and Current Supervised Injectable Heroin Treatment in Europe and Beyond*. Luxemburg: Insights, European Monitoring Centre for Drugs and Drug Addiction.

Strang, J., T. Groshkova, A. Uchtenhagen, et al. 2015. "Heroin on Trial: Systematic Review and Meta-Analysis of Randomised Trials of Diamorphine-Prescribing as Treatment for Refractory Heroin Addiction." *The British Journal of Psychiatry* 207.

Tallaksen, A. 2017. "The Narcotic Clinic in New Orleans, 1919–1921." *Addiction* 112, 9.

Terry, C., and M. Pellens. 1970 [1928]. *The Opium Problem*. Montclair, NJ: Patterson Smith.

Thobani, S. 2007. *Exalted Subjects: Studies in the Making of Race and Nation in Canada*. Toronto, ON: University of Toronto Press.

___. 2021. *Contesting Islam, Constructing Race and Sexuality: The Inordinate Desire of the West*. London, UK: Bloomsbury Academic.

Thomson, E., D. Wilson, G. Mullins, et al. 2019. *Heroin Compassion Clubs*. Vancouver, BC: British Columbia Centre on Substance Use. https://www.bccsu.ca/wp-content/uploads/2019/02/Report-Heroin-Compassion-Clubs.pdf.

Thumath, M., D. Humphreys, J. Barlow, et al. 2021. "Overdose Among Mothers: A Association Between Child Removal and Unintentional Drug Overdose in a Longitudinal Cohort of Marginalized Women in Canada." *International Journal of Drug Policy* 91.

Turner, N. 2014. *Ancient Pathways, Ancestral Knowledge*. Montreal, QC: McGill-Queen's University Press.

Venne, S. and G. Hinge. 1981. *Indian Acts and Amendments, 1868–1975, An Indexed Collection*. Saskatoon, SK: University of Saskatchewan Native Law Centre.

Waldorf, D., M. Orlick, and C. Reinarman. 1974. *Morphine Maintenance: The Shreveport Clinic, 1919–1923*. Washington: The Drug Abuse Council.

Warner, J. 2003. *Craze: Gin and Debauchery in an Age of Reason*. London, UK: Profile Books.

Whitlock, C. 2020. *Botanicum Medicinale: A Modern Herbal of Medicinal Plants*. Cambridge, MA, UniPress Books.

Winch, E. 1953. *Analysis of Provincial Goal Reports, 1944–1953*. Rare Books & Special Collections and University Archives, Vancouver, BC: University of Vancouver.

Winter, J. 2020. "Drug Users Call for Safe Supply of Heroin and Cocaine, and Show How It's Done." *The Tyee*, June 23. https://thetyee.ca/News/2020/06/23/Safe-Supply-Drug-Demo/

World Medical Association. 2004. "World Medical Association Declaration of Helsinki: Ethical Principles for Medical Research Involving Human Subjects." http://www.wma.net/en/30publications/10policies/b3/.

Wortley, S. 2021. *Racial Disparities in British Columbia Police Statistics: A Preliminary Examination of a Complex Issue*. Vancouver, BC: British Columbia's Office of the Human Rights Commissioner.

Zacune, J. 1971. "A Comparison of Canadian Narcotic Addicts in Great Britain and in Canada." *Bulletin on Narcotics*, 4-006. Vienna, Austria: United Nations Office on Drugs and Crime. https://www.unodc.org/unodc/en/data-and-analysis/bulletin/bulletin_1971-01-01_4_page007.html.

Zinberg, N. 1984. *Drug, Set, and Setting: The Basis for Controlled Intoxicant Use*. New Haven, CT: Yale University Press.

INDEX